TRAVELS IN SEARCH OF THE ELEPHANT

By JOHN FRANCIS McDERMOTT

Private Libraries in Creole Saint Louis

Baltimore, 1938

A Glossary of Mississippi Valley French

Saint Louis, 1941

EDITOR OF

Tixier's Travels on the Osage Prairies

(Translated by Albert J. Salvan)

Norman, 1940

The Western Journals of Washington Irving

Norman, 1944

Old Cahokia: A Narrative and Documents
Illustrating the First Century of Its History

St. Louis, 1949

TRAVELS IN SEARCH OF THE ELEPHANT: THE WANDERINGS OF ALFRED S. WAUGH, ARTIST, IN LOUISIANA, MISSOURI, AND SANTA FE, IN 1845-1846

Edited and Annotated

by

JOHN FRANCIS McDERMOTT

St. Louis

Missouri Historical Society

1951

TO MY MOTHER

MARY STEBER McDERMOTT

PREFACE

IN 1844 ALFRED S. WAUGH, then at Mobile, dreamt of making a collection of sketches of the memorable places and scenery of the United States which he could eventually publish with a journal kept during his travels. The following year, in the vain hope of a place on Frémont's Third Expedition, he traveled to Independence, Missouri, and for nearly a year practiced his art at that town and at Lexington. It is certain that he made extensive notes at this time as well as on his journey to New Mexico in the summer of 1846 and during his stay in Santa Fe. A period of illness confining him to his room in St. Louis in the late summer and fall of 1850 gave him the enforced leisure necessary for turning his notes into a narrative. The "first volume" of his account, entitled "Desultory Wanderings in the Years 1845-46" and dedicated to Major General Samuel D. Lucas, was completed 27 November 1850, according to the note to the reader prefacing it. An excerpt from Chapter XXIII, Volume II, of his narrative, now called "Travels in Search of the Elephant, or the Wanderings of an Artist," was published in the *Western Journal* (of St. Louis) for October, 1851. Somewhat earlier (15 August 1851) he had written to a friend in New York that the third volume was almost finished.

Of this extensive manuscript only the first volume or part is known to survive. It is written in a calfbound record book with a page twelve inches by seven and three quarters. The narrative, written on the right-hand pages, fills the volume of one hundred and forty-five pages. On the left-hand pages Waugh entered a number of explanatory notes. In addition to notes, the first thirty-eight left-hand pages are filled with copies (not in chronological order) of letters and some poems written by Waugh between 1849 and 1854. This record book comprises the Waugh Collection at the Missouri Historical Society. It has been in the possession of the Society at least twenty-five years and probably very much longer—no accession record for it has been found. There are no sketches in the collection.

The present volume brings together all available portions of Waugh's account of his travels. To the hitherto unpublished Missouri Historical Society manuscript (which begins at Mobile in 1844 and closes when the author is ready to set out for Santa Fe about 15 May, 1846) has been added a long letter written by Waugh at Santa Fe to his good friend Tisdale at Independence. This letter has been as good as lost in the files of the *Southern Literary Messenger.* I have also included as a second appendix the chapter from "Volume II," which its author had published in the *Western Journal.*

The reader will quickly find that Waugh could not spell, that he knew nothing of punctuation, and that his sentence structure is sometimes far from smooth. The manuscript, of course, has been reproduced as faithfully as possible. Occasionally I have made editorial insertions in square brackets where they seemed absolutely necessary for sense. Hasty writing and bad eyes caused the author to make unwitting faults. The notes by Waugh are all credited to him. The chapter divisions are those of Waugh except that I have broken the first long chapter into two; the chapter titles are mine. The two pieces of Waugh's writing in the appendix do not show the same faults simply because they were corrected by the editors who originally published them.

I wish to acknowledge my indebtedness for information and special courtesies to Charles van Ravenswaay and the Missouri Historical Society; Clarence E. Miller and the Mercantile Library of St. Louis; Floyd C. Shoemaker of the State Historical Society of Missouri; Nelson F. Adkins of New York University; Peter A. Brannon of the Department of Archives and History, Montgomery, Alabama; William F. Morse, Reference Librarian of the Mobile Public Library; Elizabeth J. Young, Librarian of the Lexington Public Library; General E. M. Stayton of Independence, Missouri; Mrs. Anne E. C. Peirce, Secretary to Christ's Church Cathedral, St. Louis; William N. Chambers and William G. B. Carson of Washington University, St. Louis. The index I owe to the kindness and endurance of my wife.

John Francis McDermott

CONTENTS

INTRODUCTION

"SINCE I CAME TO THE WEST I have seen a great deal of 'the world, the flesh and the devil,' but, as I hope, to some purpose, that, however, that pleases me best of all is, I have seen and crossed the great american desert—the north western prairies—been to Santa Fe for the purpose of looking at the Elephant—yes! yes! I have seen the Elephant, and now let me tell you *one sight of him* is quite enough in all conscience. But the fun of the joke is this, I am writing a history of my travels in search of that animal to be published in handsome style and fully embellished by the author. The third vol will soon be finished—what do you think of that my boy Eh? You little thought when the fellows in the modelling schools called me Goldsmith—from my resemblance to that beautifully ugly man, that I would still further resemble him by giving to the world a history of my travels. . . ."

So Alfred S. Waugh wrote from St. Louis, 15 August 1851, to his old classmate Robert L. Smyth in New York.[1] But he was to have one more sight of the elephant—one more disappointment—for he would not live to see his book of travels in print. Nevertheless, he does live today by the fragment (unembellished) of this narrative that has survived when his works of sculpture and his paintings have disappeared: the artist, save for a handful of biographical facts, is lost, but the reporter of the frontier is fresh and vigorous in his word pictures of western Missouri and New Mexico made over a century ago.

On the origin of Waugh, save that he was an Irishman, nothing has been discovered. His birthday was the first of July, but the year of his birth is unknown.[2] In 1827 (and possibly for some years previous) he was a student in the Royal Dublin Society [Royal Hibernian Academy?], Kildare Street, Dublin, where he learned to model in clay and worked in life classes. His master was named Smyth. His classmates included Robert L. and John Smyth, sons of his instructor, "Ben Hill, Mr. Alpin, Percy, Panorma, Howse, Arthur O'Leary, O'Neil, Templeton, and a multitude of others."[3] After 1827 Waugh traveled on the Continent. Reminisc-

1. Waugh Manuscripts, Missouri Historical Society. "There is a cant expression, '*I've seen the elephant,*' in very common use in Texas. . . . When a man is disappointed in any thing he undertakes, when he has seen enough, when he gets sick and tired of any job he may have set himself about, he has '*seen the elephant*'" (Kendall, *Texan Santa Fé Expedition*, I, 108-110).

2. All facts and quotations not otherwise identified are drawn from Waugh's narrative.

3. Waugh to Smith, 15 August 1851, Waugh Mss. Robert L. Smyth was probably the son of John Smyth (1775?-1834?), an Associate of the Royal Hibernian Academy. The latter was a son of Edward Smyth, also a sculptor (*DNB*, XVIII: 592).

ing on the road from Lexington to Independence in the spring of 1846, he remembered how he had "now [been] walking through the gallery of the Louvre, and then standing before the Apollo of the Vatican; then again, I was crossing the Alps, and anon, sailing up the Rhine, for I have travelled much and am familiar with antiquated scenes of the old World. . . ."

In 1833 he was in Baltimore, but when or why he came to America remains unknown.[4] The opening paragraph of his narrative informs us that he was in South Carolina in 1838. Elsewhere he makes clear that he was working in Raleigh, North Carolina, about that time. There he became acquainted with two young men he was to meet later. William Haywood Ruffin was then a senior at the university; he was to practice medicine in Lexington, Missouri. William M. McPheeters, also a student, was to take his medical degree at the University of Pennsylvania in 1840 and to become a leading physician in St. Louis. At this time (according to a writer in the *Missouri Republican* of 18 September 1848) Waugh made busts of the Reverend Dr. Joseph Caldwell, late president of the university, the Honorable William Gaston, late judge of the Supreme Court of North Carolina, and the Right Reverend Levi Silliman Ives, then Bishop of the Diocese of North Carolina.

The summer of 1842 found the artist traveling in Alabama. Considerable space in his narrative is given to an account of a duel in Demopolis on 7 July. Apparently in this season he also visited Tuscaloosa. The following summer he painted in Pensacola, Florida, a portrait of Judge Walker Anderson.[5] Probably his next move was to Mobile, a city of which he became quite fond, for he would on occasion identify himself as "Colonel Waugh of Mobile." More ambitious plans began to develop in his mind. He had "hit upon a new style of colored profiles which seemed to please people very much" and he now "formed a plan of travelling and exercising myself in my new line of buisiness which indeed, from the encouragement I met with, promised a rich harvest and a comfortable independence. I intended to go all over the union, make a collection of drawings of the scenery, battle fields, and other memorable places, to illustrate a journal which I intended to keep & which I would probably give to the world at some future day."[6]

Early in 1844 he met John B. Tisdale in Mobile. To him Waugh proposed the kind of tour he longed to make. As a test Waugh went in July

4. Waugh to Wm. J. Brickey, 31 May 1850, in *Weekly Reveille*, 3 June 1850, p. 4229.
5. Waugh to Lieutenant-Colonel W. W. Loring, St. Louis, 28 August 1851, Waugh Mss.
6. Writing in the fall of 1850, he added: "This was an other of my wild schemes which was to end in smoke."

to East Pascagoula and was reasonably satisfied about the possibilities of their "great tour." The remainder of the year they worked in Mobile (Tisdale was still a beginner) but on 19 January 1845 they embarked for New Orleans. A few months later a newspaper item reprinted from the St. Louis *Reveille* got them excited about the possibility of roaming the great plains and the Rockies as artists on Frémont's Third Expedition. "The desire of going into a region so remote and of seeing the red sons of the forest in all their native habits so occupied our thoughts that it became an all absorbing topic with us."

Hopefully they rushed to St. Louis to interview Captain Frémont but they arrived in town before he did and, acting on the advice that young Dr. McDowell was his authorized agent, they pushed on almost immediately to Jefferson City. At the state capital they missed the doctor, who had gone ahead to Independence. They decided now to wait until Frémont appeared, for it was certain he would go by boat as far as the frontier. They amused themselves by looking at the new Capitol and inspecting the little town and Waugh painted a number of portraits, including those of S. M. Bay and wife, the Reverend Mr. Hedges, Episcopal minister of the place, and Cicero S. Hawks, a North Carolinian before he became a Missourian and an Episcopal bishop.

When the *Henry Bry* appeared bearing the explorer and his party, Waugh and Tisdale boarded it for Kansas Landing. Frémont tried repeatedly to discourage the artists courteously and finally after three weeks flatly told them that he could not take them on the expedition. On 2 July 1845, therefore, they returned from the Kansas plains to the farm on the frontier of Missouri where they had been staying. Until May, 1846, they divided their time between Independence and Lexington, where Waugh was kept moderately busy doing portraits, miniatures, colored profiles, and family groups, and Tisdale was making a start at his profession.

The great bustle of overland travelers and Santa Fe traders in Independence in the spring of 1846 again roused Waugh's enthusiasm for travel. About the middle of May he left for New Mexico in a caravan conducted by Samuel Ralston and John Hill and arrived at Santa Fe on 24 June. After about six weeks in that town he left for Missouri sometime before the arrival of the Army of the West on 18 August. Traveling with George R. Clark and others from Fort Bent, he reached Council Grove on the Santa Fe Trail on 22 August. "These gentlemen were much troubled coming in, by Indians," reported the St. Louis *Weekly Reveille* on 14 September 1845. "They had one man shot down and killed in the encampment, and they shot three Indians, who were attempting to surprise them. They reported that there are more Indians on the plains than there has been for four years, and they showed every sign of hostility."[7]

Probably Waugh stopped at Independence and Lexington to see his old friends. Tisdale, whom he had left behind, he was not to see, for the young man had joined the Lexington company of the Missouri Mounted Volunteers, now in New Mexico and not to be disbanded for nearly a year longer. By the close of 1846 Waugh had set up his easel at Boonville. The *Commercial Bulletin* there on 31 December politely announced that "Col. Alfred S. Waugh, an eminent artist, is now on a visit to our town, for the purpose of miniature painting. He may be found in the Mansion House." Two weeks later (13 January 1847) the same paper gave him a puff:

"In visiting the studio of this eminent and highly gifted Artist, we have enjoyed a 'feast of reason' which is rarely our lot. The perfect specimens of a noble art and the admiration inspired by beholding how accurately are portrayed each lineament of the human face and form . . . and . . . the urbanity, the intelligence, the detail of pleasing incidents, and the inexhaustible humor, of this gentleman, render a visit to him doubly interesting. We cannot say too much in behalf of his admirable art. . . ."

Here, as previously in Independence and Lexington, he had the pleasure of talking about art. On the 21st the *Bulletin* announced that he was invited to lecture before the Boonville Lyceum on the "Influence of the Fine Arts"; a week later we read that the lecture had been "attended with a crowded house—attesting by their number and the attention paid to his Lecture, their appreciation of the author and his subject." At the close of the evening he was invited to deliver another lecture on the same subject.[8]

Presently Waugh must have worked his way down the Missouri to St. Louis. The city directory for 1848 listed him as a sculptor at 56 Pine Street. His principal activities at this time seem to have been sculpture and authorship. In the July issue of the *Western Journal* he began a series of articles on "The Rise, Progress and Influence of the Fine Arts"—no doubt the sort of material his audiences in western Missouri had listened to.[9] In the way of sculpture he had nearly finished in September a bust of Bishop Hawks. A writer in the *Western Journal*, who did not "profess

7. Dateline of the item was 8 September, p. 996.
8. For these items from the Boonville *Commercial Bulletin* I am indebted to Charles van Ravenswaay.
9. I (1848), 309-314, 383-385, 445-447, 497-500, 571-574, 627-630, 672-678; II (1849), 29-33.

to have a cultivated taste," nevertheless found it bore not merely a "close and striking" resemblance to the subject but had caught also the "characteristic air and bearing of the original." In fact, "the likeness seems to kindle up in every feature the more we look at it." In the studio at this time there was also a bust of the Reverend William S. Potts, pastor of the Second Presbyterian Church. His "more intimate acquaintances," we are told, "esteem it an excellent likeness."[10]

The articles on the arts, which had continued to appear regularly in the *Western Journal* through January, 1849, suddenly broke off. The March number carried an unhappy explanation: "Owing to dimness of sight, and consequent depression of spirits," he wrote to the editor, "I am unable to concentrate my thoughts on any subject, and will have to beg of you to do me the favor to absolve me from the duty of this month's contribution. In the next number I hope again to pay my respects to the readers of the Western Journal."[11] But no further articles appeared in any later issue of this periodical. He continued, however, to work at sculpture. By October of this year he had completed busts of Dr. Hutchinson and John O'Fallon, as well as painted "a beautiful and *unique* picture, literally; Mr. Child and family."[12]

During 1850 he talked and wrote; there are no specific references to any paintings or busts by him. In the spring he gave a series of lectures "before the young ladies of Mr. Purkitt's High School," to which citizens in general were invited. The *St. Louis Intelligencer* on 3 April reported a "large and highly intelligent" audience at the second of the talks (on

---

10. *Western Journal*, I (Sept., 1848), 517. "Epeus" also wrote to the *Missouri Republican*, 12 September 1848, about these two busts. The busts were presented to the sitters by their congregations. For Hawks see note 27, p. 13 below. Potts (1804-1852) was successively pastor of the First Presbyterian Church, 1828-1835; President of Marion College, 1835-1839; and pastor of the Second Presbyterian Church, 1839-1852 (Scharf, *History of St. Louis*, II, 1702). The following spring Waugh presented Dr. Wm. M. McPheeters, on the occasion of his marriage to Sallie Buchanan, with a copy of his bust of Potts (Waugh to McPheeters, St. Louis, 10 May 1849, Waugh Mss.). For McPheeters consult Scharf, *History of St. Louis*, II, 1528.

11. *Western Journal*, II, 210.

12. *Weekly Reveille*, 8 October 1849, p. 3058. The first named was possibly E. C. Hutchinson, D.D., an Episcopalian minister and President of Kemper College. For John O'Fallon (1791-1865), one of the notable citizens of St. Louis, consult Scharf, *History of St. Louis*, I, 343-354. Alonzo Child, born 1807, came to St. Louis in 1835. He married Mary Goodrich and in 1860 was the father of seven children (Edwards, *Great West*, 503-504).

The only other bit known concerning Waugh for this year informs us of his indignation at the funeral of Miss Brant. One of the pallbearers, "James McC——rs . . . snatched a bunch of roses from the coffin and placed them in his breast. This vandalic act aroused my indignation to such a pitch that I gave vent to my feelings" in a satirical poem entitled "Don Whiskeranzo Burro, or the chivalric Fool." This verbal lashing he sent to a newspaper but withdrew it from publication when he heard the man was not in St. Louis (Waugh Mss.).

architecture) and described the lecturer as "a self-taught man and a practical artist" engaged "in the daily and diligent pursuit of his profession." At least five lectures were delivered in this series. That scheduled for 25 April, because of the pressure of professional engagements, had to be postponed for three weeks.[13] This same spring St. Louis again had the opportunity to crowd around Dubufe's paintings of Adam and Eve (The Temptation and The Expulsion) which, in original or copy, had been touring America for many years. This time their presence caused Waugh to write three letters to his friend William J. Brickey, then absent in Lexington, in which he expatiated on the excellence of the paintings.[14] The most important accomplishment of the year, however, was the travel narrative on which he was working. Confined to his room by illness, he "kept off the visits of certain disagreeable imps called THE BLUES" by writing up the story of his travels in the Mississippi Valley and western Missouri in 1845-46. By 27 November he was able to write *finis* to the first volume.[15]

Jenny Lind captivated St. Louis in March, 1851. Waugh was so enthusiastic that he wrote a poem about the "tones of Heaven" which had been bestowed upon the Nightingale. He had it set to music by his fellow-St. Louisan, W. Rossington, and presented it to her on the eve of her departure.[16]

Three months later a "shameful outrage" occurred which called forth a letter from Waugh. He wrote:

". . . in this morning's Republican [appeared] a notice of the wanton destruction of a couple of works of art belonging to me. It was not my intention to have said any thing about so uncalled for piece of vandalism if the matter had not found its way into the public prints; but as it has come before the public with a little inaccuracy, perhaps it may be as well for me to state what I know. . . .

"The busts alluded to, together with some others, were temporarily placed under the stairs on the first landing of the Blow's building next door to Wyman's Hall on Market Street, opposite the Court House, previous to their removal from the house. About half past two o'clock in the

13. The first lecture had been delivered on 31 March. "The design of this course of lectures is to exhibit, in a popular manner, the origin, progress, and present state of the Fine Arts, both in Europe and America." The third lecture, 4 April, was on sculpture. Others were to follow on painting, poetry, and music (St. Louis *Intelligencer*, 3, 12 April 1850; *Missouri Republican*, 25 April 1850). During this year Waugh's address was 130 Market Street (*St. Louis Directory for 1850*).

14. These letters, dated St. Louis, 31 May, 7, 15 June, were published in the *Weekly Reveille*, 3, 10, 24 June (pp. 4229, 4237, 4258). Waugh had first seen these paintings at Baltimore in 1833.

15. Preface (not reproduced here) to the manuscript of his narrative.

16. Waugh Mss., 17, 24 March 1851. The *St. Louis Directory for 1851* listed Waugh as a "full length miniature painter" at 132 Market Street, upstairs.

afternoon of Sunday the 19th June 1851—the better the day, the better the deed—they were stolen from their resting place by persons, who no doubt would be highly offended were they told they were *not gentlemen,* and carried up stairs to the third story. My attention was first called to the outrage in the afternoon by seeing the bust of our excellent public spirited fellow citizen, Col. John O'Fallon placed on the top of the first flight of stairs leading from the street, horribly mutilated in the face. . . . I found that two of the other busts were missing, when I at once proceeded to remove the remainder to my room to save them from the fate which I foresaw their fellows were doomed to suffer.

"About three o'clock on the following morning the aforesaid busts were [thrown] out of the window of the center room of the third story and dashed to pieces on the street below. The room out of which they were so violent ejected, is occupied by a Mr. Gilman, and is directly over the office of the clerk of the Supreme Court of Missouri and, on that occasion must have had more than one person [in] it as the voices of several were heard to issue from its interior."

Publication of Waugh's letter immediately brought forth an answer from an anonymous friend of Gilman who insisted that the artist "somewhat exaggerated" and did "great injustice" to Gilman in implying that he had wantonly destroyed the property of the artist. Apparently they were both the victims of a practical joke played on Gilman, who may have been just a little bit drunk at the time. The facts, according to the letter writer, were these:

". . . Mr. G. had been absent from his room from Sunday afternoon until an early hour Monday morning, attending at the home of a sick friend, and upon his return to his apartment, which had meanwhile been opened by a false key, he was somewhat startled, as he entered, by what appeared, to be the 'Father of his Country,' dressed in modern fashion, reclining on a sofa, with a seedy hat on his dusty cranium. Busts of persons, to him unknown, crowded his room, which presented the appearance of an artist's studio. Wholly unconscious of their value or their owners, and seeing no speedier way to rid himself of his pale and silent uninvited guests, he threw them from his window. . . ."[17]

A visit to St. Louis at the end of July by George W. Kendall of the New Orleans *Picayune* brought back memories of the artist's travels in the southwest. He showed the author of the *Texan Santa Fé Expedition* a sketch of his "*very* [*par*]*ticular friend Don Manuel Armijo,*" a copy of

17. Waugh Mss. His letter was published in the *Missouri Republican* on 2 July 1851; the reply by Gilman's friend on 3 July.

the portrait he had painted for "that august ruler during the last days of his authority" in New Mexico. The irony, of course, was that Armijo wore the cross bestowed on him for his capture of the Texan Expedition.[18]

During the early part of this summer Waugh spent two months working on a portrait of a deceased child of Henry Stagg. The artist had never seen the child and had only a cast of its face to work from. Mrs. Stagg, their little daughter, and "little Fanny Coons" all thought he had succeeded, but Mr. Stagg, dissatisfied, refused to pay the fifty dollars promised. The picture must have remained in Waugh's possession, unredeemed, for in December it was being exhibited in the window of Daniel Spencer, gilder, on Fourth Street. A writer in the *Missouri Republican* disagreed with Stagg, for he wrote: "We almost envy Mr. Stagg the gratification he must feel in the possession of so faithful a likeness. To those who may have the melancholy occasion to invoke art's power in the procurement of similar souvenirs of remembrance, we cordially recommend A. S. Waugh as eminently successful, when aided by miniature or cast, in reproducing on canvas the life-like lineaments of the departed."[19]

About this time Waugh was seriously thinking that photography offered a more certain living than painting. It was not desire for money that influenced him so much as his rapidly weakening sight. J. H. Fitzgibbon, daguerreotypist of St. Louis, fired his enthusiasm with a description of the Hillotype he had just seen demonstrated in New York—this was a wonderful machine "by which pictures of natural scenery can be taken in all their brilliant coloring."[20] Nothing, however, came of this project.

On the first day of the new year, writing to Captain J. N. Palmer about some commissions on which he was still at work, Waugh said:

"When they shall be completed I shall then take my leave of legitimate art—as a profession at least, for I find I am physically unable to pursue painting to a profitable end, my eyesight not permitting me to work more than two or three hours per day. I do not, however, mean to abandon the pencil altogether—only as a profession; but stern necessity compels me to turn my attention to an other pursuit far more lucrative. . . . I cannot work quick enough with my pencil to make painting profitable in a pecuniary point of view. Alass! too truly can I exclaim in the language of the classic author 'non sum qualis eram.' I am no longer what I have

18. Waugh to Kendall, St. Louis, 30 July, 1851, Waugh Mss.

19. Waugh to Henry Stagg, St. Louis, 6 August 1851, Waugh Mss.; *Missouri Republican*, 10 December 1851. In this unsigned newspaper communication it was stated that Waugh had worked from a daguerreotype. Waugh declared that his regular price was $110.

20. Fitzgibbon to Waugh, New York, 2 August 1851—printed in the *Missouri Republican*, 23 August 1851.

been and must give up my darling pursuit for one that takes the fancy of 'our sovereign lord' the people, to the almost total exclusion of all those works which require the noblest faculties of the soul to accomplish them. It is rather hard for me who has spent the best years of his life in the acquisition of that knowledge which is requisite to the formation of an artist, to be obliged to relinquish it, and betake himself to the trade of manufacturing *ghost-pictures*—things which any shoemaker or tailor can learn to make in a very short space of time . . . as my sight will not allow me to pursue painting as formerly I must of necessity turn my attention to some other calling in order to accumulate a competence for the evening of my days. It is all very fine to talk about talents and honors and so forth, but let me tell you, an empty purse commands very little attention now-a-days, and the world has no respect for venerable poverty. An ass laden with gold will command more respect from mankind at large than a Raphael in rags."[21]

A month later he wrote to Colonel Loring that he "had lately learned the art of Daguerre, and when more practiced in its operations [I] will start for the South and open a gallery in Mobile."[22] Toward the end of March there is more on the same theme in a letter to Robert Smyth:

"Vainly have I clunk [clung] to my eazel—even after loosing one of my eyes; my hand still grasped the pencil in the fond hope that my sight would yet improve; but alass, so delicately are our visionary organs constructed—the sympathy existing between the living and the dead orbs, so great, that I am compelled, I fear me, to employ my impaired vision in a way that will not tax it so severely as it has been for the last four years." Worse did not come to worst, however, for a note, dated St. Louis, 14 March 1854, appended to his copy of this letter, informs us that, since he wrote, his sight had improved so much that he had resumed his regular profession.[23]

At the time these troubles were most crowding him, he was at work on five pictures for Captain Palmer and Colonel Loring which were all finished by February, 1852. Not much more can be added to the record of his life. In the *Missouri Republican* on 9 May 1852 appeared a paragraph of a letter by Waugh praising a panorama of Italy by S. B. Waugh (no relation) which edified and entertained St. Louisans for four weeks.[24]

21. Waugh Mss.
22. Waugh to Lieutenant-Colonel W. W. Loring, St. Louis, 5 February 1852, Waugh Mss.
23. Waugh to Robert L. Smith, St. Louis, 24 March 1852, Waugh Mss.
24. The letter, dated St. Louis, 5 May, was probably addressed to Robert L. Smyth, but no copy of it is found in the Waugh Mss. The omitted portion would prove far more interesting to us than the paragraph the editor chose to published: "And now,

His manuscript book contains copies of several letters written in this year but they add no information about his art or personal activities.[25] Two satirical poems appear among the correspondence in this volume. One is dated May 1854; it is an "Epitaph on an artist remarkable for his indefatiguable industry at doing nothing—except now and then he paints a horse, hence he is known as the *great animal painter*." The other set of verses, likewise, is an Epitaph "for an Artist famous for his egotism and self conceit, whose constant boast was, that he could *learn* all his brothers how to paint." Neither poem is badly turned satire.

Two more pieces of his sculpture were noticed in the press in 1855. The *Western Journal and Civilian* in June mentioned his bust of the late William Sublette, modelled from a cast ("the living subject having never been seen by the Artist"). The writer found the likeness "striking." On 4 October the *Missouri Republican* reported that Waugh had completed a bust of Micajah Tarver (editor of the *Western Journal and Civilian*) "which he executed at the request of a large number of friends of that gentleman in order that it may be placed in the Mercantile Library." He had achieved "signal success" in his undertaking.[26]

A friendly publisher might speak of success, but the Tarver bust was the last of Waugh's commissions. The pitiful close of his career was reported in the *Missouri Republican* about six months later: "Yesterday morning, Col. Alfred S. Waugh was found dead in his room over the Post Office. Col. Waugh was well known in our city as a painter and sculptor, and evidence of his genius in both branches of these arts have been attested by many of our citizens." Superior talents and a finished education, the writer thought, would have rendered him far more distinguished in his profession had he not foundered on the rock on which genius is so often wrecked. Drink had ruined him. "The mournful story that closes the life of many a poet, painter and sculptor were [*sic*] realized in this instance. Penury and want, added to a weakness that maddens the brain and stultifies the intellect and energies of the most gifted, were the inheritance of the deceased, and he sunk into his grave in silence and poverty."[27]

No busts or paintings of Waugh's have been identified: there is no way

---

as I have spoken of the arts and artists of the West, allow me to make a few remarks upon a work which has been lately unfolded to the scrutiny of our citizens . . . it comes nearer to a good gallery picture than any painting of this kind which I have met with. . . ."

25. To Captain J. N. Palmer, 2 July 1852; the Reverend John Higginbotham, 5 July 1852; Frederick Welcker, 12 September 1852—Waugh Mss.

26. *Western Journal and Civilian*, XIV (1855), 74. The bust of Tarver was in possession of the Mercantile Library in 1862 but has since disappeared

27. *Missouri Republican*, 20 March 1856. The death notice reads the 18th; the funeral was held on the 20th.

of judging his skill as painter or sculptor. Nothing remains except the narrative of his travels in Missouri and New Mexico. But this report of frontier towns and people, of life and manners a century ago, assures him of some bit of fame, some remembrance of his longing to record a way of life.

CHAPTER I

THE ARTIST IN MOBILE—NEW ORLEANS—UP THE MISSISSIPPI IN PURSUIT OF FREMONT—ST. LOUIS

SOME FEW YEARS BACK, while in South Carolina I had made arrangements to go with a party of friends to the Rocky Mountains. It was one of those wild schemes that occasionally take possession of the brain of youth whose thirst for romance and adventure never allow them to pause and reflect on the pros and cons of the undertaking, but with the recklessness of their years, they dash into everything that has the air of novelty. It never occurred to us that we would have to make ample provision for a journey over a vast desert of many hundred miles, at that time almost unknown to the white race. We fondly imagined that all we had to do was to go well armed and equipped, in order to secure sustenance by the killing of game from day to day on the road; we never dreamed of danger of any sort. Oh! it was a wild scheme, indeed, but fortunately some of the party gave up the idea, and so there was an end of our romance and adventure.

Nevertheless my mind was filled with pictures of the sublimity of that region, I thought frequently of the grand field of opperation I would have for my pen and pencil, if I could only get out there, this so engrossed my mind that it occupied my thoughts sleeping and waking, I dwelt on it by day, and dreamed of it by night. This was in the year 1838. Time rolled on and I ceased to think on the subject more. A few years afterwards, in my perigrinations, I found myself in Mobile, Alabama, and having hit upon a new style of colored profiles which seemed to please people very much, I formed a plan of travelling and exercising myself in my new line of buisiness which indeed, from the encouragement I met with, promised a rich harvest and a comfortable independence. I intended to go all over the union, make a collection of drawings of the scenery, battle fields, and other memorable places, to illustrate a journal which I intended to keep, & which I might probably give to the world at some future day. This was another of my wild schemes which was to end in smoke.

Some time in the early part of the year 1844 I became acquainted with a young man of (what is termed) smartness, he had a bold, manly, and prepossessing air, well calculated to win the friendship of most persons. He called on me one afternoon with a small picture, painted by himself, and which he wished to shew me and get some advice about the colering.

It pleased me and after some conversation I invited him to renew his visits, promising to give him all the assistance I could in an art in which he seemed born to succeed. He came again, and again, and we became friends.[1]

In consequence of the success of my new style full length sketches, it struck me that if I were to travel for a couple or three years, I might be able to accumulate a competence, which would enable me, afterwards, to pursue the legitimate departments of art at my leisure and for its own sake. Having by this time become somewhat acquainted with my new friend, I proposed to him to join me in the enterprise; to this he readily assented and we made arrangements for a start. Previous, however, to entering on our experiment, I went to a watering place on the Mississippi shore to test the plan. So accordingly on the 14 July 1844, I left for E Pascagoula, here I became satisfied from the success I met with that we might venture on our great tour. Having returned to Mobile, we selected N Orleans as the starting point. In Mobile things did not turn out quite as well as we anticipated, nevertheless we were enabled to leave with a respectfully filled purse and a goodly number of introductory letters from persons of high respectibility to others of similar standing in the famous city of N Orleans. All things being ready, on sunday the 19th Jany 1845 we embarked on board the steam boat James L. Day, commanded by a very clever fellow, Captain Charles Reynolds, an exceedingly popular gentleman, whose urbanity gained for him great favor with all, but more especially the ladies.[2]

My spirits which were rather depressed for some time previously, now rose to a pleasant pitch, but my companion's sank for he was quitting a fair young lady to whom he had engaged his heart and hand in Mobile. A game of chess, however, soon absorbed his attention and drew his

---

1. This young man Waugh presently identifies as John B. Tisdale; he is to figure considerably in the narrative. At Lexington in 1846 he enlisted as a private in Company B of Doniphan's First Regiment of Missouri Mounted Volunteers; Connelley (*Doniphan's Expedition*, 536) listed him as John B. Tisdall. Hughes (*Doniphan's Expedition*, 199) reproduced a sketch of J. W. Patton, captioned "The Volunteer," signed J. D. Tisdell; there can be little doubt that the artist was Waugh's companion. The subject presumably was John W. H. Patton, a private in Company A of the Mounted Volunteers (Connelley, *Doniphan's Expedition*, 533). At some time after the war Tisdale returned to Mobile. The city directory for 1855 (no directories are available from 1848 to 1855) listed him as employed by the Shippers' Press. In later years he served also as a deputy sheriff and as county assessor; his residence was first at Kushla, Alabama, and finally at Chunchua. After 1885-86 his name disappears from the directories.

2. Nine months later Sir Charles Lyell made this overnight trip along the channel between the islands and the mainland in the same steamer, which he described as one hundred and eighty-five feet long and drawing seven feet of water when fully loaded; berths were $5 each (*Second Visit*, II, 88).

attention for the time being, from "the little girl he left behind him," and he became cheerfull.

Next morning we reached the Crescent city, and took up our quarters at the Verandah Hotel,[3] not far from the famous St. Charles, where we remained two days, and then removed to a house on St. Charles Street, where we prepared our studio and went to work. Buisiness did not flow in upon us as fast as we wished, indeed, it was only just enough to clear expenses and no more.

We made the acquaintance of an artist of the name of Ford, from the city of Dublin, and an other with whom *he* had been in partnership named Moise,[4] both artists of talent, particularly the latter,—excentric and ingenious,—this gentleman was from South Carolina. Also a Mr. Wilson,[5] an Englishman, and one who shared his studio, with a Mr. Healy, brother to the artist who painted for Louis Phillipe of France.[6] Mr. George Cook at this time owned the National Gallery, whom I had previously been acquainted with in N. Carolina. His gallery and studio was next door to us. In his collection were several really good pictures by various artists, Chapman, Rothermede, and others of note. One by the last named gentleman, DeSoto discovering the Missippi was really a fine picture. & An interior by Cook, of St. Peter's in Rome. This picture really conveyed a better idea of the vastness of this great church than any painting of it I had ever met with, the perspective was truly fine. A very good copy of the wreck of the Medusa, in the gallery of the Louvre in Paris, by this gentleman attracted much attention. We frequently spent an hour in this gallery.[7] Mrs. Steele, the miniature painter, was at this time stopping at the St. Charles Hotel.[8] Others of the profession were here, but I did not make their acquaintance.

---

3. Built in 1836-38 on the corner of St. Charles and Common Streets, diagonally opposite the Exchange Hotel. Its dining room was locally thought "one of the most highly finished apartments in America" (*Norman's New Orleans*, 141-142). Apparently it was a bit too grand and expensive for the artists.

4. Theodore Sidney Moise, 1806-1883, portrait painter, born in Charleston, South Carolina.

5. Possibly William Wilson who "painted portraits about 1840-45 with a felicitous coloring; his heads of Porter, the editor, and of Richards, the publisher, of the *Spirit of the Times*, and others, were much esteemed" (Tuckerman, *Book of the Artists*, 68).

6. That is, the brother of G. P. A. Healy. Neither the *Reminiscences* of the latter nor his biography by his daughter mention this brother.

7. According to *Norman's New Orleans* (169-172) G. Cooke's National Gallery had been opened in 1844 at 13 St. Charles Street. For Rothermede read Peter F. Rothermel (1817-1895); Chapman was probably John Gadsby Chapman (1808-1889); for them consult Tuckerman, *Book of the Artists* (437-438, 216-222). In addition to the pictures mentioned by Waugh, Cooke had Leutze's "Deliver us from Evil," a landscape by Boddington, four landscapes by Doughty, a portrait of Davy Crockett, by Chapman, in forest costume and "as large as life."

8. Mrs. Steele, from "western New York state," at the beginning of this year had

The warm weather now set in and the citizens were leaving for various watering places, for it was expected that the coming summer would be very sickly. Things looked dull; we were in no very comfortable circumstances, our funds were not abundant, and in order to replenish the purse, we had to determine on some plan for future operations. While cogitating on our affairs, an article in the N. Orleans Tropic, copied from the St. Louis Reveille caught my attention. It was an expedition to the Rocky Mountains, under the command of Captain J. C. Fremont of the U. S. Topographical Engineers, sent out by order of the government,—to consist of *gentlemen* properly educated, and to the number of one hundred. It was stated that the expedition would be absent about three years at least.[9] I read it to my friend, who instantly proposed our joining, if possible and after some conversation I sat down and drew up the draft of a letter which meeting his views it was mailed the next morning directed to Capt Fremont at St. Louis, Mo.

Our minds became forthwith completely filled with vivid pictures of the sublime scenery of that region. The desire of going into a region so remote and of seeing the red sons of the forest in all their native habits so occupied our thoughts that it became an all absorbing topic with us. We talked with a friend on the subject, who promised to bring to our rooms, a friend of his, who had been to the Rocky Mountains where he had spent eleven years among trappers and hunters, and was well acquainted with the various indian tribes, and was conversant with several of their languages. To this gentleman I shewed our letter, on reading which, he very politely offered to add a postscript recommending us to the attention of the captain. In Col. Charles Warfield we found an agreeable acquaintance, full of anecdote and incident of travel, which he relates with much

---

been in St. Louis on her way to New Orleans; the editor of the *New Era* (4 January 1845) thought her "beautiful and highly finished productions" showed her "genius for seizing and fixing the expression of permanent and prevailing character, without which, you have not the *likeness* but merely the effigy of that likeness." J. L. Chester (Julian Cramer) met her at Davenport, Iowa, 29 July 1845: "Mrs. Steele, the accomplished . . . artist, who, after a winter passed in copying the features of the *Orleanois*, thought it best to refresh her eye by sketching the (perhaps) more inspiring features of Nature, as displayed by the 'Father of Waters' in the neighborhood of the Falls" (McDermott, "An Upper Mississippi Excursion," 21). If Mrs. Steele was the widow of Daniel Steele, she had been painting miniatures in the Mississippi Valley at least since 1837.

9. "Captain Fremont is now in this city organizing his Rocky Mountain exploring expedition. His command will consist of one hundred men, as authorized by government, to be well paid and appointed, and it is requisite that they be gentlemen and well educated. The company it is expected will be out for a period of three years, and we may anticipate valuable results from their explorations" (*Weekly Reveille*, 17 April 1845, p. 323). Actually Frémont was still in the East at this time; he did not reach St. Louis until about six weeks later.

interest. He is a young man of good appearance, agreeable manners and pleasant wit. Among the Indians he was known as Wa-pes-ta or White plume, from his habit of wearing a white feather in his hat. He gave us a great deal of information relative to the duties required of those who go on such expeditions. We were, each, furnished with a letter of introduction to Captain Fremont, by him, and as soon as we could complete our arrangements, we prepared to start for St. Louis in the state of Missouri, to have an interview with the chief himself. Having packed up all our pictures and other properties which we did not require in our travels, we gave them in charge to John B Nixon Esqr. of N Orleans, to be forwarded to Jacob Magee of Mobile, Ala, for safe keeping whilest we should be absent. Mr. Magee was brother-in-law of my friend John B. Tisdale.

On the 8th of May we embarked on board the steam Boat Superb, captain Frost, commander and quitted N Orleans on a Thursday evening. Previous to starting up the Missippi, we moved down the river, and took on board some sixty Dutch emigrants, from the ship Victoria. These imigrants had not yet set foot on American soil, for, they had just arrived from Europe, and passed without delay, from the deck of one vessel to that of the other. It afforded those on the steam boat a fund of amusement to see those awkward, clumsy creatures, sliding down planks from the lofty deck of the ship to our comparatively low craft. Their uncouth figures, clad in the uncouth dresses of their own fader-land, many of them wearing thick wooden shoes, reminded me of the pictures of Teniers, and furnished fine studies for the pencil. As soon as the transfer had been completed, we turned and passed up the river on our voyage. As we passed our point of embarkation we perceived many of our friends with whom we exchanged salutes, they were soon lost to sight for our boat was rapidly steming the mighty Father of Waters.

I should have remarked, that a short time before starting from the wharfs, an old fellow from Mobile came on board as a passenger, and seeing us standing together at the gangway, advanced and saluted my friend with, "Ah my dear friend Mr. Tissel how do you do," then turning to me he put out his hand but had scearcily began to speak when turning on him a look of contempt, I said in a stern tone, 'begone dog,' the poor miserable being, was electrified in a moment and I saw no more of him for some time. Now, this disgusting mass of mortality had engendered in me a loathing toward him, he was so hogish, crafty and mean I could not bear the sight of him, and I had, when in Mobile, ordered him never to attempt to speak to me; but, as he is a cringing, cowardly reptile, without one spark of humanity in his composition, and most probably dreading my vengeance for his villianous conduct some few months ago, thought to avert it by fawning, verifying the saying "conscience makes cowards of us all," he knew he deserved a thrashing at my hands, and feared me.

It is a remarkable fact, and must have come under the notice of many in their journey through life, that cowardise is a sure concommitant of tyrany. This fellow who has been known to seize the culinary utensils of a poor family who were tenants of his, at the very time they were cooking their dinner, because they owed him a trifle of rent, will quail before the angry glance of a mere stripling, so conscious is he of his pusilamimity.

Seeing the effect my presence had on him, I determine to draw amusement from his fears, accordingly where ever I saw him, whether walking, standing, or sitting, I managed to terrify him by appearantly hostile movements. I would approach when he would be in conversation with some of the passengers, and striking my stick firmly on the deck, would walk up with a quiet meaning in my look, regard him for a moment or two and pass on. At such times he ceased talking and generally contrived to move away as fast as his trembling limbs would carry him. Thus I kept him in continual hot water.

On one occasion when the boat stopped to wood I went on shore and percieving my *fat friend* coming down to the boat, I commenced twirling my stick in irish fashion around my fingers, as soon as I caught his eye. I was directly in his path. Instantly he ceased the air which he was humming; his face turned pale, his limbs quivered with fear and seizing a piece of fence rail which lay in his path, declaired he would knock me down if I touched him. I kept on, still twirling the stick, without speaking. When comming up to a perrogue or dug out, in which Tisdale was lolling I began to converse with my comrade without seeming to know that I had sceared old Billy Ostell, who made his way on board with the utmost speed.

The scenery on the banks of the Missippi presents nothing interesting to the traveller, except the sugar plantations, and they only in a pecuniary point of view. For miles beyond the margin of the river, the country is low and flat, indeed generally lower than the river, in consequence of which it is subject to innundation. In order to guard against this, the owners of land are obliged to raise levees or artificial banks to the stream. These are of considerable breadth and sufficiently high to keep the water within its proper channel, except on very extraordinary floods. A short time since a vast extent of country was overflowed to the great destruction of property and great amount of sickness.

The Missippi advances at the rate of three miles per hour and is very excentric in its movements. Its muddy waters are constantly boiling, and it is considered very unsafe to bathe in on account of its numberless eddies. Its yellowish color is derived from the waters of the Missouri which forms a junction with it some miles about [above] the city of St. Louis. This water we were obliged to drink. For a graphic description of this stream I would refer the reader to Joe Cowell's Thirty Years among the Players.[10]

We found the captain of the Superb a very quiet, agreeable man, who performed the duties of his station without the accompaniments of noise and bluster, formerly so peculiar to western commanders, but now so happily so rare that it is a pleasure to sail with those of the present day. His first clerk, Mr. Perkins, behaved in a very polite manner to us during the trip.

After getting beyond the state of Luisiana, the sugar plantations began gradually to disappear, then the cotton fields and were succeeded by hemp, tobacco and corn.

The scenery now began to assume a more pleasing aspect. The land undulated in a rather picturesque style. Here and there, large masses of rock rose from the water's edge with something of an attempt at sublimity. Sometimes a continuous range of strata would continue to add to the grandeur of the shore, and, with the bold outlines of the main land combined with many islands and frequent windings of the stream, present many beautiful vistas, yet not of interest sufficient to command the attention of the artist. The mineral wealth of this portion of the Union now began to make itself manifest in the various shot towers which were erected on the many rocky crags to our left.

We now came to the junction of the Ohio and the Missippi, where New Cairo flourishes in extreme loneliness. It can boast of one hotel and a few log huts some little distance out of town, occupied by germans who live by hunting and fishing in summer, and by the sale of vegitables. There are also some steam boat hotels doing a large buisiness. Passengers stop here for exchange of boats to Louisville, St. Louis N Orleans & Cincinatti.[11]

---

10. "A Bath-brick finely pulverized and stirred up in a pailful of spring water may give a conceived resemblance of its color and consistence" (p. 92). Cowell was traveling in 1829.

11. "Where the sound of a busy population should be heard, there is nothing but the hum of insects to break the pervading stillness, and the grasshopper chirps in places where commerce and industry would gladly resort . . . the only trade carried on . . . is in supplying steamboats with wood . . . Such is Cairo at this day . . . its

At length we reached our destination and were surprised at the great number of steam boats lying at the warfs of St. Louis. I am told that there are almost always, sixty, or sixty five, steam boats to be seen at the levee at the same time.[12]

On the morning of the 15th May we arrived at St. Louis.[13] *Our fat friend* who had afforded me so much amusement during the passage, still dreading my vengeance, was anxiously waiting for the boat to come to its moorings, and the moment it was made fast, he seized the first oppertunity and went ashore, after which I saw no more of the old scamp.

Although this city is rapidly growing into great commercial importance, yet it had no attractions for us, there were too many Yankeys and Dutch there to please those who know any thing of the south.

Shortly after going on shore we were going up Washington avenue, I met Captain La Vergy with whom I had become acquainted at Tuxaloosa Alabama.[14] The gentleman invited [us] to his boat which lay along side of the Superb, during our stay in St. Louis. We now made enquiries for Captain Fremont at the Planter's House and were directed to call on Colonel Brant[15] for information. The door was opened by a black servant who at first was very polite, but the moment we asked for Captain Fremont, he behaved very rudely, telling us that he knew nothing about him,

---

improvements suffering from neglect, and its whole aspect desolate and repulsive" (letter signed "B", dated Cairo, June, 1846, in St. Louis *New Era*, 10 July 1846). At this time Cairo had about fifty buildings and two hundred people.

12. Another traveler who visited St. Louis about this time wrote: "In the morning I discovered that we were in a large and rapidly improving place of forty thousand inhabitants, that our hotel was a palace, and that there was a brisk and important commerce carrying on with places up the various neighboring streams . . . and with cities, whose names even had scarcely, if ever, been heard on the European side of the Atlantic. Boats at the wharf were getting up their steam for Galena and Dubuque, bringing back cargoes of lead;—excursion boats to the St. Peter's River, Lake Pepin, and the falls of St. Anthony, touching at Prairie du Chien, and not occupying ten days, and with an excellent table all the way;—boats for Peoria and Peru, up the Illinois River;—others for Jefferson City and Independence, up the Missouri; but far the greater number were placarded about for Cincinnati and Pittsburgh, on the Ohio, whilst the largest boats were for New Orleans, touching at Memphis, Vicksburg, and Natchez. Here was an amount of business truly astounding, and I could not help saying to myself,—If there is a place in the whole of the American Union that bids fair for permanent prosperity it is this, St. Louis!" (James, *Rambles in the United States*, 144-145).

13. Arrival listed in the *Missouri Republican* on Friday morning, 16 May 1845; the boat was scheduled to leave again for New Orleans on the 19th.

14. A Captain Lavargy in February, 1846, commanded a steamboat on which Sir Charles Lyell returned from Tuscaloosa to Mobile (*Second Visit*, II, 77).

15. Lieutenant-Colonel Joshua B. Brant had resigned from the army in 1839 after twenty-seven years of service. At this time he was living on the northeast corner of Fourth and Washington. His first wife was Elizabeth Lovejoy, a sister-in-law to General Leavenworth; his second (1829) was Sarah Benton, daughter of Samuel and Mary Benton, niece of the Senator. Consult Heitman, *Historical Register of the U. S. Army*, I, 241; Edwards, *Great West*, 197-198; *Green's St. Louis Directory for 1845*.

and began very quckly to shut the door in our faces. Never was I so mortified in my life, we could not understand why such rude treatment should be offered to us. Turning away in disgust, we now directed our steps to the American Fur company, where we learned that Captain F was still in Washington City, but his authorized agent Dr James McDowell[16] lodged at the city Hotel and from him we could learn all the information we required. To the City Hotel we accordingly directed our steps. In the office of this hotel I found an old acquaintance, Mr. Theoren Barnum, nephew of the celebrated David Barnum of Baltimore.[17] He is one of the proprietors, and was very civil and obliging in giving us much information. Here we found that Dr. McDowell had left for Jefferson city about a week before our arrival, from which place he intended to go to Independence.

The following day we called upon a countryman of mine, Mr. Kirkpatrick,[18] who some years ago had been introduced to [me] by letter, in Hillboro N Carolina, with the view of becoming my pupil. We found him at the Paul House,[19] on Second Street, laboring hard at his easel, and as full of dreamy enthusiasm as ever—and not much improved in his profession.

The second interview we had with Mr. Barnum we related our adventure at the house of Col Brant and were advised to go to the Colonel's Tobacco Warehouse where we would be sure of seeing a polite gentlman. We called, and were recieved very courteously indeed, but no sooner did we make known the object of our visit, than he answered us exactly as his servant had done. Mr. Barnum kindly explained such conduct to us by saying "that so many persons were enquiring after captain Fr. that Col B

---

16. He was one of the ten children of James McDowell and Susanna Smith Preston, who were married in 1818. His father was governor of Virginia, 1843-45. Elizabeth McDowell, who married Thomas Hart Benton, was his father's sister. In 1845 young James was a practicing physician in St. Louis. He accompanied the Third Expedition only as far as Fort Bent, returning to St. Louis in the fall of 1845. Since his wife was a daughter of Colonel Brant by his second marriage, he was a great-nephew of Benton's as well as a nephew of Benton's wife. Consult *DAB*, XVI, 30-31; Edwards, *Great West*, 198; Frémont, *Memoirs*, 425-426; *Abert*, "Journal," 427; *Green's St. Louis Directory for 1845*.

17. Theron (or Theoren) Barnum, born in Vermont in 1803, was associated with his uncle David in Barnum's Hotel, Baltimore, as early as 1827. In 1840 he came to St. Louis and operated the City Hotel at Third and Vine until 1852. From 1854 to 1864 he managed Barnum's Hotel (built 1854); he died in St. Louis in 1878 (Scharf, *History of St. Louis*, II, 1442-1443).

18. His name does not appear in the city directories for the 1840's.

19. The Paul House stood on the corner of Second and Walnut, opposite the Catholic Cathedral. "The establishment, just opened, is similar in its character to European and Eastern houses, in which families and gentlemen are supplied with apartments, furnished or unfurnished, upon reasonable terms" (*Missouri Republican*, 18 June 1845).

had completely lost his patience." That was no reason why a civil question put by a stranger should not have recieved a civil answer.[20]

Next day while walking about the streets, I proposed that we should go to Jefferson city, and see Dr McDowell who, probably would be able to tell us what our chances of going with the expedition might be.

---

20. Colonel Brant had reason enough to lose his patience, if not his manners. The excitement over the expedition and eagerness to take part in it reached its height two weeks later on 2 June 1845 when Frémont was in town. The *Reveille* reported on 3 June (p. 378): "Yesterday morning we found ourselves, with others, near the enclosure opposite the Planters' Warehouse, endeavoring to hear what Captain Fremont's ideas were in relation to his contemplated mountain expedition. He was, at the time, attempting to address a motley crowd of French, Irish, Dutch and Mountain men, to the number of several hundred, who had surrounded and were importuning him to obtain the much desired 'diamond gudgeon' of this government affair. The Captain was disposed to gratify them, and accordingly mounted the most convenient rostrum, which was near,—the old rickety fence which bounds the enclosure. He had commenced and was going on with his remarks, which could not be heard, however, except by those who were immediately crowding round him, when a sudden pressure of the crowd broke down the fence, and over went the crowd, Captain and all, embracing their mother earth. About this time, a well-meaning Irishman, who had been standing on the corner of Second street, not knowing what all the fuss was about, rushed up with the idea that it was a 'big fight,' shouting at the top of his lungs, 'fair play! fair play! and be d - - d to yez—don't you see the mon's down?'

"The American Fur Company finally came to the rescue of the Captain, who, to say the truth, must have been worried almost to death by the *violent respect* of the populace, and re-assured and re-mounted upon his pedal extremities, in the body of an ox cart, he again began his harangue, of which we could distinguish but such broken sentences as these—'Those who desire to go—fifty men—good riflemen and packers—been to the Mountains before—are not such—discharge them before I get up.' We heard something about his making *something* known through the public press. We shall issue an extra as soon as we shall have been apprized of the nature of it, and we will give the information to prevent a crowd about our office. Suffice it to say, that the meeting had one good tendency, it took the *starch* out of many a good fellow, who had given up all his heart to the desire of going and giving his energies to the cause of science and his country, consequently, the mountain fever has greatly abated, the blood has fallen from fever heat to somewhat below its natural temperature, and the whole affair, among green hands at least, is considered below par value."

CHAPTER II

JEFFERSON CITY—FREMONT—THE FRONTIER

AFTER SUN-DOWN on the evening of the 17th May we left St. Louis on the steam boat Wapello, to prosecute our enquiries. The captain of this boat (Eaton) was formerly in the US army.[21] We found him a very agreeable [man]. While conversing with him upon various subjects connected with travel, I remarked, that I had never been in the habit of carrying weapons of any sort, and although I had seen much of the world, I rarely found myself annoyed. Whereupon he made this polite remark, "there is one weapon with which a gentleman is always provided, and it is the most serviceable that is known and will afford greater protection than any other, it is—politeness." This very flattering compliment I received with all due courtecy. The observation was worthy of remembrance, and so I have recorded it.

Not far from Jefferson city is a cave close to the river, where the celebrated travellers, Lewis and Clark, wintered when going to and returning from the Rocky Mountains.[22]

1845 May

About 2 o'clock on Monday the 19th we landed at the capitol of the State of Missouri, and by the recommendation of our captain, we put up at the Missouri House,[23] kept by Mr. James Herndon, a native of Virginia, but whether he belonged to one of the first families of that ancient state, we were not informed. He was a fine, goodhearted fellow however, and rendered our stay with him very agreeable. From his lady and family we recieved many kind attentions, for which we shall long remember them with great respect. We were again doomed to bear an other disappointment, for we found that the gentleman whom we sought, had, a few days

---

21. "The superior and well known steamer WAPELLO, N. J. Eaton, master, will resume her regular weekly trips from St. Louis to Glasgow" (*Missouri Republican*, 16 May 1845). Nathaniel Jackson Eaton in 1822 had entered the military academy as a cadet from Massachusetts, had become a first lieutenant in 1836, and was dropped in 1837. Except for the Black Hawk War most of his service between 1827 and 1835 was performed at Jefferson Barracks. From 1837 to 1849 he was master of various steamboats on the western rivers; in 1861 he was made Post Warden of the Harbor of St. Louis. He died 29 March 1883 (Heitman, *Historical Register U. S. Army*, I, 395; Cullum, *Biographical Register U.S.M.A.*, I, 322).

22. *Sic!* But at least they stopped to look at it. This place was probably the Tavern Rocks, above Femme Osage Creek, of which Clark wrote in 1804 "we passed a large *Cave* . . . (called by the french the *Tavern*—about 120 feet wide by 40 feet Deep & 20 feet high many different immages are Painted on the Rock at this place the Inds. & French pay omage. Many names are wrote on the rock. . . ." (Thwaites, *Original Journals of Lewis and Clark*, I, 27).

23. "The huge stone structure with spacious galleries, in the middle ground [of the accompanying view], is the Missouri Hotel. . . ." (Edmund Flagg's account of Jefferson City in Dana, *The United States Illustrated*, I, 139).

previous to our landing, gone on to Boonville, some forty miles, up the river, to purchase horses and mules. It was my intention as soon as we learned this to have taken a horse and cross[ed] the country to see him, but declined doing so on being told by a gentleman from that place, just arrived, that the Doctor had that morning left Boonville for Independence, still higher up the river and not far from the plains. Here was an other damper to our spirit. In our present position we deemed it advisable, as the river was the most probable route of Captain Fremont and party, to remain where we were until his coming, when we should then learn our fate.

In the mean time, as our funds were not by any means abundant I proposed to follow my profession and by that means replenish the common purse. In this we were rather fortunate, as I had several sitters to me in my new style of full length profiles.

In our leisure moments we wandered over the city and adjoining country, made a few sketches and examined the geology of that region. By the politeness of a gentleman, whom we afterwards learned was a judge, we were shown over the state House, in the library of which, we saw a full-length portrait of the Honl Tho's H. Benton. It was painted by a german by the name of Guerke who never got completely paid for his labor. It is considered a good likeness, but as a work of art, did not please me. It is finished too much in the style of a cabinet picture and wanted that boldness which characterizes large gallery paintings. It was to have cost one thousand dollars, and to have been paid for by subscription. How it failed I cannot recollect.[24]

---

24. In the year [blank in ms] John H. Watson Esqr son of the then Post Master of St. Louis, anxious to pay a compliment to the great senator of Missouri, asked Col Benton to sit to the artist Gercke, for a full-length portrait, which he (Mr. W) commissioned Gercke to paint. The price agreed upon was one thousand dollars. When the picture was compleated, the painter finding some delay in the payments, threatened to put up the portrait at auction in front of the Court House if it was not paid for within a given number of days. The friends of Col Benton not wishing to wound that gentleman's feelings by such a public disposition of the work, immediately took the matter in hand raised the amount among themselves and paid the artist. The above statement I recieved from the clerk of the Comn Plea court, since I wrote the notice of the state House. St. Louis, Octr 1850—WAUGH.

John Philip Gerke came to St. Louis in 1838 and died there in 1849. The *Missouri Republican* on 13 December 1839 mentioned a full length portrait of Benton hanging in Gerke's gallery: it had been "taken last summer at the request of some of his political admirers . . . when this picture was undertaken, we hinted at the propriety of the artist going on the no-credit system, and requiring his pay in advance. Our counsel, if report be true, was disregarded, and the artist is likely to have his summer's labor rewarded only by broken promises. . . . If we were at liberty to advise, . . . we would say to the artist—make the cravat a little wider, put on a pair of asses ears, and send the painting to Koch's museum, and you can make a spec[ulation] out of it." According to the *Daily Bulletin* (10 February 1840) Gerke had been commis-

The state House stands on a very commanding elevation close to the river, and present[s] rather an imposing appearance to travellers as they approach the city by water. It is built of greyish-white limestone, or marble, very substantial in the execution, but far from correct in architectural taste. There is no loftiness in its proportions, the ceilings are low, and altogether, in the interior, it lacks the characteristics of a state capitol. For the notice it recieves, it is entirely indebted to natural advantages of location. Otherwise it would appear what it really is, a low, tasteless mass of stone and mortar.[25] I made a sketch from the river back above, the most eligable point for a painting of it.

Whilst standing on the landing in company with the Revd Mr. Hedges,[26] the episcopal clergyman, I learned that the Bishop of the Diocese, the Right Revd Cicero S. Hawks, was expected on the steam boat which was then coming down the river. I was acquainted with many of the members of that dignitary's family, but had never seen the Bishop, and waited to see the youngest prelate of the protestant episcopal church in the United States, he being only thirty-five years of age at this time.[27]

Bishop Hawks is of small stature, well made, with an inclination to fulness of habit. His complexion is so like an Indian's, that he might be, nay! he *has* been taken for a descendant of that race,[28] indeed, his features

---

sioned by John H. Watson to do the portrait for the party; if impossible to raise funds by subscription, Watson had guaranteed to pay the $1,000 out of his own pocket.

25. Jefferson City had been laid out in 1823, incorporated in 1825, and made the capital of Missouri in 1826. The first capitol was burned in 1837; the new building, erected at a cost of $350,000, was occupied by the legislature in 1840-41; it was destroyed by fire in 1911. Edmund Flagg wrote: "The view from the bluffs on which the Capitol stands, and especially from the dome of the Capitol itself, is extensive and imposing. Away from the west comes sweeping on the turbid Missouri, and is beheld, gliding along the base of the cliff, mile after mile, as it rolls impetuously onward. . . . The river-reach commanded from this point, both above and below, is one of the grandest and most extensive in the West; and boats are seen from the windows of the Capitol approaching the city, breasting the mighty current or hurried along by its force, long before they reach the landing" (Dana, *The United States Illustrated*, I, 138). In the engraving (dated *circa* 1853) reproduced in the present book, "nothing of the city is here beheld . . . its streets and houses being all of them half a mile distant, along the brow of the hill, away to the left" (*Ibid.*, 139).

26. Chaplin S. Hedges commenced his labors as Rector of Grace Church, Jefferson City, on 22 December 1843; in May, 1846, he reported seventeen communicants. Bishop Hawks, summarizing his 1845 visitation of the Missouri Diocese, noted that he spent Tuesday, Wednesday, and Thursday, May 20, 21, and 22, in Jefferson City: "Here we have a substantial Church edifice built of stone, commenced years since under a former Clergyman, and now completed by our present Missionary at this station, the Rev. Chaplin S. Hedges." Consult *Journal of the Fifth and Sixth Annual [Episcopal] Conventions*, 49; *Journal of the Seventh Annual Convention*, 9, 46.

27. Cicero Stephen Hawks was born at Newbern, South Carolina, 26 May 1812, ordained in 1836, appointed rector of Christ Church in St. Louis in 1843, and made Bishop of Missouri on 20 October 1844. He died at St. Louis 19 April 1868 (Hyde and Conard, *Encyclopedia of the History of St. Louis*, II, 1003-1004).

28. Bishop Hawks, when at Niagra some time since, was accosted by an old Indian

and hair are remarkable for their "*Native American*" characteristics. He is extremely neat in his personal appearance, as becomes a gentleman, and unaffectedly courteous to all who are acquainted with him. That evening I heard him preach a sermon, which was remarkable for its truth and eloquence. This was on the 23rd day of May. The next day we called on Mr. Hedges and by him were duly presented. I took his the Bishop's likeness in the new style, at the house of S Mansfield Bay Esqr[29] who was formerly attorney general of this state, where he was staying. Mr. Bay & his lady, afterwards sat to me also. Mr. Hedges and others also had theirs taken.

Our time was rendered agreeable by the kind attention of many of the citizens, and particularly by the people at whose house we put up.

At length, on the 6th June, the steam Boat Henry Bry was descried coming up the river, and upon its stopping at the landing we learned that the renowned scientific travellor of whom we were in quest was on board with his company.[30] We no sooner had heard this than we were on board, but could not get a sight of him. The boat was now about starting, the object of our visit had not been accomplished. It had in fact moved from the landing when Tisdale proposed that we should go with her, and we would have a fair oppertunity of seeing and conversing with captain Fremont. No sooner said than done,—we took passage and after supper that evening, were introduced to the chief, who recieved us very courteously indeed, but informed us that his party was entirely filled

---

squaw who had taken her seat beside him, on a bench, with "what tribe"? the Bishop answered, "no Indian" when the squaw replied, "dont tell lies," and again asked "what tribe"? but the Bishop again said "me no Indian." The poor squaw firmly believing that he was of the red race, doubted his truth,—turned a look of contempt on him and flinging his hand, which she had taken in hers from her, uttered an emphatic pshaw and turned away. This anecdote was told me by the Bishop himself and is, as near as I can well recollect, in substance, as he related it to me, but looses much of its excellence by [my poor way of telling it].—WAUGH.

29. Samuel Mansfield Bay was born at Hudson, New York, in 1810 and died in St. Louis, 1849. He came to Missouri in 1833 and practiced law in Franklin County. From 1839 to 1845 he was attorney-general of the state. At this time he was a partner of Abiel Leonard in Jefferson City. In 1847 he moved to St. Louis. Consult Conard, *Encyclopedia of the History of Missouri*, I, 186-187; W. V. N. Bay, *Reminiscences of the Bench and Bar of Missouri*, 165-171.

30. "Captain Fremont, and his company, consisting of about sixty men, left this city on the steamer *Henry Bry*, for Independence, on Thursday evening . . ." (*Missouri Republican*, Saturday, 7 June 1845). The *Henry Bry*, built in St. Louis, owned by John W. Luke, Robert W. Ayres, James Roberts, and E. F. Chouteau, and commanded by Luke, was operating regularly in packet service between St. Louis and Weston, Missouri (*Weston Journal*, 12 April 1845). On 11 November 1845 the boat struck a snag below Island No. 25 in the lower Mississippi; Captain Freligh was in command on this trip to New Orleans. The *Missouri Republican* (15 November 1845) announced that "most of the wardrobe of Ludlow & Smith's theatrical company was on board, and is understood to have been lost."

up, an artist[31] was appointed by government, and regretted very much that our letter did not reach him until he got to St. Louis. Had it been sent to Washington instead, I might have received the appointment. He, however invited us to go on with him to the landing at Kansas, and then to his camp on the borders of the plains.

I was not a little disappointed with the manners and personal appearance of Captain F.[32] I found him a pale intellectual looking young man, modest and unassuming, seemingly more accustomed to the refinements and luxuries of life, than to the toils and dangers of the wilderness. I had pictured to myself a man of herculean frame, of a loud voice, and rough manners. What was my surprise to find him the reverse of all these—small in stature, and delicately formed,—voice low and musical, and of manners bland and gentlemanly. I could scarcely believe him to be the man who had gone through so much hardship in the previous expeditions. He had no outward indications of the mountain traveller about him; all was quiet, well bred, and retireing. His conversation was modest, instructive and unpretending, with a grace and suavity that irresistably won all who approached him. Yet in his eye, you saw something which shewed contempt of danger, and proclaimed him a man to be obeyed under all circumstances. Although he had two lieutenants[33] with him,—graduates of the Military Academy at West Point,—he alone, wore the garb of an officer,—undress frock coat. With his men he was kind and affable attending to their wants and studying their comfort. The Expedition being formed for scientific and not military purposes, it partook more of the character of the civilian than the soldier. It is true it was armed and officered by military men, but then that was for self protection along the wild and unknown route over which it had to pass,

31. Edward M. Kern of Philadelphia. "He was . . . an accomplished artist; his skill in sketching from nature and in accurately drawing and coloring birds and plants made him a valuable accession to the expedition" (Frémont, *Memoirs*, I, 425).

32. For Frémont consult Dellenbaugh, *Frémont and '49;* Nevins, *Frémont, Pathmarker of the West.* Neither these writers nor any others, including Frémont himself, have much to contribute about the early stages of the Third Expedition. Only the writer who signed himself François des Montaignes has given us any detail worth quoting; he will be cited below.

33. James W. Abert, son of Col. J. J. Abert, graduated from the Military Academy in July 1842, and at this time was serving in the Topographical Engineers. He was brevetted lieutenant-colonel 25 June 1864 and resigned because of injuries. For the next five years he was a merchant in Cincinnati, from 1869 to 1871 he was an examiner of patents, and from 1871 to 1878 he was professor of English Literature at the University of Missouri. John J. Peck, born 4 January 1821 in Manlius, New York, graduated in the class after Abert. Brevetted major in 1847, he resigned 31 March 1853. He reentered the service as Brigadier-General of Volunteers, 9 August 1861, and was named major-general a year later. He died at Syracuse, New York, 21 April 1878, where for twelve years he had been president of the New York State Life Insurance Company. Consult Cullum, *Biographical Register USMA*, II, 151-152, 158-160.

as well as for providing themselves with food when their provisions would give out. It was therefore not deemed necessary to observe the same strict etiquette as in the regular army, at least until properly in the performance of duty. Among the company were many droll characters, mostly from the Western states, with a few canadian voyageurs, who had been out with the captain on a former expedition.[34] There was an Indian of the chinook tribe, who was returning to his people. This boy captain F. had brought into the U States, by permission of his people, and now was going back with the benefits of a civilized education. He did not appear quite at his ease in the habiliments of a white man. His step was not as elastic in boots as it would be in mocasins. He spoke English very well, and appeared to be an intellegent fellow.[35] Captain F told me that when this youth would get back to his people and would relate what he saw among the whites, he would not be believed, but would be looked upon as a liar, so circumscribed are the Indians in their ideas of the powers and numerical force of the pale faces.

---

34. Aboard the *Henry Bry* "there were some twenty odd souls who, from their independent swagger and jovial carriage, appeared to belong to some party about to start for Oregon or California. They were mostly young Americans, healthy and full of fun and elasticity, yet, there were some four or five others aboard the vessel, who preserved a more serious exterior, and now and then gave utterance to some pithy ejaculation of contempt at the sayings and doings of the set of greenhorns, who they felt confident of being their inferiors in the coming profession of mountain traveling. . . . These men were Canadian men [i. e., American French], experienced in the manner and modes of exploring wild mountainous regions, or threading desert plains, of killing the wild beasts of these regions, of trading with and conciliating the barbarous inhabitants thereof, of packing animals—of everything, in fact, which is necessary to be done during an expedition among wild and savage Indians and through untrodden regions . . . the present cargo of the Henry Bry was by no means a choir of Psalm-singers, nor quakers. They ate, drank, talked, sang, played cards and smoked cigars when they pleased and as much as they pleased. When the boat stopped at a wood yard, every one of them must need go ashore and shoot at a mark. When they had no balls, they must go ashore anyhow to jump and run foot races. . . ." (François des Montaignes, "The Plains," *Western Journal and Civilian*, IX, 71-72). This writer has been identified as Isaac Cooper (Wagner-Camp, *The Plains and the Rockies*). Cooper and seventeen others of "American" name were among the thirty-three who returned from Fort Bent to St. Louis with Lieut. Abert in November, 1845 (Abert, "Journal," 7, 75).

35. "November 24 [1843].—At this place [the Mission on the Columbia] . . . a Chinook Indian, a lad of nineteen, who was extremely desirous to 'see the whites,' and make some acquaintance with our institutions, was received into the party, under my special charge, with the understanding that I would again return him to his friends. He had lived for some time in the household of Mr. Perkins, and spoke a few words of the English language. . . . Our Chinook Indian . . . accompanied me to Washington, and, after remaining several months at the Columbia college, was sent by the Indian department to Philadelphia, where among other things, he learned to read and write well, and speak the English language with some fluency. He will accompany me in a few days to the frontier of Missouri, whence he will be sent with some one of the emigrant companies to the village of the Dalles of the Columbia" (Frémont, *Report of the Exploring Expedition . . . 1842, and . . . 1843-44*, 197, 290).

The morning of the 9th we disembarked at Kansas landing.[36] Our luggage was taken out to the camp in the baggage wagons, and in the evening we accompanied the two lieutenants and the artist to Westport, where they stayed all night at the Hotel, but Tisdale, Mr. Kerns, and myself set out for the camp, where we arrived a little after sundown.

The scenery from the landing to Westport was somewhat picturesque, the ground undulating and heavily timbered, but, from Westport to the camp it was comparatively level. This distance from the river to the camp, I suppose, must have been about nine or ten miles, just far enough to qualify us for a comfortable sleep, even on the ground. When we reached the ground, a scene of great novelty presented itself. The location chosen for the camp was a gentle eminence surrounded or nearly so, with forest, and a clear spring a short distance below gave out a sufficient body of water to form a rivulet.[37] The grass was high and green, wild flowers in great variety added indescribable charm to the beauty of the scene. The camp furniture lay scattered about in rich profusion, waggons were here and there, while the horses and mules ranged at large over the prairie, luxuriating in the young and tender grass. The men were cooking supper, the smell of which was born on the evening air, to our keen olfactories long before we reached the spot. Loud talking and laughter, mingled with scraps of songs testified to the existence of cheerful hearts and willing spirits. It was a scene of happy confusion and unrestrained mirth. After smoking a pipe we prepared our bed under the body of a waggon, and, lay down to rest for the night, but scarcely had we fallen asleep when we were awakened by the violence of a storm, accompanied by thunder and lightning. The rain came down in a perfect deluge, it was useless to try and protect ourselves from its merciless fury, for we had nothing but the body of the waggon above our heads to shelter

36. "It was raining in one of those dull moods in which a hazy morning in Missouri is so frequently opened, and by the time we had carried our guns and baggage to a place of security, the wharf or landing was a complete mudhole. The horses had been taken out some three or four miles below us, and we next proceeded to take forth the barrels of flour, of sugar, of coffee, the boxes of rice. . . . Waggons arrived from Westport about eleven, to transport baggage and plunder to the camp which some said was near Westport" (François des Montaignes, "The Plains," *Western Journal and Civilian*, IX, 72). For the early history of Kansas City, which grew from a trading post established by Francis Chouteau in 1821, consult Garraghan, *Catholic Beginnings in Kansas City, Missouri*, and Miller, *The History of Kansas City*, 8-40.

37. The camp was at Boone's Fort, six miles from Westport, according to François des Montaignes ("The Plains," *Western Journal and Civilian*, IX, 72). "The rolls of the prairie before [us] seemed heaved into beautifully rounding waves or surges by some great power, and when we reached the pinnacle of a lofty eminence and beheld the American camp on the prairie before us, it seemed like some distant fleet of vessels at anchor on a heaving sea" (*Ibid.*, 73).

us.[38] Nevertheless, so much are we creatures of circumstances that we slept, and that soundly too, as soon as we had found that we could not better our condition. Although I expected as a matter of course, I should suffer a severe cold from the night's adventure, yet strange to say, I experienced no ill effects from the sound wetting I had recieved. By early dawn we were up, and having repaired to the creek made our toilet and were "dressed" for the day.

The captain who had slept[39] at the house of Maj Cummins,[40] (Indian Agent, I believe) now rode into camp, accompanied by Dr. James McDowell. I was very much struck with the appearance of the doctor. He is a tall well made young man, with rather a handsome face, of a good healthy complexion, and pleasant countenance. Having suffered his beard to grow from the time he was appointed as surgeon and naturalist to the Expedition, it had attained a very respectable size and gave its owner a really fine appearance. Captain F. introduced us to this gentleman, and he acknowledged the receipt of the letters which we bore to him from Mr. Barnum of St. Louis. These we had handed to Captain F. the day before.

Things now began to assume something like order. A couple of tents were pitched, and all hands were buisy in preparation for the long and hazzardous journey before them. Such of the men as could use the needle were set to work on the manufacture of tents and other matters of importance. Under the broad fold of the national standard, and in the presence of the commander, the bivouac of the previous evening, began at once to present the look of a regular camp.[41]

While matters were thus progressing, it was proposed that we should select some farm house on the borders, where we could enjoy the comforts of a civilized life as long as possible. Accordingly Lieutenants Peck and Abert, Mr. Kerns, the artist of the Expedition, Tisdale and myself, set out in search of quarters. After one or two trials we at length found some accommodations in the house of Lindsey Lewis, near the Little Blue, just within the boundary line of the U.S. and within twenty miles of Independence. The farm of Mr. Lewis was well managed by himself and son,

---

38. The rain began at eleven, François des Montaignes reported ("The Plains," *Western Journal and Civilian,* IX, 73); he had a rough night, lying in the corner of an uncovered wagon.

39. "Our Captain was already there" (François des Montaignes, "The Plains," *Western Journal and Civilian,* IX, 73).

40. Richard M. Cummins at this time was agent for the Shawnees, Kickapoos, Kansas, and other tribes at Fort Leavenworth.

41. François des Montaignes described camp activities in some detail (*Western Journal and Civilian,* IX, 146-148).

with the assistance of two hired hands, one of whom was an Indian of the Shawnee tribe, an intelligent and steady youth. The household affairs were under the admirable controul of his lady and daughters. I have seldom met with a more comfortable farm house.

The first evening we spent here we amused ourselves with anecdotes and glee singing. It was a fine calm evening, and the full moon shone sweetly on us, as we pursued our innocent and rational amusements. Next morning after breakfast we returned to the camp and in the evening, again repaired to the farm-house. Thus we continued to do, going and returning, for several days. During all this time we flattered ourselves that the captain might perhaps make arrangements for us in his company. Indeed I thought several times from his manner that he was disposed to take us, but then it was perceptable that there was something which opperated against our going. At length I ventured to approach him upon the subject when he informed me that the letters which we brought with us to him, was from a person who although of a good respectable family, and brave yet he did not stand high with him,[42] therefore they (the letters) were not sufficient [to warrant his] taking us, and that he was accountable to the War Department [for] the exercise of his power, and might be called to account for the abuse of it. "If," said he, "you had a letter from any public character it would be sufficient to justify my conduct in taking you." He was then on the eve of departure and I had no letters that I could make use of without writing to St. Louis, which would take up too much time. As a last recource I proposed writing to Bishop Hawks, and asked him if a letter from that Right Rev gentleman would answer. He said it would, but if it did not come in so many days we would be unable to overtake the party, for if it should be over a hundred miles it would be dangerous for us to follow him. While [I was] writing the letter, captain F. came to the tent and said: "You need not say anything of Mr. Tisdale, for I will not take him." This I did not mention to T but allowed him to add a postscript to my letter to the Bishop, who had been a school mate of his bother's. As soon as I had finished Dr. Talbot,[43] the captain's

42. Since Warfield in 1843 had led a band of Missourians and Texans in an abortive hostile military movement against Santa Fe, authorized by the Texan government, he was hardly the proper sponsor for Waugh to offer Frémont, an army officer on official duty. For a contemporary account of this expedition consult Sage, *Scenes in the Rocky Mountains*, 244 ff.

43. Theodore Talbot had gone out with Frémont on the 1843-44 expedition through the influence of Col. Abert. During the Mexican War he joined the army, serving as first lieutenant in the California battalion. On discharge in February, 1847, he re-enlisted as a second lieutenant and continued in the service until his death (as a major) in April, 1862. Waugh must have written "Dr." by mistake. Talbot's notes of the 1843-44 expedition have been published (Carey, ed., *Talbot's Journals*) but no record for 1845 by him has been found.

secretary, by my request wrote a few lines to Col. Chick[44] at Kansas landing requesting him to have the letter forward[ed] to the care of Robert Cam[p]bell Esq.,[45] of St. Louis, who was requested by Captain Fremont to deliver the letter to Bishop Hawks, and forward the answer without delay. Tisdale then went to Kansas with it and returned the next day.

I have every reason to be thankful to Captain Fremont for the kind and courteous manner he treated me in supplying me with funds in the then exhausted state of my treasury. These funds I promised to return to Col. Benton, at Washington City.

We took leave of the captain and Dr. McDowell on the morning of the 20th and went back to Westport, where we intended stopping until we should hear from St. Louis, but in three days afterward we again went to Mr. Lewis's, where, on the 29th we received the Bishop's letter of recommendation to Captain Fremont. Tisdale was not pleased with its cautious tone and remarked, "That it was just such a letter as he would expect from a parson." However, as the expedition was only two days gone,[46] we determined to see the end of the part we were playing in the matter.

After having made preparation, we started at one o'clock PM. on the 30th, mounted upon a couple of horses belonging to our host who undertook to be our guide. Never did I feel so down hearted in all my life as at that moment, in fact, I was sick in both body and mind. Our position was very peculiar, we had come out, almost, beyond the borders of civil[iz]ation, where it would be difficult to find employment in the pursuit of the Fine arts, in case we should be dissapointed in our expectations, and, to say truth, these expectation[s] now appeared to have but slender chances of fulfilment. I almost cursed my weakness in suffering myself to be thus lead into this wild goose chase, instead of quietly pursuing my profession at home in the states. Here we were, hundreds of miles away from friends and acquaintances, almost without resources and at that moment about to plunge into the ocean of praire to solicit permission to share dangers and hardships for the mere gratification of our curiosity. What could we

---

44. William Miles Chick was born near Lynchburg, Virginia, 1790, came to Missouri in 1822 and to Westport in 1836, and died in 1847. He was one of the original proprietors of Kansas City and moved there in 1843. Consult the reminiscences of his son W. H. Chick, "A Journey to Missouri in 1822" and "The Vicissitudes of Pioneer Life," in *Missouri Valley Historical Society Publications,* I, No. 1 (1921), 97-103 and I, No. 2 (1922), 207-218.

45. Robert Campbell (1804-1879), fur trade merchant (*DAB,* III, 462-463). A number of his letters have been published in *Glimpses of the Past* (Missouri Historical Society), VIII (1941), 3-65.

46. According to François des Montaignes the expedition had moved west at noon on 26 June (*Western Journal and Civilian,* IX, 366).

promise ourselves as a reward for the privations to which we should be exposed. What glories could we hope for after returning, but the mere pleasure of saying, "I have been to the Rocky Mountains." It is true I might be mentioned in the journal of the Expedition as having made such, and such a drawing of this scene, and of that Indian Chief, but, I doubt if it would have resulted in any benefit to me whatever. Two or three years would be consumed in travel which no doubt, would have contributed to the acquisition of geographical knowledge, and perhaps, improved my acquaintance with grand natural scenery, but it would be so much loss to me in the practical part of my profession. These reflections weighed heavily upon me, but having taken the trouble to go thus far I was determined to persevere and see the final result.

Nothing could exceed the placid beauty of the scenery which presented itself to our attention on all sides. Clumps and groves of trees, far and near, decieved the eye with pictures of domestic comfort. The imagination peopled these sequestered spots with the peaceful sons of toil, and all the appurtenances of agricultural life. As we advanced new scenes continually presented themselves to our notice, and, but for the solemn silence which every where prevailed, we could have fancied ourselves riding over the wide, broad lands of some extensive graziers. Now and then we could hear the distant sound of those Indian[s] who are located within the territory and, a stray horse or two told us of our proximity to the wigwams of the red men. As the Indians of the border are peaceable we felt no uneasiness, nor should we have reason to apprehend danger of any sort for the distance we expected to travel. Although the beauty and grandeur of what we saw at that time, now recals itself to my memory in vivid tableaux, yet I could not then enjoy the reality, so depressed were my feelings. Never before did I feel so absolutely lonely as at that moment, and for the first time I began to feel myself growing old.

The traveller who finds himself for the first time on the great american desert[47] feels as much at a loss to find his course across its trackless wilds as he would were he at sea without chart or compass, for there is nothing to guide him in his route. His unfamiliarity with natural objects creates a confusion of ideas in his brain. He cannot readily distinguish between one view and another where all have the same characteristics. Rocks and islands in the ocean of waters may be instantly recognised by the boldly marked or gentle outline, each differing from the other by its geological formation, but, on the great ocean of verdure he cannot so easily discrim-

47. From the time of Long's expedition in 1819-20 this had been the common designation for the Great Plains.

inate between one scene and an other where all are so much alike. Those however, who are accustomed to the prairies soon learn to make their way with as much ease as the mariner over the dark waters of the deep blue sea.

CHAPTER III

IN PURSUIT OF THE THIRD EXPEDITION—FREMONT REJECTS THE ARTIST

THE SUN WAS LOW in the Western horizon as we reached Bull creek, where our host and guide, intended to encamp for that night. Twenty three miles had been passed over since starting from his house and, without feeling fatigued we were glad to come to a halt. At the spot selected for our nights repose we found the remains, or rather the skeleton of a spanish tent which we soon fitted up for our own acco[mmo]dation, and as the architecture of a country is indicative of the taste and refinement of a people, we drew our conclusions as to the character of the persons who left these remains behind them. Now, as I was struck with the contemptitable proportions of this specimen of the frame work of a tent, I fancied it indicative of the narrowness of mind and groveling nature of the New Mexican character, just as much as the small contracted houses of some people bespeak their narrow souls. I, at once placed a very low extimate upon the character of its builders. About four pairs of saplings six or eight feet long are stuck into the ground, and then bent over so as to form a circular arch of four or five feet span. They are placed about two feet apart having others running from end to end in a horizontal position secured by strips of bark after the manner of some of the Indians. Over this slight frame work one or two blankets are spread and thus they construct their own tents. Into such an one we had to creep. Our buffalo robes were spread upon the ground over which the blankets formed a tolerable comfortable mattrass, our saddle bags serving us instead of pillows. The head of the tent was sufficiently protected by a covering of skins, and a fire near the entrance gave us at least some feeling of comfort. Having boiled our coffee we made a hearty supper on corn bread cold boiled ham and fried bacon. The pipes were now lighted and while we smoked talked over our chances of success until it was time to retire. Our horses had been hobbled to prevent them returning to their own abode and with a couple of dogs which Mr. Lewis had brought with him we felt sure of being warned in case of danger, but, yet I could not sleep, so new and peculiar was the position in which I found myself that "with all my weary watchings" I could not win the drousy god to my embrace. In a vast prairie miles away from the habitation of civilized man, close to a creek whose amphibious denizens made the night vocal with their monotonous croakings, whilst the wolves kept howling to the winds that gently swept o'er the surface of the earth, I became nervously wakeful, and thoughts of far off home and friends crowded on my aching brain.

The sky for some time previously had given notice of its vengeful tendency. To the east and west the lightnings played in fitful flashes, presently a voice not to be mistaken was heard in the distance muttering a series of hollow threatenings, large drops of rain began to fall; the breath of the approaching tempest moaned among the foliage of the neighboring woods, and was followed by a perfect deluge such as I have rarely witnessed. When the fury of the storm began we were within our wigwam, my companions on either side of me and a warm birth I had of it, with this advantage over friend Tisdale who prided himself on his sagacity, I was free from the soaking which he received. As he occupied the highest part of the floor the water from the canvass ran under his portion of the bed and gave him a cool bath to counteract the heat of the atmosphere. He had proposed to change sides with Mr. Lewis but the latter gentleman declined his civility and afterwards remarked that "an old hunter knew best how to select his bed."

Occasionly, notwithstanding the ugliness of the night, I fell into a doze from which I would be roused now and then by the barking of some prowling wolves. Once or twice we heard the yelling of Indians but it was in the far distance. Then one of the dogs coming into the tent to seek shelter roused me from another slumber. Sometimes I allowed my imagination to revel with the sounds which proceeded from the banks of the creek, and in the croakings of the frogs to fancy a regular conversation being carried on between two or more persons in an undertone. During the night the dogs growled a good deal and on one occasion they ran off at a furious rate as if in pursuit of something that alarmed them. What it was I could not tell but took it for granted that it was wolves attracted by the smell of meat at our camp.

On the morning of the first of July (the anniversary of my birth day) I was awake and out before sunrise. Tisdale, who prides himself on his acquaintance with camp usages, made himself quite at home, and undertook the preparation of our breakfast, with all the sang froid of a great artist. Our first care however was directed to our horses, one of which had freed himself from his hobble and was straying toward the road homeward, but Tisdale brought him back.

After enjoying a smoke we packed up our traps, saddled our animals and rode off. We had not proceeded far when meeting two Mexicans we learned that Captain Frémont was about one league ahead of us. In one of the Mexicans I recognized a person who had been employed by Captain F. to break mules, at his first camp on the Little Blue. We had proceeded but a short distance when we overtook some waggons on their way to

Santa Fe, from the hands of which we learned that the Expedition was but a few miles ahead of us. Coming to a clear, cool stream of water, we called a halt and made our nooning,—as dining is termed by the traders on this route,—which put us in good plight for our afternoon's ride. At length we reached the top of a hill and percieved the whole party encamped on the plain below us, whose white tents when first seen by us appeared like so many waggons at a halt.[48] Already had the duties of the Expedition wrought a change in the personal appearance of the men, they looked dirty, greasy, and toil worn, and were with much difficulty recognized by those of our party. This, I must confess, did not impress me very favourably. It was plain to me that those engaged, found it rather a different sort of thing from that of a mere hunting excursion, a party of pleasure, or a pic-nic. In a word, the poetry and romance with which I had, in my warm fancy, clothed it, fled like the baseless fabric of a dream with the light that now broke on my newly awakened sences. Not that I ever entertained the idea of its ease and comfort, but, although I knew that it was attended with many discomforts not to say dangers, yet I did not realize its true character until that moment. And if this was so perceptable at the commencement, what was to be expexted as it progressed? Nevertheless I was determined to partake of its hardships if permitted so to do by its commander.

I rode up to the captain's small waggon where I saw his secretary, Mr. Talbot, and was directed to headquarters. While approaching the camp I percieved Dr. McDowell reclining on the floor of the tent, who percieving us, raised his hand as high as his head as if saluting, which act of courtesy I immediately returned, but when he brought it, with energy, down to his knee, I saw the mistake I had made, and translated it into the following exclamation "here are those confounded fellows, sure enough." I may have been wrong in my translation, but I was led into it by a certain peculiarity of manner in the chiefs previous to our quitting them at the first encampment. This was my fancy at the time, a few years afterward I learned, in St. Louis, its reason. The doctor was talking to some person within the tent who was concealed from view. No sooner had I come up to the door than he arose, came out and shook hands with me, and was immediately followed by the captain, in whose face I read as plainly as I could in a printed book, a determination not to let us go with him. I percieved in the manner in which I was recieved although extremely courteous, that our coming was not agreable to him. I now handed him

48. From available material it is not possible to say where Frémont was camping on 1 July 1845. See note 32 above.

the Bishop's letter and whilst he was reading it, walked over to Mr. Talbot. During our conversation I happened to look toward the captain as he was in the act of folding the letter. Presently he came forward and taking me aside, asked me if Mr. Campbell had written to him, as soon as he found that I had communication from that gentleman, told me that the letter of Bishop Hawks was not sufficient and to let the matter drop. "I am placed, said he, in a very peculiar position. A great many persons have applied to me while in Washington to be allowed to accompany my party, and some too, of great distinction, both literary and scientific, who were refused, and were I to take you now, I might get myself into trouble with the Department. I regret very much that I have not the power, for I should like to have you along with me." For myself, I did not so much regret this disappointment as on account of my companion, and, knowing how much he had set his heart upon the accomplishment of this adventure, I was extremely anxious for him to go. So, I asked if my friend Tisdale could go even as an ordinary hand, but was told that none but experienced hands, and those accustomed to mountain life could be taken. Now, Tisdale is a good hunter and extremely fond of the chase, and is, indeed, as excellent fellow in a camp hunt, as can be found, besides being a good shot with the rifle, and has no lack [of] courage. If experience was one of the requsite qualifications, it could not have been rigerously enforced previous to this, for, there were certainly some in the company who had as little, if not a great deal less than my friend. Here then were our hopes blasted, the object in the pursuit of which we had expended both time and money, frustrated in a moment, and that too, when we had followed it up even into the wilderness. Notwithstanding the chagrin and mortification I felt, I could not help being pleased with the captain's politeness in inviting us to accompanying him on to his next camp and staying that night. The matter having now recieved its quietus, I took my leave & I passed over to the quarters of the officers to make my adieus and found Tisdale waiting to hear the decision of case. Well said he what news? We must go back said I. This information he recieved in silence. As we moved off he drew from his belt a small hatchet of mine, which we had brought with us from Mobile, and throwing it on the ground said "there I have no further use for that, you may have it," instantly mounted his horse and was off in double quick time. In a few minutes I followed, my feelings at that moment were not very enviable. I soon overtook him and our host. Tisdale was in a magnificent rage. I do not mean a rage that shews itself in many words, but it was eloquent however, charming us into silence for the remainder of that evenings ride. We had passed over a distance of ten miles when we came to Hickory Point[49] where we encamped for the night. I had never gone over ten miles so quickly in my life before, so occupied was I with my own thoughts. Our disappointment did not prevent us from constructing a good wide tent, nor did it spoil our appetite for supper or make a smoke after it feel less agreeable. In due time we retired but not to sleep very soundly, for I was grieved to find what a foolish part I had been playing, expended money and worst of all, lost two months of precious time. Well, there is such a thing as carrying politeness too far.

Soon after breakfast the following day we made an early start in order to avoid the heat of the day, but in a short time, we found ourselves toiling under the influence of an intensely hot sun. At the Lone Elm[50] eighteen miles from Mr. Lewis's, we made an ineffectual attempt to *noon.* No sooner had we taken the saddles off than we were obliged to resaddle them for pure mercy to our beasts. Nothing could exceed the swarms of green headed horse flies which assailed our poor animals. In a short moment they fastened themselves in countless numbers on every part of their bodies, and so rapid were their attacks that the blood flowed in frightful streams making the heart sick at the sight. Under such circumstances it would have been downright cruelty to have stayed. An hour or so afterwards, we came to halt and soon made amends for the disappointment we experienced by a very hearty dinner.

The Lone Elm derives its designation from its solitary location. In a plain of great extent a single elm tree looms up in lonely grandeur a conspicuous object for many miles around, and it is about eighteen miles from the U. States boundary line and thirty eight miles from Independence.

Three Delaware Indians now met us who were on their way to join Fremont as hunters to the Expedition.[51] I do not know how they succeeded for they were without the necessary papers from the Indian Agent, (Major Cummins). They all spoke english fluently, and appeared to be very intelligent. This tribe are in a great measure civilized, brave and honorable, and good friends to the whites. Nothing further of any interest

49. Apparently Waugh and Tisdale were now returning from Frémont's camp to Missouri. Wislizenus, traveling to Santa Fa a year later, placed Hickory Point twenty-fives miles beyond Lone Elm (*Tour to Northern Mexico*, 6).

50. "Rather a poor camping place, with bad water, scanty grass, and a single elm-tree; some brushes growing along the water" (Wislizenus, *Tour to Northern Mexico*, 6).

51. "From the Delaware nation twelve men were chosen to go with me. They were known to be good hunters and brave men and two of them were chiefs, Swanok and Sagundai" (Frémont, *Memoirs*, 424).

occurred for the remainder of the journey, which terminated at about five o'clock in the afternoon of the second day of July 1845. Thus ended all our fond hopes of visiting the sublime scenery of the Rocky Mountains.

Soon after our return we repaired to Mill Creek not far from Mr. Lewis's house, and refreshed our bodies with its cool waters. Our faces being very much sunburnt, by the advice of our hostess, when about to lie down for the night, we annointed them with some rich cream, which had a happy effect, in allaying the pain we suffered from our first attempts at prairie life.

Tisdale, who had been full of determination yesterday of joining the trading party of Mr. Bent[52] of Bent's Fork, who were about leaving, to day gave up the idea. He was so full of seeing wild life and adventure, of participating in the excitement of a buffalo hunt, in a word, of knowing something of existence beyond the bounds of civilization, that he would have done almost anything in order to gratify his taste in these particulars. For myself I felt disposed to rest content with the experience I had had, and I trust the lesson I have learned may not soon be forgotten, but there is no telling what change may come in the spirit of my dreams in the future, so much are we the creatures of circumstances.

---

52. Probably Charles Bent, who had arrived at St. Louis from Bent's Fort on 9 May (*Missouri Republican*, 12 May 1845).

CHAPTER IV

A Duel in Demopolis—The Fine Arts on the Frontier—Life and Sports on a Frontier Farm

THIS PORTION OF THE COUNTRY possesses a rich calcareous soil, producing great luxurience of vegitation.[53] The farmers on the border turn out their stock on the prairie during the summer which not only serves them for pasture, but affords an abundance of nutricious hay for the winter. In the limestone formation a variety of fossil remains are to be found well worthy the attention of the geologists. Flowers of great beauty are scattered over its surface in profusion, and the woods along the water courses abound with medicinal herbs, of great repute among the Indians.

Today is the fourth Sunday (6th [July]) since our landing at Kansas. It is a quiet, beautiful day. All around us is so still and quiet that it impresses us with a feeling of reverence. Here on the borders of a vast tract of wilderness, free from the noise and bustle of a city,—where the sound of the church going bell was never heard,—you find yourself irri[si]stably impressed with the sanctity of the day. The cessation from labor, the cattle quietly grazing in unrestrained freedom; the plow and other implements of husbandry lying where they were last used, or stowed away beneath an open shed, nay! the stillness of the atmosphere, proclaim it a day of rest. I am not superstitious, nor do I believe all things taught by preachers, but I have always, when in the country, been impressed with the sacredness of the Sabbath. Oh what wisdom is displayed in its institution. I am quite in love with this out of the way place, and wish I could lead so secluded a life as our host, but alas, that cannot be, I must return to the buisy haunts of men, and there play my part in the great drama of life.

Three years ago, this day (7th) in Demopolis Alabama, I came near loosing my life in a re[n]contre with two brothers of the name of Lane. James A. Lane, the youngest of the brothers thought proper to make some impertinent remarks about me, which coming to my ears, I addressed him a note to which he sent me a verbal reply, not at all satisfactory. I again wrote to him and this time recieved a written answer. One or two others followed without producing any arrangement of the difficulty, when I deemed it time to bring the matter to a prompt conclusion and sent a

53. The opening sentence of this chapter in Waugh's manuscript, struck out by the author, reads: "The lands of our host, Mr. Lewis, lie in Jackson County, whose fence on the west, forms part of the boundary line between the U States and the Indian territory."

message, the nature of which could not be mistaken—the law of the state making it a penitentiary offence to give, accept, or carry a challenge,—Finding an unexpected turn to the affair, for, he had heretofore firmly believed me to be a person with whom he could do as he pleased, he declined meeting me, because, he forsooth did not look upon me as a gentleman. I recollect in James' novel of Morley Erstein,[54] a remark which is applicable to the present subject, and is well worth remembering by all who indulge in offensive language, "I can readily understand a person who refuses to fight another to whom he has given no just cause of offence, to be both a gentleman and a man of courage. But, he who wantonly gives rein to his tongue, and then refuses to give satisfaction, can be nothing but a coward." In such perdicament stood my opponent. He had given an undue licence to his tongue under the belief, from my general quietness of manner that, I was one of those good easy souls who suffer themselves to be trampled upon with impunity. He saw his mistake rather late, and tried to get out of a scrape by subterfuge. If he did not consider me a gentleman, then why did he meddle with me? Had he have been what he denied me to be, he would, being the agressor, have instantly complied with the demand I made upon his magnaminity. The gentleman who acted as my friend on the occasion, replied instantly, "Then you cannot refuse to meet me." Whereupon Mr. Lane was compelled to accept the courtesy of my friend Thomas B. Prichett, Esquire, Councillor and Attorney-at-Law.

Upon recieving this information—I inwardly resolved to let no man fight my battles, and at once decided upon my plan. Some few hours after this, while thinking over the matter, my friend Prichett came to me in a great hurry, and taking me into a room, told me there was nothing more for me to do now than to publish Mr. Lane. "That is exactly what I have determined to do said I, and the sooner it is done, the better." A plackard was there and then drawn up, of which I made two copies, one of which I posted on the door of the Post Office and the other on a post at the corner of Farenholt's store. Previous to putting them up, I had procured a couple of duelling pistols from a medical student, who loaded them himself. At first I had intended using a stick in case of an attack, and had actually taken the pistols out of my pockets and returned them to their owner, but was induced to take them back. The papers being put up in public I stood at one of the doors not far from the post. Several persons read it and Nathan Lane, the elder brother, deliberately removed it, and repaired to

54. G. P. R. James, *Morley Ernstein, or the Tenants of the Heart* (3 volumes), first published in 1842.

the office of his brother, with said document. He had not been long gone when the brothers accompanied by a colonel, somebody, I don't know who, came to the corner door, entered the store and awaited the action of James A. Lane, who advancing to the door outside of which I was standing, and placing himself behind some packing boxes, addressed me by saying, "Now Sir, you have descended to the meaness of posting me as a coward, I now pronounce you no gentleman." To which I replied by saying in a cool and deliberate tone, "You are a d - - - d liar." Lane while speaking, had his right hand in the mouth of an umbrella which he held in his left. No sooner were the words out of my mouth than he drew a pistol ready cocked, from the umbrella, and the moment I could see the weapon I flung my stick at his head, which no doubt disconcerted him for he missed his aim. I instantly ran into the store by one of the corner doors, a few steps from where I was standing, and while doing so I drew a pistol from my right hand pantaloons pocket. It was not my intention to kill him, but only to wound his in the leg. Having to ascend one step, it raised the pistol higher than I intended and the ball entered the left side in the region of the lungs, after having passed through the fleshy part of his left arm. I now stepped into the street and recieved his second fire while in the act of cocking my other pistol (I had but two, while he was armed with four, and a large bow[i]e knife under the collar of his coat) which [*i.e.,* his second fire] striking the guard of my pistol caused it to explode into the air, thereby saving the life of Nathan, who after having fired at me from behind, came in front and stood before me. In a moment my weapon was leveled at his breast, but finding that I could not draw the trigger, I drew back, recocked it, and again drew the trigger but without effect. On discovering this, I struck him on the forehead with the pistol when he fell to the ground. All this time I was not aware that my pistol was empty. By this time I saw his friends carrying off James, who had fainted.

Turning round to look about me, I percieved a young fellow of the name of John Carlos, a clerk in Farenholt's store, advancing toward me with two four pound weights in his hands, with the intention, no doubt, of murdering me, for as he subsequently proved, he was a sneaking, treacherous rascal, full of cruelty and deceit. With this fellow I had scearcely an aquaintance, why he should attempt to assault me I do not know, as he professed no friendship for the Lanes, and had no cause to hate me.

I now stood alone in the middle of the street, when Nathan came up to me, his face and clothes covered with blood from the blow he had recieved, and for some moments looked me steadily in the eyes. Seeing that he had no weapons offensive, or defensive, I refrained from touching him, which he percieving he walked quietly away. The battle being ended I went to the office of Jule Martiniere, a justice of the peace, with a view of surrendering myself into his hands. Not finding the squire at home, I walked to the corner of the street opposite the scene of the rencontre and touching him on the shoulder, startled him by my announcement of surrender. While going to the corner, one of the citizens of the town met me and said, "Mr. Waugh keep out of the way until the excitement is over and nothing will be done with you, as you are in the right." I declined taking his advise however, having determined to let the law take its course.

With Mr. Martiniere, I returned to his office, but subsequently repaired with him and a guard, to the back room of the Post Office, where I remained until an other magistrate, (Mr. Martiniere declining to act on account of being a brother Free Mason, he suspected that my opponents, they being strong anti masons, would charge him with partiality in the matter) had made arrangements to give my case a hearing. The court was held in a room over the store where the affray had taken place, and the first witness, Mr. Farenholt was so confused in his evidence that no one could understand the true state of the case. John Carlos and the Missippi colonel swore that I made the assault, one saying that I drew first, and the other, that I fired first. This testimony was rebutted by twelve honest men who swore to the truth. Notwithstanding the magistrate who was a Dutchman, demanded five hundred dollars bail, myself in three hundred and two securities in one hundred each. When asked who my securities were, and before I could reply Mr. Anderson, a lawyer, and Dr. Robert Gale offered themselves. The matter being settled for the present— I retired in company with the doctor and was his guest that and the three following days, when I paid a visit to Genl Andrew C. Pickens at his plantation about nine miles from Demopolis, and for the first time had chill and fever.

The following Oct we were all tried at circuit court, James Lane, to the astonishment of all having recovered. By agreement the parties were allowed to sever, the Messrs. Lane taking their trial on Friday, were found guilty and fined two hundred and thirty dollars each, and the next day my case went to the jury, when I was fined one dollar.

I have dwelt longer on this subject than perhaps I should have done, but recollecting that I had no written account of it, I thought I might as well put it down. It was an unpleasant affair, and one, that I would have avoided, but the foolish fellow brought it on himself. When he believed himself dying, he sent me word that he entirely acquitted me of all blame.

Indeed, my conduct was viewed by the community at large, and even by his near relatives, as perfectly justifiable. I am glad he did not loose his life. But to return.

It is said that before the Fine Arts can be duly appreciated, mankind must have progressed through all the stages of civil life. Their advances are from the necessaries to comforts, from comforts to luxuries, and from luxuries to refinements, until these have been passed the Fine Arts recieve no real encouragement. In all newly settled countries the first care of man is to provide for his absolute wants, nor, does he dream of refinement until an abundance of the mere necessaries of life creates a desire to render these more pleasing to his taste,—a taste thus created by a superabundance,—the gratification of one desire invariably begets an other, and with the increase of wealth he indulges in the gratification of intellectual pleasures, hence those arts which speak to the mind find favor with him. Architecture, Painting and sculpture, music and Poetry being the offspring of the imagination, springing from, and speaking to itself now claim that attention which he could not have bestowed while toiling for mere existence. They are the last to come forth, and then only, when a community have duly advanced step by step, from the lowest to the highest state of moral culture.

I do not know of a wider or finer field for the exemplification of the above remarks, than is to be found on the continent of North America. Over its vast surface the human family occupies every position, from the savage to the most refined, and offers to the mind ample food for reflection and deduction.

The untamed denizen of the wilds, like the early children of the world, contents himself with a mere shelter, and relies upon the spontaneous productions of the ground or the precarious fortunes of the chase, for a subsistence. The newly arrived settler resembling man somewhat advanced from primitive simplicity, constructs his habitation of logs—at once a shelter and refuge in case of danger—and cultivates the earth, that in due season he may reap the kindly fruits thereof. The merchant, living in communities in a state of still further advancement, and depending, not so much on manual as mental labor, builds for himself a substantial dwelling, whilst the prosperous citizen erects a marble palace, glowing in all the splendors of architectural symmetry, and adorns its walls with the miracles which the magic wands of the painter and sculptor hath wrought.

In each progressive stage we see the march of mind, advancement is the result of civilization, and excellence the test of refinement. The traveller, as he passes over a country can form a correct estimate of the character of its inhabitants by the prevailing style of buildings—private as well as public, for the mind invariably communicates its tones to all works of art.

On this portion of our vast continent mankind have only just emerged from the toils of a new settlement and are not yet sufficiently advanced to seek the luxuries, to say nothing of the refinements of society. They are still laboring for the necessaries, but look forward to the comforts at some future day. At present they have neither wealth nor leisure to bestow on mental culture. The *utile* and not the *dulce* alone finds favor with the good people of the border. A cow, a sheep, or a hog, is, in their estimation, a far more beautiful object than the finest picture that ever came from the eazel of Raphael or Titian.

Here then were we thrown by adverse circumstances, into a region where the noblest genius would fail to support himself by the exercise of his art, he would find himself looked upon as a useless member of society, a drone in the hive of humanity, whose highest aspiration would be viewed as evidences of insanity or the effervessence of a disordered fancy.

Having tried in vain to be employed, I returned from visiting some of the neighbors perfectly depressed in spirits, for I met with some adventures which disgusted me. At one house l was asked by a short, vulgar looking fellow, who evidently considered himself a wit, "if I could take the likeness of a hog?" It was not the question that annoyed me, but the peculiar impudence of the manner that was offensive. He evidently intended to show off at my expense, but I turned the laugh against him when I replied, "yes, I can take yours."

The natural objects around us are not sufficiently interesting to claim the homage of a sketch, yet I have made some drawings which may hereafter serve to remind me of my sojourn here.[55]

Fishing has become quite a favorite amusement with us, to which our success in the Waltonian pursuit has mainly contributed. One evening while speaking of our achievements with the rod and line our host very kindly proposed to take us up the creek where we could realize the truth of the saying of "killing made easy." Two of his horses were immediately placed at our service, and crossing part of the prairie in front of his house, we wound through the devious path of a beautiful forest glade for some time, when coming to a cool sequestered spot, dismounted, and having tied our horses prepared for our finny friends. Scearcely had we

55. None of these sketches have been found.

commenced opperations than we were assailed by countless mirriads of mosquitoes. In vain we moved from one part of the creek to an other, in order to escape their attacks, still the bloodthirsty little wretches followed with a perseverance worthy of a better cause. They gave us not one moments peace, which in a great measure destroyed our angling, and brought us to the sage conclusion that we were enjoying anything but sport, and had better beat a retreat from an enemy whose guerrilla warfare we could not endure. So, as the sun had withdrawn his beams from our portion of the globe, the fishing tackle were collected, and with sorry spoils of a short campaign, as trophies of our valor, we again mounted our steeds and were retracing the path we came. Mr. Lewis being anxious to get out of the reach of the enemy as soon as possible was the first in the saddle and was off before either of us was ready. Tisdale who was detained for a few minutes in adjusting the trappings of his horse did not start with me, I rode slowly however which enabled him to overtake me before I had gone far. Well knowing his intuitive knowledge of woodcraft and his skill in traversing the forest, I gave him the lead. For a moment we halted to ascertain the route our host had taken then spurring on briskly and crossing a small creek mounted the opposite bank and in the right track. No sooner had we reached the top than we heard Mr. Lewis' voice, as we supposing giving us notice of his whereabouts—a practice not infrequent with those who are accustomed to sylvan sports,—but scarcely had we replied to the sound when we caught sight of the old gentleman gallouping at full speed, bare headed, and cheering on his dog Fip [Tip?], one of the two who were with us in our pursuit of the Expedition. In a moment Tisdale was off as fast as his horse could carry him. I was at a loss to make out the cause of all this great excitement, but hastened after then with all speed. I saw they were very much excited and urging the dog to seize some creature that had taken shelter in a clump of brushwood. Just as I reached them I saw a large animal leave the shelter and make for a tree up which it very leisurely began to climb. As it clung to the trunk its character at once became appearant. It belonged to the feline family, was about the size of a large beagle, but longer in the body, with a short stumpy tail and a head very much like a tiger. Its prevailing color was dun, or muddy yellow. As there were at that moment no fire arms in the possession of our party, recourse was had to such missiles as nature presented. Three times in succession Tisdale came very near giving the *critter* its quietus with a hard stone, well aimed. The *varmont* finding himself rather too close to his enemies changed his position, and mounted to a loftier limb, while the attacking party repaired to the creek to collect amunition with which to commence a regular siege. The ordinance munitions being deposited in two piles a short distance from the besieged tree, missile after missile flew fast and furious round his devoted head, but, with the cool affrontary of one who, from his elevated station, fancies himself secure, [he] looked down with contempt on his assailants as they strained every nerve to lower his pride. Occasionally, as a well aimed stone came rather too close, he would growl out his defience and change his quarters, still increasing the distance between himself and the earth, no doubt, thinking that "the better part of valor was discretion." Finding this primitive assault not very effective, a resort to civilized warfare was decided upon, the old hero taking upon himself the task of furnishing a reinforcement and the engines of war. There was a momentary cessation of hostilities in the absence of our host, of which the besieged took the advantage to raise himself still higher in the world, and, from his topmost round to survey us with calm indiference as he stretched himself at full length on a very lofty branch. I could not help admiring the coolness of all his motions, he seemed to have too high a sense of his own dignity to move at a rapid, vulgar rate, and could not be induced, even, to appear as if he feared us. Short was his repose however for,

"The war that for a space did fail
But doubly thundering swelled the vale,
And *Milton* was the cry,"

as we espied the son of the gallant old man galloping toward us, his long hair streaming in the air like the wings of Mercury's cap, and holding the rifle aloft in his right hand. On dismounting he handed over his acoutrements to Tisdale, who to his chagrin found when he proceeded to load the gun that he had every thing necessary, except powder. It was amusing to see the effect this dilema produced on the countenance of our friend. For a moment he lost that command which he usually had over his temper and indulged in language and gestures far from practical. The night was fast closing around, the young moon's beams were yet too feeble to afford light sufficient for our storming purposes, which led us to apprehend that our devoted prey might escape in the increasing darkness. As matters now stood, Milton returned to the house and brought back a good supply of amunition with the addition of two youths and a couple of horses. This increase of the sinews of war threw an air of interest over the proceedings which the onset wanted. Now the attack began in right good earnest, shot, after shot, waked up the echoes from the surrounding woods and might in other places have alarmed the settlers. The two youths being armed with shotguns took their stations at the foot of the tree, while the rifle sent forth its solitary ball from a distance. By this time night was so far advanced that if the locality of the *tarnel critter* had not been known he could not have been found, their aim was therefore directed to one spot, but owing to the general gloom that prevailed they were unable to tell whether their shot took effect or not. During all this time, I remained only a spectator, and not an actor [of] the drama which was being enacted. Finding that I could render them no service, for they proposed remaining there all night or they would have their prey, besides the insects were extremely annoying to me, I came away and soon was discussing a hearty supper. I had scarcely risen from the table when Tisdale made his appearance for the double purpose of allaying his hunger and procuring a fresh supply of powder and balls, as they intended to keep up the siege during the night, and have him in the morning. As it was the intention of the party to make their camp there, he took with him buffalo robe and blankets, besides a pan of burning coals to kindle a fire, and a good supply of pipes and tobacco. In the morning on looking out of my bedroom window, I saw our host very busy undoing the trappings of two of the horses of the party just returned. Going down to the gate I asked permission to mount one of them and make a visit to the field of opperations. I had scarcely proceeded more than a quarter of a mile when I met one of the hunters, his horse loaded with the bedding, and bearing before him in tryumph, the carcase of the deceased catamont, for such it proved to be. Seeing the others, Tisdale and Milton Lewis advancing on foot I tarried their coming and learned from them that after expending a few more shots after I had retired from the field the night before, they had kindled four fires in different places, one of which was at the root of the tree and an other at the one adjoining and then lay down to sleep while a sentinal was posted to guard the camp and see that the enemy did not make his escape. When the morning broke Tisdale was rather surprised to see the animal apparently in quiet repose in the fork of the tree. Impatient to secure him, he immediately began climbing, his surprise increased as he advanced for the catamount moved not, and on reaching the object of his pursuit he found to his amazement that his prey was already dead. It met its death during the night, but in consequence of the darkness it could not be ascertained whose shot had put an end to his troubles.

I was desirous of stuffing the skin, we set to work, as soon as we had breakfasted, and flayed the body. I made an opening in the belly not greater than half the animal's length and took out the body. The decayable parts of the head were carefully removed to prevent decomposition, and the skin turned inside out, stretched with twiggs, and without any preservative whatever exposed to the sun's rays to dry. In examining the carcase we found a number of buck shot and only one rifle ball, the death wound was in the abdomen and caused by small shot. Thus ended the hunt of the catamont but the excitement which it caused furnished food for conversation for several days afterward. The length of the animal must have been about three feet six inches, or more. I did not measure it, and only speak from recollection.

Three weeks passed away without producing any material benefit to us, either professionally or otherwise, and, when we have our time unemployed, its lengthening shadows fall gloomily upon the mind, making it seem interminably long indeed. Of books there were but few to occupy our attention, newspapers we seldom saw and whenever a stray one fell in our way, why it was old and well stricken in days. We were in a measure shut out from the buisy world and knew little of what was going on around us. Placed in such circumstances, it is not to be wondered at that every trifle should be seized on, wherewith to fill the void. In order to satisfy my craving for employment of some kind, I set to work, and sketched the likenesses of the whole of Mr. Lewis's family and presented them to him in token of our regard. Tisdale helped the old gentleman in the construction of a light waggon and proved himself a tolerable mechanic.

Sometimes we would amuse ourselves under the shade of the good trees, in telling our adventures, conversation, smoking, or playing off some practical joke on an innocent character. One morning while thus employed, we were joined by a Shawnee Indian brave, who, with his small keen eyes looked at our gambols for some time in silence. I saw that his attention was particularly directed to friend Tisdale, whose eyes seemed to fix his closest study. Curious to learn the reason of the scrutiny, I looked enquiringly to the Indian and recieved for an answer an eloquent pointing of his right hand in the direction of the object of his regard, at the same time pronouncing the words "*Wau-nee-saw-caw-whay-wau*", "Look him eye," said the Indian, "him *prairie wolf.*" At this we commenced quiping Master Jack, who, not by any means, pleased with his new title, declares his rejection of the honor. He says that the prairie wolf is the meanest of all that rascally tribe and prefers being called "*Lay-yah-ki-the-ta-whay-ware,*" or *white wolf*, as more becoming his qualities.

In the cource of the day, being struck with the simplicity of an apparatus for manufacturing soap much used in the country parts of the U. States which occupied a prominent position on the premises of our worthy host, I made a sketch of an "Ash Hopper," as it is called and greatly astonished the good lady of the house at my want of taste in selecting such a nasty, ugly looking thing instead of the handsome brick house of good old husband. In the evening I went down the creek and made a sketch of the grist and saw-mill of Mr. John Cummings. I have rarely found a subject so well arranged for pencil, particularly as regards the distribution of light and shade, as this simple little mill situated on Indian Creek, and surrounded with quiet forest scenery. At some future day I will paint a picture in oil colors from it.

The next morning (22 of July) we left for Independence, at about half-past-five o'clock, accompanied by our friend Mr. Lewis, who furnished us with horses and acted as our guide. The distance—twenty miles—was shortened two miles by crossing a sequestered part of the country, and at half past eleven A.M. we reached our destination.

CHAPTER V

Independence—Portrait Painting—Some Leading Citizens and Some Oddities

This town is the county seat and contains between eight and nine hundred inhabitants.[56] It is pleasantly situated on a very slight eminence surrounded by a well timbered and handsomely undulating country, about three miles, or so, south from the landing at Wayne City. It is a great starting point for the traders to Santa Fe, and the emigrants to Oregon and California.[57]

In the center of a small square, enclosed in a wooden fence, stands a low, square, two story brick court house, with no attractive features about it to draw your attention or, claim the slightest homage from the lovers of architectural beauty.[58] Around are a number of irregular buildings used by small traders and dignified with the lofty sounding title of *stores.* At present a Mr. Wood Noland, or Uncle Wood as he is familiarly known, is building a large house at S W corner of the square which he intends to occupy as a hotel,[59] and, as the worthy old citizen is very public spirited, he is ambitious of rivaling the Planter's house of St. Louis, in the splendors of its accomodations, and as he intends to shew that some things can be done in one place as well as another, it is his intention to procure a french cook from the commercial capitol of the state, to tickle the pallates of traders and their very refined teamsters. I am told that he looks forward to the time when Independence will be the capitol of the United States, and his large house, no dout, will be used for federal legis[la]tion. There are a couple of hotels beside whose accomodations are not very remar[ka]ble for their ellegance. The methodists, the presbyterians, the baptists, cumberland presbyterians, and cambellites, or as they

---

56. On the page opposite the beginning of this chapter is a note in Waugh's hand: "Write on the conduct of the Mormons in this portion of the country previous to their being driven away." However, no such paragraph appears in the manuscript. Probably his impressions were largely derived from those of his particular friend, General Lucas, who had commanded the Missouri militia in the "Mormon War."

57. Independence was laid out in 1827 and its first landing place was established at Blue Mills, six miles away, in 1831. The landing at Wayne City was washed away in the flood of 1844. During the latter part of that year the construction of a good road between Wayne City and Independence was a matter of local concern. Consult Conard, *Encyclopedia of the History of Missouri,* III, 349-350; *Independence Journal,* 12, 19 September, 3, 24 October 1844.

58. This was the second courthouse, built in 1838.

59. S. V. Noland's Washington Hotel had been destroyed by fire on 19 February (*Weston Journal,* 1 March 1845). For a description of the new hotel see note 130 below.

very modestly call themselves, *The Christians,* have each a place of worship.[60] Blacksmiths, waggon makers carpenters and gunsmiths are abundant. In the stores every article requis[it]e for traders and emigrants are to be found fully as cheap as in St. Louis. Old traders prefer making their outfit here, and it is advisable for those who make their debut on the plains to wait until they come here, to make their purchases, as all the really useful articles are constantly ready. Many things are provided by emigrants in their ignorance, who find them quite useless on the route and by waiting until they reach Independence they avoid many unnecessary expenses. It is a striving, pleasant little town, and in the spring, presents quite a novel appearance to a stranger.[61]

When we reached here Mr. Lewis introduced us to a very worthy fellow of the name of Macguire who claims to be an Irishman born three months after he came to the United States, and as good a hearted man as can be found anywhere. Tom, as all his friends call him, took us over to the court house, and introduced us to General Samuel D. Lucas, clerk of the

60. The first Presbyterian Church, Old School, was organized at Independence 21 November 1841 by the Reverend J. L. Yantis; it owned no place of worship until 1852. The Independence Cumberland Presbyterian Church was organized in 1832; a brick church was built in 1840. Among persons Waugh mentions in his narrative Samuel D. Lucas and his wife were original members; Robert Sloan was a pastor. Pleasant Grove Baptist Church (Old School Baptists) dates apparently from 1837 and the First Baptist Church of Independence was organized 3 April 1845. The first Church of Christ was organized in 1835; among its members were W. F. Dewebber, John Maguire, and Lilburn W. Boggs. For these churches consult *Vital Historical Records of Jackson County,* 199, 211, 28, 60, 121-124. A description of the Christian Church by George S. Bryant is given on p. 121; no Methodist church information for Independence is listed in this source.

61. "Boarding in the taverns [is] $2 50 to 3 per week, private boarding $1 50. . . . There are four saddlery and harnessmaking establishments, nine blacksmiths' shops, some of them working four and five fires, and seven wagon makers' shops, all actively employed in preparing for the wants of the ensuing summer season. There is also one tinner and whitesmith's shop, one gun smith, one hatter, two jewellers, one druggist and about a dozen stores for the sale of general merchandise. There are also two excellent taverns, though it requires 'the biggest kind of a house' to accommodate the crowds who are frequently here in the summer season—a house, such as no one has yet had the public spirit to erect, but which (if there were one of the kind I have named), would be a general benefit to the place, and would pay a rent that would be a handsome interest on the investment. There are several brick houses now in progress of erection, and contracts already entered into for the building of many store and dwelling houses in the ensuing summer. . . . There are here four places of worship, one Catholic, one Methodist, one Reformed, and one Cumberland Presbyterian; a new church is about to be commenced by the New School Presbyterians. . . . The principal building of this place, at present, is the Jackson County Court-House, which was built in 1838, at the expense of some six thousand dollars.

"The tone of society in this place is decidedly of a high order—that observance of the moral and religious duties of life which tends to elevate the character of its people, and secure for them the respect and esteem of those who are accidentally thrown among them. . . ." (Viator to George R. Gibson, editor, *Weston Journal,* 1 March 1845).

circuit and county courts.[62] We were much pleased with the courteous reception given us by this gentleman, who, upon learning our profession, as well as our desire to sojourn in the town for a short time, was good enough to offer us a room in the court House where we could set up our easel and he would introduce his friends to us. This kindness was duly appreciated, the room put in order, and everything got ready for commencing opperations in face making. For some years I believe, before our coming, there were no artists in this section of the country, from which we were told we would be likely to do a good buisiness. The first likeness I made was of the general, it was in the new style, and gave so much satisfaction that sitters came in sufficiently fast, to allow us to make some outlay for our comfort. One sitter amused me not a little, he was a yankey clock pedler, and quite a character in his way. He was dressed true yankey style and could be taken for nothing but a yankey. Being pleased with what he saw in our studio, he took a fancy to have his *pictur took*, but true to his nature he proposed a *swap*. I took him at his word, gave him his *pictur* and put a silver watch in my pocket in exchange. The operation occupied about an hour and a half. I now painted a miniature on ivory for a south carolinian of the name of George Pringle who had come to Independence in the early part of the year, with the intention of going to Oregon, but subsequently declined.[63] This was in exchange for a very good rifle, and a large bowie knife. John Henry Harper, who afterwards filled a large space in the public eye, now sat for his also and paid me fifty dollars in hard cash for it.[64] I was now commissioned to paint in my new style, the lady and four children of Samuel H. Woodson, Esq. for which I recieved fifty dollars, and it gave general satisfaction.[65] We now felt, from the success we met with, tolerable comfortable in our

---

62. Samuel D. Lucas, as major-general commanding the Fourth Division of the Missouri Militia, played a leading part in the so-called Osage and Mormon Wars of the 1830's in western Missouri. He served for many years as Circuit Clerk of Jackson County.

63. George Pringle served as private in Company A, First Regiment Missouri Mounted Volunteers (Connelley, *Doniphan's Expedition*, 533).

64. In 1844 the office of Harper and his law partner J. R. Palmer was on the north side of the public square, one door west of Washington Hall (*Independence Journal*, 12 September 1844). Harper murdered William Wirt Meredith in May, 1846; see note 143 below.

65. Samuel H. Woodson was born in Jessamine County, Kentucky, in 1815 and died at Independence in 1881. After a visit to Independence in 1838, he settled permanently there two years later. He served in the state legislature and in Congress, and on the Circuit Bench from 1875 to 1881. He married Margaret, the daughter of Dr. M. Q. Ashby, of Mt. Sterling, Kentucky, in 1838 (Conard, *Encyclopedia of the History of Missouri*, VI, 519). At this time he and Hugh N. Smith were law partners, with an office on the south side of the square (*Independence Journal*, 10 October, 1844).

circumstances, and enjoyed ourselves very much. Nothing could exceed the kindness extended to us by General Lucas and family, he seemed to take as deep an interest in our welfare as if we were old acquaintances instead of mere strangers, and for him we entertained a deep respect. Indeed it could not be otherwise, for his disinterested kindness commanded that which we most freely gave. At all times and under all circumstances he was bland and courteous, not only to us, but to all who had any thing to do with him. Frequently has he been known to turn back, even when on his way to dinner, to attend to some small matter in his official capacity worth ten cents or a quarter, with as much politeness as if his client was a magnate of the law and his fee the greatest that the law allows. Between poverty and wealth he makes no difference, alike attentive to all, he performs the duties of his office with a grace that won all hearts and made him justly popular. His eldest son John-Samuel, who assists him in the office rendered himself particularly acceptable to us and contributed in no small degree to our comfort. This young gentleman, possesses an excellent, kind heart and a most obliging disposition. Of him and his brother James, I made separate full length likenesses, cabinet size, and presented them to their mother.[66] Also a miniature of the youngest daughter, besides sketching the balance of the family in a group.

If we can judge by the kindness which we recieve on every hand, we are decidedly popular here, Tisdale especially so among the young portion of the inhabitants.

Like all other small country places Independence has its *characters,*—originals in their way—who from their talents or excentricity are considered privelleged in the community. Having now been sufficiently long in this town to have become acquainted with some of them, I shall attempt their sketches as well as I am able. To begin then, I shall first take the gentleman who was the first to pay me for my professional services. I shall not easily forget our introduction to each other.

Jonathan Palmer[67] is a tall, spare going man, with looks beyond his years, his age is only twenty four, but might pass for thirty, & cannot be considered handsome, by any means, but his countenance bears the impress of genius and a certain bearing in his manner and conversation

---

66. J. T. and James Lucas served as privates in Company A, First Regiment Missouri Mounted Volunteers (Connelley, *Doniphan's Expedition,* 532); they may have been sons of General Lucas. Charles D. Lucas, born in Independence 5 May 1834, succeeded his father as recorder of deeds in 1867 (*History of Jackson County, Missouri,* 806-807).

67. Palmer served as a private in Company A, First Regiment Missouri Mounted Volunteers (Connelley, *Doniphan's Expedition,* 533). See also note 64 above.

shews him to be a man of very superior intellect. Of quick perception and great clearness of thought, he is enabled to read character almost at a glance. A liberal education has assisted his natural fine talents, to develope themselves, and, before a court and jury he displays a depth of legal knowledge far beyond some of his elder brethern. In conversational powers he has few superiors among those his own age. On every subject which he touches, he is interesting and instructive, and all who know him acknowledge his powers. With him I was very much pleased and frequently enjoyed his sallies of wit and satire. In his dress he is rather slovenly, showing very little respect for the fashion of the day, and perfect indifference to the world's opinion of him or his ways. To him, am I indebted for some of the most amusing annecdotes relative to the members of the Bar.

His partner in the practice of Law, is rather the reverse, being neat in his personal appearance, rather handsome, and very flowery in his speech. Without the talents or genius of Palmer, John Henry Harper, is perhaps a greater favorite with the people at large, and is just such an one, as would be selected to make a Fourth of July oration, or an address to an assembly of young ladies. He has a fine voice, and executes several negro melodies in admirable style. It is a pity that so good a voice should be directed by so bad a taste. A few months ago he ran away with a beautiful young lady and got married by a justice of the peace in a wood a short distance from town. As soon as the father of the bride became aware of the fact, he took [her] to the East for the purpose of placing in a boarding school for a couple of years—she is very young,—rather too young, being only fourteen, but not liking the idea of so long a separation, she returned to her father's house, when the old gentleman wisely making a virtue of necessity had them married over again by a minister of the Cumberland Presbyterian, and then gave the happy couple permission to take lodgings at a Hotel.[68]

Another member of the legal profession figures here in high relief, and is known as Talladega Hall, from the circumstances of his possessing a walking stick which was cut on the Talladega battle ground in Alabama, and from which he derives more celebrity than from his legal knowledge or moral rectitude. Jacob Hall is a large gross man, with taste and feelings as gross as his body, and no more honesty of purpose than is sufficient to make him steer clear of *that* law which he so arrogantly presumes to use as his profession. Without the slightest qualms of conscience

68. The girl was Fanny Owens, a daughter of Samuel C. Owens. See also note 143 below.

he will practice at the bar—of a grocery,[69] drive a drove of hogs to a market, sware himself into a Masonic lodge, altho' under expulsion in Kentucky, and then have the affrontary to defend himself in the papers after being published by the fraternity.[70]

Richard R. Reese Esquire, although small in stature is a considerable man in many respects, and very much esteemed for his good qualities. As master of the Masonic lodge he is upright in his dealings, in travelling on the level of time is not above attending to his duties, and in his intercourse with his brethern and the world at large his actions are so squared that all the work that comes from his hands, is creditable to him as a faithful and able workman.

Perhaps the ablest lawyer in this town is Samuel H. Woodson, a native of Kentucky and descended from a good Virginia family—but he does not boast of it, indeed, I believe he has no particular respect for the *first* families of the Old Dominion. He recollects the anecdote of the english governor Lord Dunmore, and a lady who wished to take precedence of all others, aye! even the governor's lady, and that too, at a party in Lord Dunmore's own house. After bearing with her imperious demands for as long a time as he could, he directed his secretary to bring him the New-Gate Calander, from the library. And when he had looked into it for a few moments, he raised his voice and bowing to the lady said, "Yes Madam, you are entitled to precedence here, for your grandfather was the *first* convict who was transported to this colony." She certainly was of the *very first family* and accordingly was entitled to great respect. Mr. Woodson's grandfather was an english gentleman of much learning, who after having passed through college with the celebrated Dr. Samuel Parr, the great greek scholar, emigrated to Virginia while it was yet a colony, and purchased the services of several members of the *first families,* literallv verifying the saying the last shall be first, and the first shall be last.

At the house where we lodge there are a few specimens of the class mammalia genus homo, who amuse me not a little, but the greatest character of the group is Major Robert A. Rickman, whose philanthropic spirit has reduced its owner to poverty in his old age. He is a dreamer, and lives in a world of his own creation, and like all such persons he is an aerial

69. That is, a dramshop or saloon.

70. Jacob Hall came from Kentucky to Independence a few years ago, [visited?] the Lodge and mingled with the fraternity for some time as a mason in good standing. After a while, the lodge in Independence was regularly notified by the brethren in Kentucky, of his expulsion for gross unmasonic conduct. This was published by the lodge here, and Jacob had the hardihood to reply to it in a public newspaper, and asserted that it was all a lie.—WAUGH.

architect. His mania is for railroads and internal improvements and so firmly convinced is he that Independence is the center of the continent of North America, that he believes it will ultimately become the greatest and most important city, not only in the Union but,—the world. His gigantic mind is at present engaged in planning a railroad across the plains, from this place to the Pacific Ocean in order to trade with China.[71] The major has been to California and his travels form an unceasing source of conversation between himself and all who choose to listen to him. When we came to this house, he politely selected me for his audience, and I became the object of his most unremitting attentions. All his travel history was related to me, with a minuteness of detail that was truly instructive. In me he found a patient listener, not only as an act of courtesy but because I percieved that I had a great original to deal with. He was frequently heard to express himself very much pleased with me, and spoke in exalted terms of my looks and manners, "any one can tell," he would frequently say—"any one can tell that the colonel is a smart man by his very appearance." His odd ways and quaint sayings, amused me, and his singular phraseology came upon my ear like a new and distinct language, and until his store of information became exhausted I continued to listen, but the moment he began the same volume over again the interest ceased and I ceased to be patient,—nay, more, was ill natured enough to quiss him on his foibles, which caused a coolness between us, and finally we ceased speaking to each other. In a short time his opinions underwent a change, I was lowered in his estimation, I could lay no claim to talents or smartness whatever. Our misfortunes sometimes turn out to our benefit, from the rapid change I passed through, from the highest pinnacle of esteem to the lowest depths of his contempt, I learned to place no value on personal popularity, but to act independent of smiles or frowns. From that time we heard no more of railroads or California until a couple of pedlars came to board with us, when poor Rickman glad to get on a chance of holding forth once more, seized upon the new comers and again burst out in all his effulgence.

In, or rather close to town lives a certain W. Wilkinson who dubs himself doctor, and enjoys a very unenviable notoriety. When this man came to Independence he caused it to be given out that he was the doctor Wilkinson who had an affray in Louisville Kentucky with some persons there,

---

71. This was written in July 1845, and although the Major was looked upon as a wild visionary and his road plan laughed at, yet the present movement among the citizens at large makes me look back to the remarks of the poor old major as prophetic. —Waugh. This note is dated "St. Louis Oct. 1850."

was tried before a court of justice and triumphantly acquitted. This was done with a view of lionizing himself, but Mr. Woodson, who knows the parties well, and speaks of *that* doctor in very exalted terms, soon tore the mask from off the false hero, and declares *this* to be an arrant paltroon. Of this would be doctor there are many tales told which, if true, are far from creditable to any man. One day, while engaged in our studio in the court House Mr. Doctor Wilkinson did me the honor to call, with the view of patronizing us, and engaged my services for his own, his lady's and children's likenesses, and began his patronage by sitting to me at once. When it was finished he called and took the likeness with him to shew his lady, but forgot to pay me for it, nor did I hear of either the picture or himself for a fortnight. Thinking that he had forgotten the matter altogether, or was so professionaly occupied that he could not find time to see me, I wrote him a note but recieved no answer. In a few days I again wrote, but with no better success than at first. This irritated me, for I could not brook such conduct from a man who evidently tried to shun meeting me, and I sent the following note and had it delivered into his own hands

"Independence, Oct 25 1845.

"Sir, As you have not had the politeness to answer my former notes, I now demand that you instantly return the picture which you put me to the trouble of painting

Alfred S. Waugh

To Dr. W. Wilkinson."

To which he returned the following

Independence Mo Oct 23

Sir last night at 10 I Reced the first note from you this morning a nother Demanding the Picture I now send you the Picture & money I think *suficent* to pay for the Troble if it was convenient I— would send you the Balance

Yours

W. Wilkinson

Mr Alfred S. Waugh

The above is a litteral copy of his elegant answer, with its orthography and punctuation as in the original. The price of the sketch was five dollars, and the amount which *he* thinks *suficent* was three dollars. I shewed the note to my friend Mr. Woodson, who advised me to keep the money, and dispose of the likeness in any manner I deemed proper. So I pocketed the cash and nailed "the counterfit presentiment" to the wall of a public room in the Court House, in the doing of which a nail went through the ear. There was no mistaking the resemblance, in a few hours every one in the town was aware of the exhibition. Jonathan Palmer who loves a bit of mischief, in a very serious manner, informed the doctor of the disposition I had made of his likeness, and of the indignity *he* suffered by having his *ear* nailed, as it were, to the pillory. At this he seemed surprised, threatened to tare it down, and play the very devil with me, for my conduct. But before proceeding to put his threat into execution he visited Mr. Woodson for the purpose of obtaining legal advice in the matter. Mr. Woodson told him that the picture was mine, that being the master of it, I could do as I pleased but the resemblance, which no body could possibly mistake, was *his*, and he might go and take it down when ever he saw proper. Or he might obtain redress in single combat. This last hint he declined taking, as he said, he was now suffering from the effects of a wound which he recieved in an affaire of honor, and did not wish to be engaged in any more such scrapes. When I put it up in the way I did, as a matter of course, I expected to be called to account, for, if the same treatment was offered through my likeness to me I would most undoubtedly have invited the perpetrator to fight. The sketch remained where I placed it for a long time, nearly a month, after I left Independence and was finally taken down by Tisdale and Samuel Lucas. The doctor saw it once or twice but did not touch it.

An other small creature vegitates here and is called Dewebber.[72] He is a yankey, a cambelyte, and a very small man in every sense of the term. He has a very little body and a mind beautifully less. He keeps a shop for the sale of dry goods and writes himself merchant. This little creature belongs to a numerous class, who fancy they are doing God a service, when they talk religion, where ever they can find an oppertunity—either in season, or out of season. Such people do more harm, than good to the cause of religion. When ever I hear a fellow who is engaged in the pursuit of Mammon, interlarding his discourse with pious remarks and quotations from Holy Writ, I most decidedly set him down for, either a knave or fool, and shun him accordingly, for, he will cheat me if an oppertunity ever presents itself to do so with impunity.

The third in this unholy trinity is Burford, Druggist and Apothecary, Note shaver and money lender, gratuitous director of public works, and Paul Pry in general to all the good citizens who do, or do not, wish to be talked of throughout the country.[73]

But the greatest character yet remains to be sketched, and is, I fear,

72. W. F. Dewebber. For a typical merchant's advertisement see his in the *Independence Journal*, 12 September 1845; among other items he offered dry goods, boots and shoes, Latin, French, Spanish, and English school books, and hemp.

73. Miles Washington Burford settled in Independence in 1839; in 1871 he moved to Indianapolis and died there in 1877, aged seventy-two. For a letter about him by his son see Webb, *History of Independence*, 146-151.

beyond the power of my humble pen. However, as I am a bashful Irishman, the reader will have the kindness to overlook my blundering for, it cannot be expected that I can do justice to so exalted a personage, so now with your permission I shall do myself the honor to introduce to your notice J Brown Hovey, Esquire,[74]
Councillor & Attorney at Law &c. &c. &c.

The subject of my present sketch was born some where in the state of New York, and at an early age, was "bound prentice" to a chair maker, but, whether he displayed genius in that line or gave satisfaction to his boss is not recorded. That it was not his vocation is sufficiently proven by the fact that he discovered a wider field for the exercises of his colossal powers. Nature, it seemed had endowed him with a soul too mighty to waste its energies on such common place matters as chairs. Fate had designed him to occupy, a higher—a nobler sphere,—the divinity stirred within him,—his spirit soared aloft on the pinions of the bird of Jove, and by Jove, he longed to give the world assurance of what he could do. What better field for the display of genius could possibly present itself than that of law. In a fit of heavenly inspiration he rose up "regenerated, disinthralled and free" and with the energy of a Hercules, dashed down the base tools of mechanism,—hurled the chairs to the devil, and at once felt himself superior to the occupation of a grovelling drudge. The Bar, and the Bench displayed themselves in all their attractions before his far seeing eye. Honors and distinctions sparkled refulgently as he looked into futurity. Fame held the ermine in one hand, while with the other she pointed to her temple, the assent to which, to him was but child's play. Instantly the commentaries of Blackstone opened their pages to his enquiring mind, their legal wisdom transferred itself to his brain and in due course of time he presented himself before the constituted authorities, stood his examination, and obtained licence to practice law. During his studies his preceptor frequently tapped him on the skull with a gold snuff box, to recal his wandering thoughts, or, as is supposed, to endue him with a proper respect for the precious metal. Of this golden age he delights to speak, and by his fondness for money shews that at least, his training has not been lost upon him.

Like all other great men whose minds are solely occupied with their own lucubrations, he is subject to fits of abstraction, the world and its vanities become lost to him for the time being, and without regard to

---

74. The card of J. Brown Hovey, attorney-at-law and solicitor in chancery, gave his address as Colly's Building on the northeast corner of the public square (*Independence Journal,* 12 September 1844).

what people may think, will, on the spur of the moment, when his researches call for it, run from his office, to the court House, in his bare feet, or, perhaps with only one slipper on. This may be thought to savor too much of premeditated excentricity, but the world is very censorious, it can make no allowance for the peculiarities of genius, they cannot see that, at that moment his mind is deeply absorbed in some very important subject on which the fate of an estate, or, it may be, life itself is dependent upon the perfect concentration of all his faculties, regardless of such small matters as the mere decencies of life. What to him are the remarks of the mere mass? They are no [more] to be noticed than the buzzing of so many flies, or the murmering of the idle wind. In his forensic displays, his oratory more than equals the thunder of Demosthanes,—it surpasses it, for the piercing glance of his eagle eye, is the lightning that accompanies the unearthly tones of his superhuman voice. Talk of your ancient and modern orators as much as you please. Laud to the skies the wisdom of Solon, and the eloquence of Cicero. Praise the learning of Adams, the genius of Webster, and, collect into one vast despot, all the talents of times past, present and to come, and with one accord, the crown of immortality will be placed on the brows of the immortal Hovey, for he surpasses them all in wisdom, wit, and valor.

Oh! how have I stood entranced, listening with an actual intensity to the flow of the most profound aphorisms, as they came from the mouth of this prodigy of wisdom. In the charmed circle which his eloquence had thrown me, I remained a chained captive, bound by the magic of his genius and learning, and, carried away by the irresistable force of his transcendant talents, involluntarily exclaimed, "He *is* a man, take him for all, in all, *I* ne'er shall look upon his like again." Like most other great men, "on whom every god hath set his seal," he is accompanied by that sure concommitant of inate brilliancy,—ex*centr*icity, but wrapt up in the majesty of his own originality the shafts of envy hurt him not, nor does the contempt and ridicule of his less gifted brethern annoy him in the slightest degree. Alike, above and below the malice of the world, he neither turns nor falters in his *forward* course, but with an eye steadily fixed on the goal, tis impossible to divert him from his purpose.

One of his amiable excentricities, is to turn abruptly on his heel, after having made a speech at the bar, retire to the main body of the court room, and then continue to walk backward and forward, appearantly lost to every other consideration but the case in hand, until his turn comes round to speak again, when he then proves to the hon'l court and jury what a consumate blockhead Sir William Blackstone must have been to write on what he did not understand, and how extremely foolish are all those who take so great a booby for authority in law and equity.

An other of his foibles is to look out for rascals, no matter how great they may be, and fee, or no fee, undertake their cause, which by taking advantage of mere quirks and turnings in legal phraseology,—he gains,— to the increase of his reputation as a great criminal lawyer.

An other peculiarity belonging to his character, is a thorough belief in his own greatness of conversational power. In his estimation no other human possesses half the amount of information on *all* matters as himself, for, he derives more heartfelt pleasure from hearing his own voice than in listening to that of any other on the face of the globe. Narcissus like he has fallen in love with his own shadow, and makes his likeness play the part of a regal embassador in affairs of the heart. When he deigns to honor a young lady with delicate attentions, his picture is despatched to the residence of the fair one for the purpose of creating an impression in his favor, e'er the original presents himself before her admiring eyes. Thus he contrives to econamise his valuable time, and saves himself the trouble of acting like every common son of earth who is foolish enough to court in the usual way. In fact he does nothing like other men, for instance, he took it into his head to cow-hide a methodist preacher, who had remarked to his congregation, when interupted by the great *J. Hovey*, "that if some persons were as soft in the heart, as in the head, he, (the preacher) might hope to make a favorable impression on them." The little great man at first could not be made to understand the observation was intended for him, but as soon as he became thoroughly convinced of the fact, he purchased a cowhide and proclaimed to the whole town his designs upon the insolent preacher. After having gone over the entire limits of the corporation, he at last met the object of his vengeance in the store of the Director general of public work, Burford; and with the handle of the thrashing machine sticking out from the breast of his coat, stood before the doomed soul saver, looking for all the world like a little fi[blank in ms.] dog before a quiet mastiff. The preacher aware of the threats held out, seemed in no way alarmed, but cooly looking the mighty one in the eye, said, "Mr. Hovey, I am aware of your threatinings and regard them as idle talk; your little tongue may wag as much as you please, it is an unruly member and very harmless. I shall not notice it, but let me advise you to guard your actions, for the moment you lift a finger against me, that moment I will [give you] the prettiest flogging you ever recieved in your life, *verbum sat* —you know the rest, good morning Sir." Here discretion became the better part of valor and Hovey retired without taking the shine off his cowhide. The Irish blood in the preacher's veins, was ready for a scrimage.

Not long since I was summoned by the sheriff to serve on a jury, to try a man for negro stealing. The prisoner, Samuel Drake, was defended by J. Brown Hovey. It was the first time I had ever been called on to be a juryman, and paid particular attention to the merits of the case. The testimony went strongly to prove the defendant guilty of the crime laid to his charge, and at the conclusion of the evidence, my mind was fully made up as to the criminality of Drake, as well as from the charge of the judge. On this occasion I was thoroughly disgusted with the conduct of Hovey, not only to the prosecuting officer, but to the court itself. He was constantly interupting the bench by handing up books and papers and then snatching them away in a rude and insolent manner. For some time Judge Ryland[75] bore his impertinence, but at length the patience of his honor ceased to be a virtue, and he remarked with a peculiar smile which conveyed a profound contempt for the pigmy, "Why! the boy not only instructs the solicitor, but would instruct the court," whereupon *J. Hovey* replied that he merely wished to draw his Honor's attention to the law, and was in the act of handing up a volume of Reports, when the judge remarked in a tone of voice not to be mistaken. "Mr. Hovey, I read that law before you were born." This reproof which would have made any one else feel mortified seemed to produce no effect on him whatever, although it raised a laugh of scorn among the assembled crowd.

In addressing the jury he observed no respect toward us, and spoke of Col. Smart[76] (the solicitor) in language at once gross, vulgar and insulting, but that gentleman who very well understands the nature of the little creature, paid no attention to him at all. We now retired to the jury room, but being unable to agree were permitted to go to our several lodgings, with a strict charge from the bench to suffer no person to converse with us on the case nor to listen to remarks of any kind bearing upon the trial and to present ourselves again before him in the morning.

That evening while sitting with some friends in a store on the public square, talking of common place subjects, this little fellow came bouncing

75. John Ferguson Ryland was born in Virginia, 2 November, 1797. He moved to Kentucky as a boy and read law there. Moving to Howard County, Missouri, in 1819, he served as Circuit Judge in western Missouri from 1830 to 1848 and was appointed to the State Supreme Bench in 1848. He died in 1873. Consult Bay, *Bench and Bar of Missouri*, 271-276.

76. Robert G. Smart was born in Montgomery County, Kentucky, in 1819 and came with his father to Missouri in 1828. After representing Jackson County in the legislature, he served as circuit attorney in the 1840's. He died in 1862. Consult Bay, *Bench and Bar in Missouri*, 407-408.

in, but without any preface began making some allusions to the days proceedings in opposition to every thing that was fair and honorable. Annoyed, tho' not surprised at this unmanly conduct, I turned toward him and said, "Mr. Hovey, I have seen a great many courts of justice both in this country and in Europe, and I must say that I have never witnessed such proceedings as I did to day. Had I been the judge on that bench most undoubtedly would I have sent [you] to prison for contempt of court. Were I a lawyer and had have recieved such language as you used to Col. Smart, I would have tweaked your nose for your insolence, if not in the Court House, at least out of doors. Were you in the South and would conduct yourself as I have this day witnessed, you would most certainly get yourself well cow-hided or your brains blown out,—that is provided you had any. At all events, *there* you could not live over one week, for, your conduct would not be tolerated among the high minded sons of the South." Whereupon he moved to the door, exclaiming as he made his exit "I was right." The next morning he saluted me as if nothing had occured and that evening he again came to where I was, when I gave him about double as much as on the preceding one.

Before I take leave of this gentleman I must not omit to mention a very good anecdote which was told me of him, one which will give as good an insight into his character as anything I could say, here it is.

On one occasion he either was called on, or volunteered his services, to make a speech before a primary school. The future citizens were there in their hollyday suits, and clean washed faces, glowing in all the freshness of happy childhood. Their friends too were collected in goodly numbers, for many an anxious mamma waited for the moment when her darling boy would astonish the audience by his precocious talents. Select pieces of declamation and oratory, were repeated by the embryo statesmen and senators, and every thing went off to the satisfaction of the parents, guardians, and patrons of the institution, when the time came round for the great man to make his valedictory. All eyes were now turned to the speakers stand, expectation was on tiptoe, and smiling glances beamed out from the face of many a fair and lovely creature as the lilliputian figure of councillor Hovey popped up from behind a table on the rostrum and bowed to the assembly with all the grace of a wooden cuccoo on the top of a dutch clock, when that sagacious little bird makes his congé while proclaiming the time of day. A smile of perfect self approbation sat upon his lips, and he looked the very picture of benevolence when he opened his mouth and said,

"My dear young friends. This is the happiest moment of my life, and I the proudest man in existence, because I have now an oppertunity to do that which few can do so well as myself; yes my dear little children, I am about to illumine you juvinile minds with bright lessons of glorious wisdom. You who now sit before me in all the simple innocence of uninformed ignorance, will e'er many years shall have passed over your infantile heads will be called upon to take part in the duties of citizens of our great and glorious, and happy, and most transcendantly prosperous country; it will be therefore incumbent on you to mark, learn, and inwardly digest the important truths of my experience during my progress through life, from the time I was no bigger than yourselves up to the present moment of my station among men."

"Born at an early age, in obscurity I was thrown by the adverse winds of adversity into the turbulent stream of poverty—a beardless boy at the green age of six years—to battle with the buffeting billows of tempestuous strife on the tide of time and the current of contrary waters on the faithless ocean of uncertain life. When I entered upon the great stage, which you e'er long are doomed to tread also, I knew no more than yourselves, but by the force of my natural character & perseverance of an indomitable will, I have raised myself from oblivion, made my way through the cobwebs of society to an enviable station in an honorable profession. And now, in me, you behold what genius struggling with adversity can do in claiming and asserting her rights against the contending armies of poverty and indigence. Yes, my little friends, in after years, when misfortunes overtake you, you must not suffer yourselves to sink under its incumbrous weight, nor give up to despair, but brave all as I have done,—only think of me,—of what I was—of what I have gone through—and what I *am* and you will be able to overcome every obstacle which may beset your path."

The above is the substance of what he said to his young friends and needs no comments on its merits or demerits, and is given as near as I can recollect in the way it was said to me. I do not endorse it, but only give it as I recieved it.

CHAPTER VI

LECTURES ON THE ARTS — A NATURAL BRIDGE — ANECDOTES AND ADVENTURES ON THE ROAD TO LEXINGTON

THE LITERARY ASSOCIATION, not having had a meeting for some time, some of its leading members made an effort to resuscitate it, and thought by getting up a lecture to which the public would be invited might aid their cause very materially. Accordingly they paid me the compliment, through a committee of four members, of inviting me to give a lecture on the subject of the Fine Arts at such a time as might suit my convenience.[77] To which I returned the following answer.

Independence, Missouri,
August 14, 1845.

Gentlemen

I have the honor to acknowledge the receipt of your very polite communication of this morning, informing me that you were appointed a committee on behalf of the Literary Association of this place, to request me to deliver before that body, an address or lecture on the subject of the Fine Arts.

The calmness attendant upon the pursuit of the beautiful Arts, and the quietude of the studio rendering those of our profession unfit for public speaking, would deter me from appearing before an audience, but I trust more to your politeness, and the interest of my subject, than my own poor abilities for the due performance of the task you are pleased to assign me. I therefore cheerfuly comply with your wishes when and where you please.

Accept for the Association which you represent, and yourselves individually, my highest consideration, and believe me to be, gentlemen,

Your obedient sert
Alfred S. Waugh

To Hugh N. Smith,[78] Geo.W. Buchanan, J. H. Harper, and J. R. Palmer, Esquires, committee.

---

77. Waugh was fond of lecturing, but if we are to judge from his published writings, his talks must have been filled with large generalizations. See "The Rise, Progress and Influence of the Fine Arts," in the *Western Journal* (St. Louis), I (1848), 309-314, 383-385, 445-447, 497-500, 571-574, 627-630, 672-678; II (1849), 29-33. Probably his failing eyesight explains why the series was not completed.

78. Hugh N. Smith went to Santa Fe as a private in Company A of the First Regiment Missouri Mounted Volunteers (Connelley, *Doniphan's Expedition*, 533).

On Tuesday evening the 19th a large and highly respectable audience assembled in the Court House, all the beauty and fashion of the town were there. Lawyers, doctors, and divines, merchants, traders, and even the great J. Hovey himself deigned to be present. I need not say that I felt somewhat embarrassed as the critical moment approached. I was about to appear before people who were strangers to me and, I to them, and I could not, and did not feel as much at home as I would do where each was known to the other. I am not now pretending to a feeling of modesty, no such thing I assure you, but, although the town of Independence is, as one might say—on the borders of civilization,—there were several highly cultivated persons,—citizens of the place—whose education in other states, qualified them to adorn any community into which they might be thrown,—such person[s] I was aware would be present on this occasion and I doubted my ability to deliver myself as I should. I was not accustomed to public speaking—knew none of the clap trap tricks of speech or manner and, in a word, did not know how to win the public ear. However I was willing to try what I could do in the way of talking so down stairs I went, was recieved courteously by the president and took my seat on the rostrum, while the preliminary ceremonies were being gone through. Before me the judges desk was covered with a blanket, a couple of tallow candles stood on either extremity and a pitcher and glass of cold water waited my call upon their service during the evening. Jonathan Palmer, the president of the Association, now rose and presented me in due form to the audience. How I got along after this I cannot tell, but I know this, that I was very patiently listened to for one hour, at the conclusion of which the usual courtesy of a vote of thanks was tendered me, and the next day the papers spoke of it in very polite terms.

Not long after this while shewing my sketch book to my friend Samuel Lucas, he told me that if I wished to see an object worth looking at, that he would take me to a natural bridge, the sight of which would amply repay me for the trouble of a ride to its locality. Thankfully accepting his politeness, I accompanied him the following morning "in search of the picturesque."

Our route from Independence lay in a southernly direction along the state road to Harrisonville, for more than nine miles, until we came to the farm of the Rev. Robert Sloan, whose house stands within a few hundred yards of the object of our pursuit.[79] Here we tied our horses, and crossing

79. Robert Sloan was born in Tennessee in 1801 and died in Cass County, Missouri, in 1869. He married Margaret Davidson Ewing (born Todd County, Kentucky, 1807) in 1826; they had twelve children. In 1845 he settled near Lee's Summit, Jackson County, Missouri (*Memorial and Biographical Record of Kansas City and Jackson*

his lot under the direction of his son, soon came to a ravine deeply shaded with hickory, hazle bushes, and sumac. Through this we descended to the dry bed of the creek (Sedar creek) and pursuing our way along its rough channel suddenly found ourselves standing at the entrance of a low arched cavern of compact limestone of some fifty feet wide and about twelve to fourteen feet high; almost forming an equilateral triangle and bearing the same proportions throughout its entire length—a distance of about fifty yards or so. I was very much pleased with the effect of light produced by the sunshine. As we stood at the west or lower entrance an exceeding fine effect, resembling that produced by the sun streaming through a stained glass window in some gothic cloister, attracted our attention by its monastic appearance. The opening in the extreme end was shaded by foliage, through whose partly colored leaves the sun came into the cavern and mocked the ingenuity of man by the beauty of its many tinted rays. A wide gap in the roof of the cavern, near its eastern extremity, admitted a full flood of light from the north and divided the interior into rich masses of light and shade, and affording to the artist one of the most charming studies that can well be imagined.

This freak of nature is formed by two huge blocks of limestone, here and there encrusted with carbonate of lime in small stalactites very much resembling *brocoli*. About the centre of the roof, a fissure, varying from half to five or six inches, completely divides it into two distinct masses, whose rough uneven surfaces, in many places, give indication of decay; and whole strata seem ready to add their most prominent parts to the broken rugged floor, whose present elevation has, no doubt, been caused by the falling of detached pieces at different periods. As we stood now at the upper entrance and looked down to the western we again encountered an other charming effect as we did when we first looked through the cavern. The mouth was shaded with foliage presenting the same illusion of stained glass as in the eastern termination. Toward the east a large gap is formed on the north side of about a dozen yards in extent through which the daylight streams in sufficient volume to render the interior sufficiently distinct for every purpose of exploration. Beyond this the arch is again complete, and the stream, when there is water in the creek, enters by a sharp angle in the ravine and falls over a ledge of rocks into a bason formed by its own impetuosity. Within this last named arch large fragments of the roof and wall have fallen down, leaving the south side almost perpendicular. Having sat down on a mass

---

County, 57). In Independence he served as pastor of the Cumberland Presbyterian Church (*History of Jackson County, Missouri*, 658).

of flat rock, I made a sketch of the interior, as far as the eye could take in the view at a glance, then turning to the right, made another introducing the figure of my friend Sam Lucas, quietly reposing at the entrance, in order to give the relative proportions of the scene. After enjoying the refreshing coolness of this secluded retreat for a while, we once more emerged into the upper air and beheld a fine undulating country on the borders of a prairie, finely diversified with clumps of trees, and mantled over with a most luxurious vegitation. A broad road, wide enough to admit two wagons abreast, conducts to an elevated ground finely timbered, over which the traveller might pass and repass, without being aware of the existence of a bridge of any sort in the vicinity, so concealed are its sides by trees, whose tops, just rising a few feet above the ravine and looking so much like brushwood, entirely prevents the passerby from detecting the presence of such a specimen of Nature's own architecture.

I now made a sketch of the road across the bridge with the accompaniments of surrounding scenery and then returned with my friend to the spot where I had made the first sketch. Our ride having furnished us with most excellent sauce to the creature comforts contained within our saddle bags, we made a very hearty dinner, after which we lighted our cigars, mounted our steeds, and returned to town well pleased with the days excursion.

This singular natural curiosity is not, I find, generally known to the citizens of the county, for, when ever I spoke of it, I was invariably told that its existence was unknown, never having heard of it before. At present there are no names either written or cut upon the rocks, from which it may be supposed to have few or no visitors. Altogether I deem it well worthy of consideration and feel much gratified in having the good fortune to be the first artist to transfer its beauties to the pages of my sketch book, and draw the attention of the public to an object that must ultimately become one of the lions of Jackson county.

Under this impression that I might gratify the good people of the county by making it known, I wrote to the editors of the Expositor, a letter on the subject of my visit which they politely published. Immediately after the appearance of the letter, a party of ladies and gentlemen paid a visit to the natural bridge, taking with them the published account, and while there read it over, and then placed the newspaper in a crevice of the rock with a note appended, requesting all new comers to leave it where they should find it for the benefit of future visitors. After this several other parties went out to it and now it is tolerably well known.

Our little friend J. Hovey who is great upon all matters, thought I had made but a bungling affair of the description, and promised, as soon as I had left Independence, to pull my poor bridge all to pieces but as he did not do it, I suppose he must have had more important work on hand. He is great,—very great,—in his own estimation.

In the whole of this country, as far as I have seen, the forest abounds with every variety of oak, and one species in particular, struck me as remarkable of which I have no recollection of having seen a specimen before; it is called the Burr oak. Its acorn in a great measure resembles the base of the scotch thistle just as the fibres are beginning to grow. Of the walnut, I noticed two varieties in great abundance. This wood is in common use by the farmers for building purposes, aye, even for burning. I could not help thinking how valuable the splendid tree is in many other places, while here it is thought almost nothing, being used for the commonest purposes. Shell bark hickory, and a variety of this, called the Pignut, Hackberry, or as it is sometimes termed, huckleberry, Linwood, Hazel, and Ash, with a variety of shrubs peculiar to a northern latitude, but not a specimen of the Pine is to be found in all this section of the country. The Linwood is used as a substitute in carpentry, but has one great defect which renders it less useful than the Pine; it becomes, when wet so very soft that nails can be drawn from it by the fingers with great ease.

Finding general Lucas to be a Free Mason, I was introduced to the Lodge and found in the members thereof a warm hearted band of brothers in whose breasts were cherished all the enobling principles of this time honored institution. The general's lady is a sister of the order, being a Heroine of Jericho.

As the September court drew near, I was again invited to deliver an other lecture before the Literary Association. The Bench and the Bar honored me with their presence. My subject this time was one that did not admit of the same scope as my first on "the Fine Arts and their influence on society," being confined to architecture alone, and, with which I was not so familiar as with painting and sculpture. Frequently did I regret the choice I had made for my theme,—became out of sorts with it and myself and when I came to deliver it, felt very indifferent about its success and anticipated no applause whatever, but what was my surprise to find that it was considered even better than my first,—well! I am glad they liked it, I did not. It only shews that the things we sometimes are pleased with are not always agreeable to the public as some that we ourselves, esteem of less value.

Friend Tisdale having spent a week at the house of our good old friend

Lindsay Lewis returned to town rather unwell and next day was confined to his bed with congestive fever. The moment general Lucas was aware of his illness he had him removed to his own house, where he received all the kindness from the motherly care of Mrs. Lucas as he would were he under his own paternal roof. In a short time Jack recovered—and in grateful remembrance of this kindness—for what ever is done to my friend, is done to me, I took the likenesses of the whole family in a group, and presented them to the general.

Having been previously introduced to several gentlemen from Lexington in this state, and having also completed all my orders here, I merely finished the heads of the general's group, intending to complete it, after I should reach Lexington. I intended to leave on the 20th of Oct., but was induced by Col. Jacob Hall of whom I have already spoken, to stop and paint the likenesses of himself, his lady and child. These I treated as in the other group, and were to be finished at my next halting place. The following Sunday morning the 26th, at about half past nine, I mounted the horse which I had purchased on the first of the month and given to Tisdale, and set out to pioneer the way for our future campaign. I left Tisdale engaged on a miniature on ivory of Jonathan Palmer, this by the by, was the first piece of work which he undertook professionally, and for which he was to receive fifteen dollars. As soon as it was completed he was to join me again and lend his assistance to me in the business of face making.

I had scarcely started when I was joined by Mr. J. B. Slaughter and in a very short time we overtook Colonel Samuel Owens.[80] Both these gentlemen are citizens of Independence and were going on a visit to the town of Liberty on the other side of the river distant from Independence about twelve miles. Mirth seemed to take possession of us all, for, we were mutually entertained with each other's anecdotes. It was a delightful day, every thing around us bore a pleasant appearance, and contributed in a great measure to our exhiliration of spirits. Col. Owens was in his finest mood and gave us many anecdotes in a style peculiar to himself, one of which, I must here relate. It appears that at some country hotel, where situated I don't recollect, the stationed methodist minister boarded. He was without a family, and although perhaps a well meaning and

80. Samuel C. Owens was born in Kentucky in 1800, settled in Franklin, Missouri, in 1818, became manager of James Aull's store at Independence in 1827, was a partner of Robert Aull from 1836 to 1844. He commanded the Traders Battalion in Doniphan's Expedition and died at the Battle of Sacramento in 1847. For much information about him consult the index to Ralph P. Bieber (editor), *Southwest Historical Series*, the Magoffin *Diary*, and Connelley's *Doniphan's Expedition.*

sincere man, he could boast of very little common sense for, he was continually displaying his exuberant zeal on every occasion. At the public table the dishes grew cold under the inordinate length of the blessings which he invoked and, so indefatiguable was he in the discharge of what he considered his imperative duty, that the opposite effect resulted from his labors. The sanctity which should accompany the performance of religious ceremonies, was lost sight of by those whom he thought to convert; his overwrought zeal seemed to lie too much on the surface, and like the bubbling and noise of a shallow brook, had no depth beneath. The very means he employed to do good, were the source of evil to those around him. His sighing and groaning were laughed at as hypochritical. His long face and self rightious air, were held up to the ridicule of every body and, instead of making men correct in their language, curses followed his prayers, almost as invariably. The landlord, who was irritated beyond measure with his pious boarder, had been, for some time, devising plans to put a stop to the annoyance which the rest of his boarders experienced in this man's conduct, at last hit upon one which he proceeded to put in execution on the arrival of a traveller, one wet and disagreeable evening in the autumn of the year, 18——. The new comer was past the meridian of life, of a spare and attenuated frame, and a certain rigidity of the muscles of his face, shewed him to be of an irritable temper. The moment the host saw him alight from his travel stained but powerfully made horse, he selected him in his own mind for the instrument by whose means he should veto the preacher's proceedings in the future without coming to an open rupture with the divine.

The traveller enjoyed the comfort of the fire in the bar room for some time after supper when, feeling strongly inclined to sleep, retired to his chamber, leaving the rest of the company behind him. Weary with his long and dreary ride, no sooner had he ensconed himself within a comfortable bed than he fell into a pleasant, refreshing sleep. He had not been in bed more than an hour, when he was awakened by some one in the next room praying in a very loud, and, by no means musical voice. To this, at first, he listened with respectful patience, but finding it continued longer than, he thought, was necessary and hearing many repetitions of—worm of the earth,—vile sinner—lost soul,—bottomless pit, and everlasting hell fire, he lost all patience and heartily wished the speaker to the devil. But as every thing has an end, at some time or other, the voice ceased and our traveller fell into a doze.

The morning came, and with it the irritated traveller also. He looked gloomy and discontented; eat his breakfast in silence; rose from the table with a vexed air; ordered his horse and called for his bill. In glancing over the items, his eye rested on one that seemed to puzzle him a great deal,—he could not make it out at first, looked again, and again when at last he became satisfied of its true reading. Hallo landlord, what the h—l do you mean by this "fifty cents for prayers." I never heard such a thing in all my born days! Are you in earnest in making such a charge? "Yes Sir, said the bonneyface we always have prayers in this house, every night sir, and they form an item in the bill of every travellor who stops with me." The preacher, who was sitting by the fire, now heard himself cursed for a roaring jack-ass, who ought to be sent to jail as a pest to society, and the landlord came in for his share of abuse for keeping such a nuisance in his house. Instead of paying the damn fellow, he would be served right to give him a good cow-hiding, and "I tell you what it is, landlord I will publish you and your d——d house in the newspapers, for the public ought to be made acquainted with such rascally conduct. You needn't say you'll scratch it out of the bill, I will have it remain,—There sir I will pay it but depend upon you will never hear the last of it." O! sir, said the landlord, I am very sorry that prayers are not agreeable to you. They please every body else that I know of, but you are the only gentleman who ever refused to pay me for the use of the prayers, here's your fifty cents back, sir.

As the traveller black with indignation was about to mount his horse, the host stepped up to him and in low tone, said that he did this in order to put a stop to the prayers for the future, as the noisy preacher was at that time sitting at the fire, and he wished to give him a hint. An immense burst of laughter followed in the presence of the poor soul saver, who, from that moment out was never known to pray aloud. By this trick of the host, he, and his guests were saved from any further annoyance on that score.

There are a great many persons who through ignorance or, a mistaken notion of the service of God, do a vast deal of mischief to the cause of religion. We do not like to have opinions or doctrines crammed down our throats whether we will or not, nor do we like to see sectarianism brought in upon every occasion. Religion is too sacred a thing to be profaned and thrown about like party politics in every hole and corner. There is a time and place for all things and it is not always judicious to force it on the attention of people at an undue time or season.

We thus passed our time along the road until the current of our thoughts was changed by an unusual number of persons both in carriages and on horseback, hurry toward town to hear the celebrated Alexander Cambell,[81] founder of a new sect which bears his name, who was expected to preach there that day. As we rode on the concourse of horsemen and carriages increased, it seemed as if all the country was in motion on, on they came, drest in their best, and looking as if they expected to be highly benefited by hearing and seeing this great fountain of new light. A few carriages now came in sight, and from the unusual bustle by the occupants of some five or six others that formed the escort of the one in advance, it was pretty evident that some person of great importance was advancing.

At length the cortage passed us and we beheld the great man himself seated in the first carriage. He was leaning back on his seat with the air of a magnate and a ruler in Israal. It was very evident that he was a man of no common mould, his very air and bearing shewed that he himself thought so, for he bowed to us with a most patronizing grace, as we passed.

There goes a great man, said Owens, a d——d smart man and no mistake. He and Joe Smith understand human nature very well; they were both baptists, but feeling that they were idling away their time, without any chance of distinguishing themselves, they held council together, and determined each, to shine as a star of the first magnitude in the firmament of genius. Accordingly they broke off from all connections with their old church, and each set up on his own hook. Joe founded the Mormons, and Alexander the Christian church. Joe Smith has run his race, but he has laid the foundation of, it may be, an empire which may ultimately become as flourishing as that of the Ottoman. Cambell has more scholarship than Smith, but the later is fully as learned in human nature and was equally well qualified to command.

At the forks of the road, six miles from town we separated, Owens and Slaughter taking the left, and I the right. I now felt my spirits sink, and for the balance of the day continued rather melancholy. About one o'clock P. M. coming to the 10 mile house, kept by a Mr. Hambright, I halted for dinner and at three again resumed my journey. This delay threw me into the night, and two or three times I was tempted to seek quarters at some of the snug houses I saw along the road-side. Thinking however as I had been told that the road was a plain one and could not be missed, I continued to ride on, in expectation of reaching Lexington some time before morning. About nine o'clock I saw a light ahead of

---

81. Alexander Campbell (1788-1866), born a Presbyterian, came to America in 1809. A few years later he was baptized by a Baptist minister and became one himself. In 1826 his Disciples of Christ became a separate denomination (*DAB*, III, 446-448).

me along the road, to which I soon came up and found it to proceed from a waggoner's camp fire. My sight was so dazzled that I could not see my way so I gave the reins to my horse, who, finding himself at liberty to take his own road, took me too far to the right, and we became lost among the scattered undergrowth of some open ground, where we wandered about completely bewildered for more than an hour. Not knowing exactly where I was in the dark, I did, two or three times, think of kindling a fire and camping out for the night, but at last I made up my mind to return to the waggoner's and ask to stay there. I knew I could not be far from my destination, but, far or near, I did not know where I was, or how I should proceed, therefore my best plan would be to return to the fire on the side of the road. Slowly I wended my way back to that light which now served as a beacon to guide me to repose. Alas! alas! how often are we disappointed in our hopes and expectations, I had made sure of a hospitable reception at the camp to which I was returning. I had pictured to myself a rough but, a hearty welcome from the hardy sons of toil and never once dreamed of anything like a repulse. Having now reached the ground I called out and was answered by some person from within a tent; in a moment a rough unprepossessing figure of a man emerged from beneath the canvass and stood before me at the other side of the first. He looked sour vinigar at me for disturbing him from his slumbers, "What's your buisiness stranger" said he in a harsh, uncivil tone, "What do want rousin me at this time o night." In a few words I offered an apology for the intrusion, and stated my case by way of an excuse for so doing, and asked permission to stay by his fire all night. Without waiting for an answer I dismounted, took off the saddle and trappings, tied the horse to a tree, and came back to the fire with saddle and saddle bags in my arms, and at once proceeded to make preparation for repose by disposing of my saddle for a pillow and spreading a piece of buffalo robe on the ground for a bed, lighted my pipe and stretched myself on the couch to enjoy a quiet smoke e'er I should resign myself to the arms of *Murphy*. The waggoner who during my preparations, kept eying me rather curiously remarked that he had no accommodations for strangers, as he had neither corn nor fodder for my horse. Make yourself easy on our account, my good sir, said I, we both have dined, and as I know what it is to camp out, I can put up with a hard bed for one night at least. Still the fellow seemed uneasy, why? I could not tell, he talked of the plainess of the road, its short distance to Lexington, and wondered how I could have missed my way. In vain I tried to explain my dilemma to him, he could not understand it, and was surprised that I did not select some house on the road instead of a waggoner's camp for a night's lodging, and in verry surly manner retired within his tent. While ruminating on my novel situation, my horse commenced a disturbance with his neighbors; this called me up, and I shortened his rope; but no sooner had I lain down than he began again, when my host ran out once more and in a loud voice called up his hands desired them to make up a blazing fire and see that all his horses were safe. It now occurred to me that some suspicion was attached to me from the manner of my coming to his camp, and my rigmarole story of loosing my way when the road was plain enough to any person who could see, and besides there were plenty of houses along the road where I could have stopped. This I must confess gave him a coloring of suspicion against me. Finding however that I was not a welcome visitor, I determined to relieve him of my presence, and although myself and my steed were weary I would seek a more hospitable abode. In accoutering my horse for a start, which I did at the fire, I purposely displayed all my equipments in order that he might see that I carried away only my own property, I happened to let fall the piece of buffalo skin which covered my splendid bowie-knife, and while talking to the man, slowly hung the weapon upon the horn of the saddle. The sight of this formidable weapon, no doubt, confirmed him in his previous suspicions of me, and, it is more than probable, that he thanked his stars that he was about to get rid of me. Everything being ready, I advanced to the fire, and standing erect before him, took off my hat and in a style and voice, strongly smacking of the stage, asked him if I looked like a gentleman? "Why Look here stranger," said he, "you have a very respectable appearance, but I don't know who you are, or whar you come from and I can't tell whether you are a gentleman or not, It's so tarnation hard to judge by appearances." Whereupon I told him in a very pompous manner, that I was Colonel Waugh of Mobile Alabama and too much of a gentleman to stay where he was not welcome. "Look here Kurnel" said he, did you ever live in old north caroliney. I answered in the affirmative when, he continued "Kase why I knowed Kurnel Waugh of Wilks County and a mighty fine man he was too, and no mistake," he is a particular friend of mine, I replied, but no relation. "Well see here now, stranger I'm from the old north state myself, and I'd like to be civil to any body coming from thar, I think I can accommodate you with me, so don't go," but I declined his rather late civility. Mounting into the saddle, I took off my hat, wished him good night and was in another moment retracing my steps to a house which I had passed some mile and a half back. The poor colonel (the horse) walked slowly away, thinking no doubt that he was an ill used horse, but we had to go. On we went until we came to the house, here dismounting I knocked at the door, and enquired for lodgings for the night, but was told by a man, who answered from within, without opening the door, told me that I could get no quarters there, and advised me to turn back about a quarter of a mile and probably Mr. Graves would accommodate me. Here again was I in a nice predicament, neither camp nor house would take me in, so, I once more took to the road without the slightest desire to add to my adventures. Arrived at the residence of the aforesaid gentleman, I knocked at his door for a long time before anyone answered my summons, but my steady perseverance in this line at last drew some attention to the knocker. I was asked by some person within the window of a side room, what I wanted. I replied that I was a traveller and wished lodging for the night! How came you to travel at so late an hour? asked the man from within in a voice that evidently belonged to a person who was very drowsy. I told him recieving no answer to my urgent solicitations to be let in that I determined, as a last resource, to make my bed in the porch, but sleep came not to my weary eyelids. Feeling rather cold toward morning I became anxious for a smoke, but refrained as it occurred to me that the people of the house, if they saw the light, might fancy me an incendiary. Just as the dawn began to appear in the east I rose from my couch and went down the steps to see how the colonel was doing, when a negro man came forward and politely asked me if I were cold, requested me to warm myself at the kitchen fire. Finding my body in a more comfortable condition, and daylight beginning to spread itself over the face of the earth, I returned to my chamber in the porch and sat down to enjoy my pipe which I had kindled at the kitchen fire. By the time I was beginning to feel its soothing influence, and forget the eventful passages of the previous night, the hall door opened, and an elderly gentleman, with a candle in his hand, came out, to whom I expressed my regret at being obliged to disturb him at so unseasonable an hour, but excused myself by saying that I was compelled to do what I did, as I had no other resource left to me. After examining me from head to foot, he began appologizing in a very handsome manner for having kept me in the cold all night,—spoke [of] being very sleepy, and of the great number of trifling characters who were in the habit of disturbing him at all hours, which prevented him from opening his door after dark unless he knew who it was who wished to come into his house, then in a very courteous manner requested me to enter and took me into his own room and placed me before a good fire, and again expressed his regret at the circumstance of any gentleman being kept outside his door all night. Breakfast was now announced and as I was taking off my great coat previous to going into the parlor, the masonic badge of mourning on my button hole caught his attention, he now spoke to me as a brother, and asked me why I did not make myself known, when the door should have flown open to me, instantly. In the course of conversation he invited me to call on him and spoke engaging my professional services. In his eldest son I found a gentleman to whom I was introduced by Samuel Lucas at Independence. I now took my leave and in company with Desha Graves,[82] my new acquaintance, I started for my destination where we arrived at half past eight o'clock on the morning of Monday the 17th of Oct. 1845.

---

82. Desha B. Graves served as second lieutenant of Company B, First Regiment Missouri Mounted Volunteers. He was born in Fayette County, Kentucky, a grandnephew of Governor Desha of that state. He came to Lafayette County, Missouri, in 1839, and died there—a farmer—in 1850 (Connelley, *Doniphan's Expedition,* 539).

CHAPTER VII

LEXINGTON—MANNERS OF THE LEXINGTONIANS—SOME LEADING CITIZENS —A LECTURE—CHRISTMAS AT INDEPENDENCE—BACK TO LEXINGTON

FREQUENTLY since the adventure spoken of in the last chapter, have I drawn in my own mind, the great contrast between the south, and the west. In this state, the people are selfish and suspisious; in the South they are generous and unsuspecting. Here almost every man is viewed as a rogue until he proves himself an honest man,—there it is the reverse, every man is taken to be a decent fellow until he shews himself a rascal. Here the highest characters in the community will take pay from a traveller for a nights lodging, but in almost every part of the south, the wayfarer is entertained with great kindness and no charge made, except where he lodges at houses set apart for the accomodation of the public. I will venture to assert that I might have travelled in any part of the South and no man would have refused to open his door to me. As for the waggoner, he was but a sorry specimen of the old north state. The north carolinians, like my own countrymen abroad, must not be taken as samples, for, few of the better class of either country are amongst us, here in the west. Reflections like the foregoing continually occupied my mind during my ride into Lexington.

This town is stretched over a great extent of ground and, in a partial resemblance of ancient Rome, occupies as many hills. The houses are not few and far between, but are scattered about with a profuseness that bespeaks a stirring, active population; they are mostly built of brick, generally neat, and some of them in very good taste. It is divided into two parts, called the old and the new town; the old is about a mile from the landing and is chiefly occupied by the working classes, while the shopkeepers and professional men, dwell in the New.[83] In the last-named

83. The "old town" was laid out in 1822; a city charter was granted Lexington in 1845 (Young, *History of Lafayette County, Missouri*, I, 310). The *Missouri Republican* for 15 January 1846 described Lexington at the close of 1845: "This town still continues to flourish, and to extend its commerce, aided by the rich country which surrounds it on every side, and by the energy, and industry, and thrift of its inhabitants. The 'Express,' of the 6th inst., publishes some of the statistics for the year 1845, from which we derive the following information. There were thirty-three brick houses erected during the year ending 15th of November, at an estimated cost of $62,400. But in addition there were twenty-nine frame houses also erected, at a cost of $8,700. At the end of the year there were in Lexington, twenty-five dry goods and grocery stores; four apothecary and drug stores; twelve ware-houses; two pork-packing establishments; three saddlers and harness makers; three cabinet makers; two turners of wood and one of iron and steel; seven blacksmiths; five coopers; one steam flouring mill, with four pair of French burrs; one tobacco stemmery; two cigar

division, the City Hotel, a good, substantial brick building, is situated; it consists of a basement and two upper stories, with a yard and out offices. To this hotel I directed my steps as I had a letter of introduction to the landlord J. J. Burtis, of whom I shall speak by, and by.[84]

The hemp buisiness occupies the attention of many of the most substantial citizens, and to some extent pork packing is carried on profitably. The usual array of shopkeepers and coffee houses, as in other places make up the picture. A very large proportion of the citizens here are from Kentucky who have selected it with a view of bettering their delapidated fortunes.[85] Before leaving Independence I was told that it was quite an aristocratic place with a population remarkable for the refinement of its manners. In expectation of seeing good society I provided myself with introductory letters to several heads of families, who were considered the leaders of the town, but out of nine which I delivered I had the honor to be called on by four of the recipients. The Revd. Mr. Yantis[86] was the first to pay me a visit and to give me an invitation to his house, Mr. Wm. Russel,[87] a whole soulsman [*sic*], was the next to shew me courtesy, and the Hon. Judge Ryland, the third, but beyond there, I received no household invitations, nothing beyond mere common place civility. In giving my opinion of the social habits of the Lexingtonians one evening, to the

---

and tobacco stores; nine tailors; four shoemakers; three bakeries; two barbers; one tin and hardware store; two printing offices; nine or ten joiners' shops; three ropewalks; and various other shops and places of useful employment. There were also ten practicing physicians in the town, and fourteen lawyers."

84. His advertisement in the *Lexington Appeal*, dated 13 January 1847, reads:

"City Hotel
Main Street
Lexington, Mo.

"The undersigned having taken the above establishment, hopes by his attention to the comfort and accommodation of travellers, to receive a liberal share of patronage. The building is new, large and commodious, and one of the best Hotels in the Interior of Missouri. His table will always be well supplied with the best that this abundant country affords, and his rooms always comfortable: indeed no pains shall be spared, to insure the comfort of his guests." A card offers his services as "resident dentist" with an office on "Main Street below the New Bank" (*Ibid.*, 7 April 1847). A letter signed "Johnson County" in the *Appeal* for 15 February 1848 proposed Burtis for state senator.

85. The town was named for Lexington, Kentucky.

86. John Lapsley Yantis, born in Kentucky, 4 September 1804, married Elizabeth Montgomery of Lincoln County, Kentucky, on 21 August 1828, and died 28 May 1882. He is credited with organizing the First Presbyterian Church, Old School, at Independence on 21 November 1841. He served as Presbyterian minister at Lexington from 1841 to 1847; the church there was erected in 1844. Consult *History of Jackson County, Missouri*, 657; Young, *History of Lafayette County, Missouri*, I, 163; *Portrait and Biographical Record Lafayette and Saline Counties*, 126.

87. Probably William Hepburn Russell (1812-1872), overland freighter and pony express founder. He was born at Burlington, Vermont, and married Harriett Elliott Warder at Lexington, Missouri (*DAB*, XVI, 252-253). Not to be confused with William Henry Russell who went to California with Bryant in 1846 (see note 112 below).

Revd. Mr. Fackler,[88] the Episcopal rector, I remarked that they were not a very social or friendly people; there seemed to be no free or pleasant intercourse between families, nor were the young people disposed to cultivate a better feeling among themselves. The old ones appeared to be taken up too much in buildings, and the young ones in gambling to have any leisure to cherish the refinements of life, and altogether, they were not a people with whom a stranger could feel pleased. "Why Sir," said my friend, "I was more than a year in Lexington before any one, even among my parisheners, thought proper to extend to me an invitation of any sort." This then was a confirmation of the opinion I had expressed; for if a clergyman can be suffered to remain twelve months in a town before he is asked to take a cup of tea by any of its inhabitants, I think that its character is at once told, and that too in a few words.

In a day or two after my arrival I prepared my studio in a front room of my hotel and received visitors. A prospect of success was held out to me, and practice to a great extent promised in miniature painting. But although everyone seemed to be in the notion of having their likenesses painted, yet they were in no hurry to give me the first sitting. This talking without working gave me a feeling of disappointment. I could not be satisfied, and began to think of leaving for a wider and fairer field of operations and wrote to Tisdale to stay where he was until he should hear from me, as I did not think arts were in any estimation among the citizens.

This is a singularly strange town indeed; every day I have the most fashionable persons to call on me, who talk loudly of getting this, that, and the other done by me, yet with but one exception only, have any of them sat. One lady,—I would be afraid to call her young,—who talks well on most subjects, and is moreover, somewhat of a bluestocking, has been to see me several times, about a picture which she says she wants painted, for her sister. This lady, Miss Martha Boyce, consider[s] herself, and is considered to be, the very queen of elegant society; her opinion on subjects of literature and art is supreme among the fashionables; her sanction is necessary before any move can be made in the beau-monde,

---

88. St. Michael Fackler in May, 1846, reported twenty-four communicants at Lexington. A year earlier Bishop Hawks, then on a visitation of his diocese, spent 16-18 May at Lexington. He wrote: "This is a spot where I desire very much to see the Church established upon a firm foundation. Before leaving the place I gathered the friends of the Church and induced them to make an effort towards obtaining a suitable lot and erecting a Church edifice. The edifice has proceeded so far as to enable them to purchase the lot, and, with some assistance from abroad, I trust they may in a little time have a suitable house in which to assemble and worship." Fackler resigned his charge in 1847. (*Journal of the Seventh Annual Convention*, 25, 9; *Journal of the Eighth Annual Convention*, 9.)

I was therefore advised to pay court to her, or I could not expect to succeed. I am averse to every thing like todying whether man or woman, but, am fond of the society of intellectual ladies, and, although I am an old bachelor, I am capable of appreciating the female character. Having recieved an invitation from Miss B. I did myself the honor to call one morning, and found her to be exceedingly interesting and well informed, but deeply dyed in the tint aetherial. The interview terminated by being told that her father would call and arrange with me about having a picture painted, but I heard nothing further on the subject.[89]

I do not like the habit they have here of saying "O! before you go I will get my likeness taken," it is not exactly the thing an artist likes, he wants to be employed. Not at all pleased with my prospect, I wrote to Tisdale, "If you have any thing to do in Independence, remain there until I see my way clear here, for it is cheaper and you are more comfortable than if you were with me at present. It is true I feel very lonely, but I do not wish you to join me until I see whether it will be advisable to remain in Lexington or not." Again in an other letter I wrote the following, "Of late I have had a great many visitors without procuring me a single order, and I begin to think it useless to remain longer among a people who care so little for the Fine Arts." There is nothing so unpleasant to an artist's feelings as this thing of being kept in expectation, without a consumation of his hopes. His time is his only estate by the proper farming of which he can live and enjoy life.

A few days after my arrival, I had the pleasure of meeting an old and highly valued friend, whom, I had not seen since I left him a senior at the University of North Carolina,—Doctor Wm. Haywood Ruffin[90] is now located in this town, is a noble fellow and stands deservedly high in the estimation of the citizens. Much of my leisure moments were spent in his company and very much to my benefit, in an intellectual point of view. To him am I indebted for many a happy evening. To a naturally fine mind his education has opened all the lore of classic antiquity, and the refinements of really elegant society hath bestowed all its charms on the conversation and manners of this true, and gentle son, son of good old North Carolina. In person the doctor is what every well bred gentleman should be, a perfect model of neatness. A dandy or fop he can never be, for he possesses too much self respect to put himself on a level with every brainless creature who fancies himself a *gentleman* because he wears the

89. This lady rather doubted my abilities to paint, and believed that the pictures in my room, were the work of some other artist not mine own.—WAUGH.

90. A card in the *Lexington Appeal,* 7 April 1847, gave his office address as the northwest corner of the public square.

newest fashions in his apparal. Having a mind of his own, his actions are governed by a sense of inate propriety, and a decent respect for the usages of the world around him. A gentleman in the strict sense of the term, requires no written code of ettiquette to govern him in his intercourse with his fellows. Real politeness is based upon goodness of heart and needs no arbitrary laws to keep it with a certain pale. A ready acquiessence with the usages of those with whom we are brought in contact, is oftener the characteristic of the truly well bred, than the closest adhesion to the elaborate rules that were ever laid down by Chesterfield. There was more politeness in one simple act of the prince of Wales than that superficial nobleman was capable of concieving. On one occasion, when a lady had the misfortune to pour her tea into the saucer, a smile of contempt on the lips of others more fashionable displayed itself to her mortification; which the gentleman prince percieving, without one moment's delay, [he] exercised the power which he possessed in the world of ton, & at once gave the stamp of fashion to the poor lady's blunder by quietly pouring his own tea into the saucer. In his intercourse, either professionaly or social, the doctor creates the impression that he is in reallity a gentleman of sterling worth, and like the prince just spoken of he exercises a happy influence on the community at large.

Although I have not been very favorably impressed with the Lexingtonians there are some among the citizens who can lay claim to something like intellectuality, and are fine scholars, but few are to be found who have cultivated tastes. Individuals, most excellent in themselves, you will find, but strictly speaking, *society* does not exist in Lexington. It looks as if every man and woman in this town forms a separate and distinct class in themselves. Mrs. A will not visit Mrs. B because A is better of[f] in the world than B. Mrs. C who is a methodist will not be familiar with Mrs. D because the later lady is a baptist, and Mrs. E whose husband is a professional gentleman, cannot think of being acquainted with Mrs. F as *her* husband is only a mechanic. How positively absurd is all this, and the fun of it all is, there are no persons here who can lay any claims whatever to the most distant approach to aristocracy either in descent or wealth. A young lady whose father is an honest carpenter, takes it into her head that she belongs to the first class, turns up her nose at the sight of a mechanic, and refuses to recieve the addresses of a lover below the grade of lawyer, doctor, or merchant,—God save the mark, she means by this last title, a shopkeeper,—and now stands a very good chance to live and die an old maid. Well may we exclaim with Richard the Third, "Poor thing what pains she takes to curse herself." If according to

Shakespeare "all the world's a stage and men and women are only players"—be true, this portion of uncle Sam's dominions is a thespian society and, the members only play comedy, and broad farce.

This place has its characters too, who stand out in bold relief, and by their strongly marked outlines give great force to their originality. Foremost in the group stands Robert Aull,[91] a citizen of some consideration on account of his wealth. In matters of *taste* he is decidedly the reigning *spirit,* for, if he pronounces a barrel of bad whiskey to be good, it becomes at once a favorite beverage with all who wish to be considered as members of upper life. An other spirited individual who has "more flesh than most men, therefore more fraility" is an ex-schoolmaster of the name of Plunket. This gentleman who seems to be the very personification of old Sir John Falstaff, occupies a large share of public attention, and is the very life and soul of the young bloods about town. Sir John as he is now familiarly called, like his great prototype, is in his glory when, surrounded by a circle of wild youths, he recounts his "deeds of valor" by day and night, and, with a coloring that would astonish the fat knight himself, his pictures of adventures in the champs-de-mars, and sphere of venus, dazzles the sight of his admiring auditors. That he is a man of great learning all can see by the numerous quotations he makes from various authors, particularly Burns. Indeed, his erudition is very extensive,

"Lands he can measure, time and tide presage
The story ever runs that he can guage

* * * * * *

In arguing too, the parson own'd his skill
For e'en when vanquished he can argue still."

When detected in a faux-pas, he manages to creep out with, "by the Lord I knew you all as well, as he who made ye." On one occasion while speaking of the various actors of the present day, he declared his ability to play Hamlet better than Macready. Falstaff, you mean said one of the company, when turning a look toward the speaker which would have done credit to Hackett, replied, "No more o' that, Hal, and thou love'st me."

Plunket figured here for some time after my coming, but determining to "repent while in some liking" he has escued [eschewed] all their potations and betaken himself to the country where he lives cleanly, like a gentleman.

---

91. Robert Aull, born in Newcastle, Delaware, 1807, came to Missouri in 1825 and died in Austin, Texas, 1878. For the Aull brothers consult Bieber, "Letters of James and Robert Aull," and Atherton, "James and Robert Aull—A Frontier Missouri Mercantile Firm."

Today, 25 Nov'r the following letter was handed to me by Dr. Ruffin.

Lexington, Mo. Wednesday morning
Nov 18th 1845

Dear Sir,

The undersigned, in consideration of the wish manifested by the citizens of Lexington, in the matter, and of your known ability to do the subject justice, hope that you will consent, at some convenient time, to deliver one or more lectures on the Fine Arts. And participating in the desire to hear you upon that subject, they trust you will not feel at liberty to decline the invitation.

With assurance of the highest respect and esteem, we have the honor to be

Your obedient Servants

J. L. Yantis
St. M. Fackler
W. P. Ewing
W. D. Digges
J. M. Butler
S. J. Mills
W. T. Yeomans[92]
W. H. Ruffin
W. T. Wood[93]

To Alfred S. Waugh Esq.

To which I replied

Lexington, Wednesday 8th Nov 1845

Gentlemen:—I have the honor to acknowledge the receipt of your very polite letter of invitation of this morning, acquainting me with the wishes of the citizens of Lexington, that I would deliver before them, at some convenient time, one or more lectures on the Fine Arts.

I need hardly say how deeply I feel the compliment paid me by such a request, coming as it does from men, eminent for the pulpit and forensic eloquence—whose learning and talents would make me shrink, at the mere thought of opening my mouth before them; but aware of the interest of my theme, at once humanizing and enobling, I am emboldened to undertake the task you are pleased to assign me, and cheerfully comply with your wishes.

As I intend to leave for Jefferson City on Saturday next, permit me to

92. In 1845-1846 W. T. Yeomans was the proprietor, with James R. Pile, of the Lexington *Telegraph* (Young, *History of Lafayette County, Missouri*, I, 293).

93. W. T. Wood was born in Mercer County, Kentucky, 25 March 1809, the son of William and Sallie Wood. He was settled in Lexington by 1839, moved to St. Louis in 1856, and returned to Lexington in 1865, where he died in 1902. He was married three times. Consult Young, *History of Lafayette County, Missouri*, I, 256; *Portrait and Biographical Record of Lafayette and Saline Counties*, 495-497.

name Thursday the 27th, for the delivery of a lecture on the Fine Arts, and their influence on Society.

Do me the honor to accept my highest consideration and esteem, and believe me to be

Gentlemen; your obt serv't
Alfred S. Waugh

To the Rev'd J. L. Yantis; Rev'd St. Michael Fackler; Dr. Ruffin; Dr. Digges; Col. Wood; Col. Ewing; Major J. M. Butler; S. J. Mills; and W. T. Yeomans, Esquires.

On the appointed evening I deliv[er]ed the lecture before an attentive and respectable audience. The Rev'd Mr. Yantis conducted me to the pulpit and introduced me to the assembly. The weather was extremely cold and the result was a severe cough the next day. Although it may seem egotistical to copy laudatory remarks, yet I will presume to give the following from the editor of the Telegraph of the 9th Dec'r 1845.

"The Lecture—The lecture of A. S. Waugh, Esq., "on the Fine Arts and their influence on society", delivered in the Baptist Church in this city, was a most beautiful production. Although the night was excessively cold, there was a very considerable audience, who were delighted with the lecture" &c &c &c

By some chance it went abroad that I had come here to spend the winter, and the people concieving that they had plenty of time, were in no hurry to get any thing done. I therefore purposed going to Jefferson as the convention was in session there and wrote to that effect to my friend in Independence who sent me the following reply.

"I will advert to the most important part of your letter at once, viz. your projected departure for Jefferson City. I will give you my opinion on the project, and 'tis not only *my* opinion—The inhabitants you know to be not a picture loving community. The members of the convention, when not engaged in buisiness at the House, will pass most of their time frolicking and spreeing, those who are of a generous turn will open all their money in this way, and those who do not so pass their time are close fisted farmers, and probably look upon the Fine Arts, as did the man Wilburn,[94] whom you met while at Mr. Lewis's—such is the opinion I have concieved of the members—consisting as does this convention, of men, probably met for the first time and, probably the last—what can you expect but that, (vieing with each other in sociability and good fellowship, as they undoubtedly will from their relative position) spree

94. See page 34 above.

will succeed to spree, frolic be succeded by frolic, and each night's debauch be but the precursor of a greater the following."

From the above it is very evident my friend Tisdale entertained but a poor opinion of the august body then assembled at the capitol of the state, and indeed when I began to reflect upon what he said I was of his way of thinking, and became confirmed in it, by the recipt of a letter from General Lucas and an other from Mr. Woodson who both expressed the same views, so I concluded not to go there. But even if I had not relinquished the idea, the commissions which now began to flow in upon me would have detained me in Lexington, and I requested Mr. Yeomans to state in his next paper (The Telegraph)[95] that I would remain some time longer in town.

Tisdale in the mean time had completed the miniature of Palmer and afterward painted one of a lady. Both these productions of friend Jack gave much satisfaction, and I was highly gratified by hearing them spoken of in terms of praise. I learned from my friends in Independence, that for a time, he was doubly diligent, but the cold weather coming on, he amused himself by hunting. When I wrote to him to come immediately, he was so much absorbed in the sports of the season that I began to fancy some thing had happened to cause his delay. His absence was in consequence of a visit he had to make to a very agreeable family of the name of Hamilton.

The weather at this time was so very cold that the water froze in my pencil, although my painting apparatus was close to good fire in my room. The day after his arrival I accompanied Mr. Hugh N. Smith[96] to the residence of his father, about five miles from town for the purpose of taking sketches of that gentleman's family, for a painting of a group. On the following Sunday, the 21st Dec., we set out for Independence to eat our Christmas dinner with our excellent friend the general, who had kindly made us promise to do so, e'er we left him in the Fall.

That night we stopped at the residence of Mr. Graves, the gentleman at whose door I had slept, and next morning left for the residence of Mr. Samuel Hamilton, known as the *six mile.* Here I saw a *good,* well formed and spirited horse which Tisdale told me he was anxious I should purchase. We found the family of Mr. Hamilton very agreeable, particularly Mrs. Hamilton who converses very well, and entertains liberal views on

95. A Democratic newspaper founded in 1845; it ceased publication in 1860.

96. This gentleman was, after the entrance of our troops into Santa Fe made attorney general of New Mexico, and is now in Washington city as a delegate from that Territory.—WAUGH. See also notes 65 and 78 above.

most subjects. The hospitality of this family is right royal. On Wednesday 24th we reached Independence.

Christmass—that season so dear to young hearts. Oh! how the approach of that festival used to look to me in my young days, so frought with happiness. Dear happy childhood, how the bright the world looks through thy young eyes. When I think of my early days and all its innocent pastimes I am redy to burst out in the words of the song

"Oh would I were a boy again"

but what's the use of sighing. Our friend made the day look like Christmass at home.

As I wished to visit a old North Carolina friend of mine who resides near Platte City, I set out to Wayne City with the intention of crossing the frozen river but on seeing the bad state of the ice I declined running my life into danger and returned to town and then proceeded to Mr. Lewis's, where Tisdale had proceeded me the previous day. When I reached there I found that my friends had, had a wolf hunt the day before. Their descriptions were so eloquently told that I felt anxious to witness one, and was gratified in my wish the following Monday, but as I am not accustomed to field sports, and they were getting into I thought a breakneck sort of a chase, I forbore taking part in the game, and I could see nothing after they had started, I returned to the house to await the termination of their sport.

Towards evening whilst standing in the stable yard, a horse with saddle and bridle came across the prairie toward the farm, very much resembling the one that Tisdale had ridden, and as this was without a rider, it occurred to me that probably my friend had been thrown, and I hastened to meet the animal, but to my relief it turned out to be a stranger horse. I caught him and tied him to a tree to await the coming of his owner. Soon after this the party was seen advancing slowly, one of the horses carrying double. The gentleman who rode behind the saddle was very much bruised, and bleeding in the face; his horse had fallen with, and I believe on him; he was not seriously hurt however, and claimed the stray horse which I had caught.

On Tuesday the 30th we once more took leave of good old Lindsay Lewis,—for he is most decidedly, a good man. He is, what I should like to see in every man,—an acting, not a talking Christian, and returned to Independence, there dined and again was on our way back to Lexington. Twelve miles [*sic*] from town we stopped again with Mr. Hamilton. As Tisdale was anxious for me to buy the horse, I rode him back to his owners, and was fully satisfied with his action and brave spirit. Come

Jack said I, supose you purchase this horse and present him to me. Eh!—after a little thought he said he would, very well my boy now be industrious. This I did in order to give an incentive to stick close to his studies. Jack was a philosopher and took things very easy.

We spent a couple of days with the Hamilton's and reached Lexington on the evening of New Year's day 1846. Next morning I went to work in good earnest and finished a miniature on ivory of Sam'l J. Mills, who although now engaged in the very unpoetical pursuit of selling family groceries, is himself an amateur artist. Some others in the chartemnography occupied my attention closely and buisiness, as some smart young men say, buisiness was pretty good. And in the evenings we were richly entertained by witnessing vaudevilles by the Brittingham Family.[97] By the by this man B is a character,—a genius in his way, and his eldest daughter has quite capivated the hearts of the young men. Tisdale who is very gallant, put himself under the tuition of Mr. B. to learn the polite art of dancing, in order to have the pleasure of dancing with the daughter of his instructor; but there were others in the school who pleased the fair maid better than Jack. Quite a sensation is produced by the arrival of this very *interested* family. The young fellows are vieing with each other in the costliness of the presents which they make to the daughters, while the father smiles at the attention that is paid to his dear, good girls.

---

97. Probably Mr. and Mrs. Robert Brittingham who appeared at the Chestnut Street Theatre in Philadelphia, 1838-39. Miss Brittingham made her debut as a child actor in 1835 at the Walnut Street Theatre, Philadelphia. In 1852 the daughter was playing Louisville and the parents were living in retirement in that city (Brown, *History of the American Stage;* Wilson, *History of the Philadelphia Theatre*).

CHAPTER VIII

Sac and Fox Indians at Lexington—Thespian Society—The Theater and Religion—Some Lexington Ministers

I ought to have mentioned a few pages back but overlooked it in my notes, of a visit our town received from a party of Sac and Fox Indians.[98] While enjoying the company of Messes. Mills and Yeomans in my room on the evening of the 23rd of last November Mr. Thomas Mills came in and told us that a party of two hundred Indians were coming on shore from the steam boat Amaranth and would encamp for the night on the banks of the Missouri. Pleased with the idea of seeing so many red men in a body, I proposed to my friends that we should go down and see them. As we approached their landing place, nothing could surpass the picturesqueness of the scene which presented itself. Although the night was very cold and the ground frozen hard, we, somehow did not seem to feel it, for the pleasurable excitement produced by the novelty of our visitors kept us from thinking on the weather. On reaching the foot of the hill and turned to the right, looking down the river, we saw a number of fires, faintly glowing before us, the smoke from which thickened the frosty atmosphere, and spread a dull, greyish pall over every object around us. It was a curious sight to see the dusky forms of these aborigines, gliding noiselessly about in every direction like spectres in an ancantation in some opera. Around the numerous fires were seated really handsome squaws and beautiful children, interspersed with noble looking warriors, over whose heads, on the branches of trees, hung their belts, powder horns, shot pouches, bow and arrows, and pieces of blue and red drapery, giving to the bivou[a]c an effect of great interest to the artist. While here and there a number of fine looking youths, with forms of great beauty, so beautiful as to serve as models to a sculptor would be collected in groups, and in attitudes at once easy and graceful, because natural. At one fire we saw some five or six men and a couple of squaws, playing with a pretty child of about two years old. The little creature had nothing on but a short tunic of calico, fastened around the waist with a wampum belt, its plump little legs and feet were naked regardless of

---

98. The *Western Expositor* (Independence) of 6 December 1845, as quoted in the *Missouri Republican* (St. Louis), 15 December 1845, reported that between five and six hundred Sac and Fox Indians had "passed through Independence, a few days previous. . . . They traveled on cheerfully, notwithstanding the mercury in the thermometer stood 5 degrees below zero." Waugh saw this party at Lexington, not Independence.

the cold. The arch little thing looked at us; and smiled sweetly in our faces as if he recognized us as old friends. An old Indian of fine commanding appearance, began humming a low monotonous chant to which he beat time with a short stick on a log beside him, the child came forward and having reached a mat in front of the fire commenced dancing, at first slowly, as if fearful of not being able to sustain the part he was called upon to play, but gradually loosing his timidity, he warmed up and entered into the spirit of the exercise with animation. Although his dancing could not be said to be the poetry of motion, we were very much gratified indeed, and testified our approbation in loud plaudits. It was very evident that the Indians themselves were gratified with the child's performance, for they looked pleased, and spoke to the boy, from time to time, encouragingly. For some time we watched the culinary opporations and found that some of the viands were cooked in a way that would do no discredit to a *grande artiste* among the whites. We now turned to an other group, and there beheld a lovely creature of a girl, whose finely moulded figure and really classic features were sufficient to endow a very venus. As she stood before our admiring eyes, wrapped in a scarlet blanket, her face and figure brought into fine relief by the blazing fire, it was scearcely possible to conceive a finer study for the pencil. Her attitude was natural, and graceful, and, her blanket was drawn around her form in such classic style, that, in its full, massive folds, we were taught a lesson in the disposition of drapery, far beyond that of some of the finest specimens of ancient sculpture. Much as we may be inclined to look upon these children of the forest, with a feeling allied to contempt, we cannot but admire the artless arrangement of their simple toilet, and some of our most brilliant belles might see in the daughters of the red men, the same love of finery, as they themselves display. Although civilization has refined the articles of ornament, worn by the softer sex among us, yet, the same spirit is manifest in the poor Indian squaw as in the noblest dame. Whilst ostrich plumes wave from the jewelled brow of one, that of the other is adorned with glass beads and tinsel trinkets. From the ears of the courtly beauty, depends diamonds of the first water, —a brass ring or a piece of shell hangs from the other. Bracelets of costly material and exquisite workmanship, sparkle on the fair arms of a duchess, & a few strings of pottry beads, encircle those of the squaw, the same spirit actuates both and, extrinsic display marks one of the characteristics of woman in civilized, as well as in savage life; in the wild woods and the gay saloon, an inate and innocent love of external finery is appearant in the sex, but the only difference is in the manner and style of the exhibition.

We saw a fine looking youth trying his musical powers on the jew's harp. When he percieved that we were noticing him, he doubled his exertions with a view of shewing us what a genius he was; but with all his skill his greatest effort produced only a good sound—nothing more although no doubt he felt himself to be a genius of the first order.

Many of the warriors and braves wore large medals, one of which, from where we stood, looked like that of Washington.

Pleased with this romantic and novel scene we came away, with the intention of paying them an other visit in the morning, and see what they looked like, in the clear light of day. As we were retiring, and just at the outskirts of the camp, a young Indian, hastily drawing his blanket around him, came forward and asked us for *whisk,* but as he seemed to have had more than was good for him, his request was denied.

When the morning came we again went down to see our red brethren, but I must confess that much of the romance and poetry with which I had invested the Indian character was dissipated by the light of day. Although in phisical conformation they are a noble looking set of fellows, yet there was such an air of degradation and filth about them that the charm was at once broken and they stood before me a miserable set of creatures. I found them in enclosures composed of mats made of bull-rushes, without anything to serve as a roof overhead. After spending about an hour and a half among them I came away rather disappointed with the day exhibition.

A short time after dinner, my attention was attracted toward the upper end of town, by a large body of warriors on foot advancing in a very rapid manner in the direction of where I stood. These were followed by a squadron of horsemen, gaudily decked out in all the finery of red, blue, green and white blankets, with their faces all daubed with vermillion. I must confess, it was a very imposing spectacle. On they came whooping and yelling and flourishing their tomahawks and other weapons in a wild and really fearful manner. I can scearcely say what they looked like, but could fancy for the moment, as the sun beams glanced from their brightly polished blades of their knives, spears, and hatchets—a legion of devils incarnate, just let loose on the sinners of earth. Here I must acknowledge that I was struck with admiration of this body of mounted warriors, for they looking very imposing in all this array of war paint and gaudy trappings. As they approached, I remarked to a gentleman beside me, "here Sir, is the real native American party," "and no mistake," said my friend, "they have a greater right to dislike the whites, than a certain party who have usurped that name, have to dislike the foreigners to come to our shores; we have behaved worse to them than any europeans who come here by our invitation, can do to us." As they passed, I noticed several of the men and boys, with their faces blackened, which I afterwards learned was done by order of the chief as a punishment for misconduct. The warriors and braves amounted to about three hundred. Immediately after them came the squaws and papouses, mounted on small horses, followed by a great number of pack horses bearing the meats, cooking utensils and other camp furniture, besides infants in their cradles tied to the saddles. Some of the merest children were mounted on poneys with the reins in their hands exercising full authority over their steeds. Two of the chiefs sat on their horses in front of our hotel and reviewed their troops as they passed before them. One of them was Keokuck,[99] the principal chief and the other was, the heriditary prince or grand chief of the nation, He is a man of great abilities as a ruler, and very much respected by his people. Keokuck is not, as I supposed, the son of Black Hawk. This chief is a great friend to the whites and was opposed to the war in 1832. Big Horn[100] is the hereditary chief, but the government of the United States, appointed Keokuck to the sovereignity, why! I do not know. A son of the renowned Black Hawk I instantly recognized, by the resemblance he bore to his father; he is a man of fine commanding appearance, and positively his manners seemed courtly.[101] When all their people had passed, the chiefs followed at a slow pace.

In a piece of bottom land about half a mile from town, in the neighborhood of a very extensive bed of bituminous coal, hilly and picturesque, this native American party, pitched their tents for the night. Their wigwams were scattered about as fancy dictated, generally, under some young trees. Their lodges were formed by placing a number of saplings in the ground, and arched over; their sides were strengthened by others running horrizontally, bound together with strips of bark, and a couple of ridge poles on top, a few inches apart, served as an opening through which the smoke might pass when all was completed. This framework was then covered over with mats and [the] lodge was ready for its occupants. Over the entrance, a piece of drapery of some sort was hung which served insted of a door. It is a curious sight to get a peep into one of these

99. The most extended sketch of Keokuk is that in McKenney and Hall, *Indian Tribes of North America*, II, 115-149. See also McDermott, "Another Coriolanus: Portraits of Keokuk, Chief of the Sac and Fox."

100. In note 103 Waugh gives this name as Long Horn, but under neither appellation is he identifiable.

101. Catlin painted two sons of Black Hawk at Jefferson Barracks in 1832: Náh-se-ús-kuk, the Whirling Thunder, and Wa-sáw-me-saw, the Roaring Thunder (Donaldson, *George Catlin Indian Gallery*, 30). In note 103 Waugh lists both these names (spelled slightly differently) but does not identify their owners.

domiciles and see the Indians wrapped in their blankets, sleeping, or sitting around a fire of small branches of trees, in the centre of the lodge, every object dim[m]ed with smoke.

"The fire water" had played its part this evening, for almost every man of them was under its influence. We saw some two or three who were very drunk, tied hand and foot, lying at the outskirts of the encampment, as a punishment for being so; each one was attended by a squaw who saw that the poor fellow wanted for nothing, consistent with the nature of his peculiar position. In the tent of Big Horn, a large party were engaged at cards among whom were several degraded whites gambling with the Indians. There was a Mohawk travelling along with the party, he was from New York, and spoke english remarkably well, he was dressed as well as any white man, and was a fellow of great intellegence. With this man I entered into conversation, and found in him a bitter spirit of revenge against the pale faces. The agent, Col. Vaughan,[102] who is conducting the party to the waters of the Kansas, told me that this same Mohawk was a dangerous fellow to have along with him, but he cannot be got rid of. He has intruded himself without permission, and it is feared he will create mischief along the road. These Indians came from Iowa. The next day the whole body left for Independence.[103]

An acquaintance of mine, german confectioner, who is an amateur artist, wished to have the likeness of Black Hawk's son, and had to pay that *prince* the sum of ten dollars for the privellege of copying his illustrious face and figure. It is very plain that avarice belongs to no particular race, and that a man who is red in his skin, can place a value upon his likeness as well as a white man. When my artist friend, told me the premium he had to pay for the honor of having a sitting from Master

---

102. Possibly Alfred J. Vaughan, Sub-Agent on the Osage River of the Ottawas, Pottawatomies, and Sacs and Foxes.

103. This emigrating party consisting of 473 of the tribes of Sac and Fox Indians are under the direction of their agents Messrs Vaughan and Clements, passed through the principal part of this city yesterday, on their route to their new home on the waters of the Kansas, west of Fort Leavenworth and west of the Kickapoos. They are from the Desmoines, in Iowa, and are well provided with camp furniture and horses. They are elated with the excitement of travelling and seem pleased at a change of location. The whole party look well, and are in excellent health, except one man who is believed to have been poisoned. Over this man, the "Medicine man" of the tribe, with his assistants, perform daily some secret ceremony, a sort of incantation perhaps, to restore him to health. They appear to be highly gratified at the visits of the whites, and are particularly delighted when ladies visit them.

The principal chief of the party is Long Horn; the others, are Young Keokuk, Wa-som-e-saw, Nash-a-ash-kuk; Black Neck and Black Snake. A son of Black Hawk is one of the chiefs, and is a man of some thirty-five years of age, with a remarkable fine, commanding presence.

To this party was added an other of some two hundred more of the same tribes. WAUGH.

Tommy Hawk, I could not help thinking of a certain Dr. Wm. T. Hamilton of Mobile Ala., who wanted me to give him a miniature on ivory, for the privelege of taking his likeness for my own collection.[104] This learned D.D. placed a higher price upon his own head, then the Indian did on his whole figure, *he*, only charged ten dollars, while the reverend gentleman asked fifty, that being the amount I charged for a miniature on ivory. Not feeling disposed after such a *modest* request, to minister to, either his vanity or his purse, I repectfully declined the honor of taking his head off. I would have taken more interest in the decapitation of the red chief's son, then in opperating on the learned doctor of divinity. One was a handsome, noble looking fellow, the other, to use his own words, "had an ugly face, and an ungraceful figure," and I was too polite to contradict a clergy-man, and too honest to deny a fact, so there the matter rested.[105]

---

104. Mat Field consulted the Rev. William T. Hamilton (1796-1884, minister of the Government Street Presbyterian Church of Mobile) when he was considering abandoning the theatre for the ministry (Carson, "Diary of Mat Field," 95).

105. It should have been mentioned here, that a second call was made upon me to speak in public. The following is copied from the Lexington *Telegraph* of the 13th of Jany 1846.

"At a meeting of the board of Directors of the Lexington Library Association, the following resolution was unanimously adopted:

Resolved, That for the purpose of increasing the funds of the Association, and therby becoming enabled to increase the number of books in the Library, as well as affording an oppertunity to our citizens, to listen to the lectures of some of the most eminent men in the State—a course of lectures be immediately commenced, and that Robert Aull, John F. Ryland, and Edward Winsor be a committee to carry this resolution into effect.

In pursuance of the above resolution, the committee addressed the following letter to Col. A. S. Waugh, as an invitation to deliver the first lecture of the course, on Tuesday, 13th inst, at 6 o'clock, in the Christian Church.

Lexington, Jany 3d 1846.

Sir—We the undersigned, have been appointed a committee to request, on behalf of the Board of Directors of the Lexington Library Association, certain gentlemen, each to deliver a lecture or lectures for the benefit of said Association.

We therfore, in pursuance of the object of our appointment, do now take the pleasure of requesting Col Waugh to deliver a lecture on some interesting subject of his own choosing, before an audience in Lexington, in the Reformer's church, on Tuesday evening, 13th inst. at 6 o'clock.

We respectfully request an answer.

Yours most respectfully
John F. Ryland
Robert Aull } Committee
Ed Winsor

To which the following answer was returned

Lexington, Mo. Jany 3d 1846

Gentlemen:—I beg leave to return, through you to the Board of Directors of the Lexington Library Association, my respectful thanks for the honor which they have conferred upon me, by their request that I would deliver a lecture on some interesting subject of my own selection, before an audience in the Reformer's Church, on Tuesday evening the 13th inst. for the benefit of said Association.

A number of young gentlemen have lately formed themselves into a Thespian society, and have performed with great credit to themselves, and amusement to their friends.[106] It is under the presidency of Dr. Ruffin, who is admirably fitted to fill the office. He occasionally takes part in the performance, and plays tragedy in an able manner, his personation of the stranger in Kotsebue's piece of that name[107] has drawn down rapturous applause from all who witnessed it. My friend Tisdale made his first appearance on any stage, here, and performed to admiration. It is an innocent and really rational way of amusing ourselves and friends, and when properly conducted, tends to improvement in many respects, particul[ar]ly in acquireing a correct pronounciation, and gesticulation. That such amusements sometimes are turned to bad account, cannot be denied, but when properly conducted, much good results from them. The Rev. Sidney Smith, speaking of theatres, said, "There is something in the word playhouse which seems so closely connected in the minds of some people with sin and Satan, that it stands in their vocabulary for every species of abomination. And yet why? Where is every feeling more aroused in favor of virtue, then at a good play? Where is goodness so feelingly, so enthusiastically learnt? What so solemn as to see the excellent passions of the human heart called forth by a good actor—animated by a good poet? To hear Siddons repeat what Shakespeare wrote? To behold a child and his mother—the noble and the poor artisan—the monarch and his subjects—all ages and all ranks convulsed in one common passion, wrung with one common anguish, and with loud sobs and cries, doing involuntary homage to the God that made their hearts? What wretched infatuation to interdict such amusements as these! What a blessing that mankind can be allured from sensual gratification, and find relaxation and pleasure in such pursuits!

As it was my intention to have given three more lectures on the Fine Arts, I cheerfully comply with your polite invitation, and shall deliver one on the Art of Painting at the time appointed

Do me the honor to accept my most respectful consideration, and believe me to be,

Your ob't serv't
Alfred S. Waugh

To
Hon. John F. Ryland
Robert Aull
Ed Winsor Esq
} Committee

At the time and place appointed, the lecture was delivered before a very select audience, indeed the most intellegent of the citizens were there. The president, Judge Ryland, introduced me to the assembly.—WAUGH

106. The Thespian Society continued to be active after Waugh's departure. The *Lexington Appeal* for 15 February 1848 carried a notice of a forthcoming production of *The Drunkard's Fate* and *Hunting a Turtle* for the benefit of the Episcopal Church.

107. A. F. F. von Kotzebue's popular play, *The Stranger*, was first printed in 1799.

I entirely coincide with that excellent and talented divine, in the above. Of Theatres as they are generally conducted, I am no advocate, but [of] the legitmate drama, and a well regulated playhouse I am a warm friend. I am sure more good is produced by good plays, perfermed by good players, than from some scenes which I have witnessed under the name of revivals of religion. I have never yet heard, in any theatre where I have been, a single sentence uttered which could be construed into any thing like irreverence to God or his religion, while—and I am sorry to say it—I have heard the character of the deity most dreadfully misrepresented and that too, in places set apart for religious worship. I can stand almost any kind of exhibition when of a moral tendency, but my conscience will not permit me to be present where the religion of Almighty God is turned into solemn mockery, nor hear the great Omnipo[te]nt ordered to do the dirty bidding of every brainless fool who fancies himself a minister of heaven.

These remark[s], gentle reader, may be taken just as you please, I do not write to gratify any man or, any set of men, but from honest conviction of the truth of what I say, so, if you do not like them—just have politeness to pass on to others that may please you better. I am, according to the notion of some,—a man without religion—because I am not a communicant of any church,—but I do assure you, I am far, very far from being irrelegious, for, I have too much heart-felt reverence and love for the God who made me, to believe the idiotic fancyings of some who stand in a pulpit.

I was induced one evening to attend one of these meetings called a revival, but I had to come away,—I was so disgusted with the whole proceedings. I look upon all such doings as well calculated to lead to infidelity, I often think that old Nick has employed the persons who set up such meetings for the express purpose of rendering religion ridiculous for they certainly tend to divest it of that sacredness, which should ever accompany the worship of God.

The people of this town are sadly preacher ridden, so much so indeed, that life is stript of its charms, There are no private parties, no friendly interchanges of the courtesies of life, no open, generous comm[un]ing, one with the other. If they meet at each others houses, gossip and scandal are the themes that principally occupy their attention. A person can hardly do the most simple thing but it is known in every house; between this and their constant attendance upon church their time is fully taken up. Charity they have none, for they deal damnation round the land on all who differ from them on matters of faith. How apt the quotation may be applied here, "Si quoties peccant homines sua fulmina mittat Jupiter, exiquo tempore solus est."[108] Oh if the great creator were to be as severe on us, as we are upon our fellow sinners, the world would shortly be depopulated. In making these remarks, I must not be set down as an opponent to godliness; far be it from me, I am only aiming my shafts against cant and hypocrisy. The world is moved impulsively, every thing has its day, and religion in its turn has now become fashionable. Formerly, it was a very strong evidence of a man's sincerity for him to attend divine worship, because, it was not then considered fashionable to be seen too often at church, and a degree of scorn was shewn to the devotee which frequently debarred him from worldly preferment. Then it was, when a man proved his sincerity by braving the odium of piety. But now-a-days it is so much the fashion to be a church member, that the veriest scamps will assume the garb of religion in order to be successful in worldly affairs. I am not speaking irreverently or without a foundation for what I say. I have seen, alas! too much of the world to think all men good who *profess* to be religious, and have too much of the seemingly pious, to trust in either the dress or talk of the *would make believe saints upon earth.* A good man where ever found, regardless of his creed or church, I most sincerely reverence, but a hypochrite, I do most cordially abominate whether in, or out, of communion with any sect or party. Now, here is the revered Mr. Yantis, of the presbyterian church, a really true and sincere man, with charity enough to cover a multitude of sins, even in other men, let alone in himself, him, I respect for his quiet, unobtrusive piety, and that rare virtue, leinency to the faults of his fellow mortals. This most excellent quality in any man, more especially in a preacher, was fully exhibited on one occasion lately. A poor fellow—a returned volunteer from Mexico,—died from the effects of the campaign and a previous irregular life, and was buried with the honors of war by his comrades of B company of the first regiment of Missouri mounted Volunteers. Mr. Yantis was requested to perform the funeral service over his grave. After the earth covered the mortal remains of poor Magruder,[109] this reverend gentleman delivered an oration, in which he gave an interesting account of the life and adventures of the deceased, painting in strong colors the virtues of the departed, and wound up by saying, "if he had faults, let them rest with him in the tomb—remember only his virtues."

108. "If every time men sinned Jupiter was to hurl his thunder, in a short time no one would be left."—WAUGH

109. John S. Magruder was born in Virginia and died in Lexington in 1848 of wounds received at the Battle of Sacramento (Connelley, *Doniphan's Expedition,* 538). He was a member of Company B, First Regiment Missouri Mounted Volunteers. It is to be remembered that Waugh was writing his narrative in 1850.

From that time out I honored Mr. Y. A few years ago, I attended the funeral of Judge Sewell of Raliegh N. C. and heard a little bandy leg's fellow of the name of McOsborn—a presbyterian preacher—tear the character of the deceased, all to pieces, and that too, in the house of the late judge, and in the presence of his widow and orphans. I would advise all such people to study that magnificent description of charity, given by St. Paul, and then they would be less apt to think evil of their neighbors, and behave themselves "not unseemly" in their intercourse with the world.

Among the Episcopalians, The Rev. Saint Michael Fackler, is an other excellent specimen of what a Christian should be. In the discharge of his clerical duties, he is a model of meekness, and true forbearance. Modest, and retiring, he meddles not with matters, not properly belonging to himself, but in his walk through life, shews himself a truly good man. This gentleman, besides being a fine scholar is, deeply versed in natural and experimental philosophy, and very scientific as well as something of a practical mechanic. He occupies a small room in a cross street, where his books rest in a bookcase made by himself, and here he spends time in the pursuit of knowledge, almost unknowing and unknown in the little world of Lexington. I had the honor of his acquaintance, and spent many a pleasant and instructive evening in his company, from which I never retired without feeling that I had been a gainer in knowledge. His congregation, which is quite small, allow him a salery of three hundred dollars. On this pittance he manages to live and is "surpassing rich on forty pounds a year," sixty I should have said, but that would have marred the quotation. Three hundred dollars being about or, rather more than sixty pounds sterling.

In contrast to him figures a certain spare, consumptive looking man, of the name of Ashby[110] who has charge of the Methodist church, and although a *weak* man in more senses than one, is capable of making his voice be heard at the distance of a mile or upwards. I never heard him preach, except *at a distance,* but, if noise is a requisite qualification in a preacher, then most decidedly is Thomas T. Ashby a splendid preacher.

One Monday morning just as I was coming from the stable where I kept my horse, I met this son of thunder, who complained very much of the indisposition which he felt. "Why! Mr. Ashby said I, I do not wonder at your illness, for, a man who roars as loud as you do, cannot but feel unwell. I am surprised that a man of your good sense should deem it

---

110. He was a brother of Major Daniel Ashby of Chariton County, Missouri. According to a card in the *Lexington Appeal,* 14 April 1847, he was then agent of "the Grand Lodge of Missouri . . . for the collection of subscriptions to the Masonic College."

necessary to raise your voice to such an ungodly pitch. You must surely have but a poor opinion of the judgement of your hearers, when you substitute *sound* for *sense.* You ought to recollect that a man is a rational creature, and you must appeal to his reason instead of playing upon his senses." "I wish said he, that I could speak louder and longer," Why? I asked, because said he, "I see so many of my fellow creatures going the downward road to perdition, and *I* wish to save them." Then my good sir, I replied, you have made a mistake in the means you employ,—*noise* is a poor substitute for sober, quiet argument, You may, for the time being, scare some of your audience into a momentary belief in what you say, but depend upon it, on the return of calm reflection your talk will be found to have produced no other effect then disgust toward themselves for allowing their passions to be worked upon instead of their reason. "God is a spirit, and should be worshipped in spirit, and in truth. Man who is made in the image of his maker, should be reasoned with, and not frightened. Such proceeding as yours produces more harm than good."

CHAPTER IX

RETURN TO INDEPENDENCE—SANTA FE TRADERS AND TRAVELLERS—FOR OREGON AND CALIFORNIA—THE ARTIST PLANS TO VISIT NEW MEXICO

I DO NOT KNOW why some people should think it necessary, in order to serve God, that they should make us reject every innocent and rational amusement. What a poor opinion they must entertain of the great Being, when they suppose dancing offensive to Him. If such a pastime be a sin, what in the name of mercy, has become of our progenitors. Ah! what a thought! surely we are not better than they were! Indeed I doubt if we are half so good, with all our austerity, nay! I don't believe we are so near the mark as they were. This vetoing of innocent pleasures is certainly productive of much evil. When young men are debarred social intercourse with the other sex, they do not place that guard over their actions or conduct as they would if under the gentle guardianship of the ladies. Cut off from their society, they become reckless of the world's opinion, seek in the bar room, or at the gambling table, other sources of amusement not so condusive of their spiritual, or temporal welfare, and thus, by a mistaken idea, many a fine young fellow is driven to his own destruction. This town proves the truth of these remarks.

Tisdale having taken it into his head to try the world by himself, laid out a plan which, if it had no other merits, was decidedly an original one. He conceived the idea of visiting various states on the great highways of the rivers, in a canoe furnished with every thing requisite for living, by flood and field. So well were all his plans laid out in theory, that he could sleep in his canoe or pitch his tent on the banks of a stream as convenience or fancy might dictate. He was to be amply provisioned for the voyage, and with a good dog and shooting apparatus, he intended to guard against the chance of want by his skill in shooting, fishing &c. A regular journal of his adventures, was to be kept, from day to day, and his sketch book was to be filled with scenes and views to illustrate the pages of his diary. When ever he came to a town, or city, he intended to paint likenesses of such persons as wished themselves *committed to paper*, and thus combine buisiness and pleasure at the same time. When he first broached it to me, I opposed the scheme, but, as Jack prided himself on his argumentative powers, nothing could please him better than my opposition. Finding, as was usual with him, that he got stronger in proportion to the obstacles thrown in his way, I surrendered at discreation, and he was deprived of further chance of shewing off. Altho' I shrudely suspect he never seriously entertained an idea of embarking on such a voyage, he appeared to be quite in earnest, for, he began to make preparations for a start,—that is as far as talking to a carpenter about building a canoe, getting a rifle and shot guns, &c. and writing to some friends in Independence for introductory letters to persons along the route he intended going. Or, it is more than probable, he wanted to try the strength of my attachment to him and was rather disappointed when he found that I gave my consent of his leaving me, after so long travelling together.

On my part, I turned my attention to my old residence in Raleigh N. C., where I had no doubt, a warm welcome awaited my return to that pleasant little city. "Now, Jack, said I, you are going to travel by water, and I by land, the horse which I gave you can be no further use to you, let me have him again. I think he may as well be in my possession as in that of that scamp Wilson to whom you are about to sell him." So I got back the horse. I now ordered a cover for my paint box, so contrived that it could be secured by straps to the back of the saddle, purchased a good sized pair of saddle bags, finished all my buisiness in Lexington paid all demands against me, took receipts for the same, shook hands with my friends and started for Independence on the 14th of March 1846, where I intended to spend some time with my friend General Lucas e'er I should make a final start to my old home in the south.

No sooner had I arrived at Independence then I was warmly recieved by all my friends there, particularly, the general and his family. As soon as it was known that I was in town many citizens commissioned [me] to paint pictures for them and this occupied so long a time that the season came round for the Santa Fe trader[s] to assemble here, previous to their start across the plains. Emigrants to California and Oregon this year were numerous, indeed to a greater extent than was ever known before, which [gave] to this flourishing little town an exceedingly bustling appearance.[111] Almost every nation on the face of the globe had sent its repre-

111. At the close of June Josiah Gregg estimated the California and Oregon emigration at 2,000 men, women, and children, and 400 wagons—without counting the army (Fulton, *Diary and Letters of Josiah Gregg*, 1, 201). Edwin Byrant about six weeks after Waugh returned to Independence described the town as follows: "Its population is about one thousand; and at this season, every man seems to be actively and profitably employed. It has been for some years the principal outfitting point for the Santa Fe traders, and will probably continue so. Many of the houses around the square are constructed of brick, but the majority of the buildings are frames. I noticed, among the busy multitudes moving to and fro through the streets, a large number of New-Mexicans, and half-breed Indians, with their dusky complexions and ragged and dirty costumes. They were generally mounted on miserably poor mules or horses, and presented a most shabby appearance. Long trains of oxen, sometimes as many as ten or fifteen yokes, strung together and pulling huge tented-wagons, de-

sentatives to this starting point. The streets were alive with quadrupeds and bipeds. The neighing of horses, the braying of mules, the lowing of oxen, the cracking of whips, with the systematic swearing of teamsters, made its otherwise quiet thoroughfares, most inharmoniously musical, if one can call any thing musical which lacks harmony. The rich and the poor; the mechanic and the farmer; the trader, the speculator and gambler; the pious christian and profane unbeliever whose every other word is an oath; the visionary who sees in the distance whole cities growing up under his superior guidance,[112] the artist,[113] the naturalist, [114] and man of letters;[115] and though last, the gentleman of leisure[116] who was amply

---

signed for some Santa Fe trading expedition, were moving about the streets, under the direction of numerous drivers, cracking their whips and making a great noise" (*What I Saw in California,* 13-14).

112. Col. Wm. H. Russel, a very worthy gentleman from Calloway County, who went off to California with bright hopes of becoming a man of consideration in that far off land, but so visionary that he entertained the idea that he could form a colony there and be its ruler. He is a goodhearted fellow, but extremely visionary. He was, immediately after the occupation of California by our troops, secretary of state under Fremont.—WAUGH

William Henry ("Owl") Russell (1802-1873) was born in Kentucky, the son of Robert S. and Deborah Allen Russell. He settled in Callaway County, Missouri, in 1831 and from 1841 to 1845 was United States Marshal for the District of Missouri. In May 1846 he left with Edwin Bryant and others for California; out there he served as major in Frémont's California Battalion. In 1849 he returned from the West Coast. He was named consul in Trinidad, Cuba, in 1861. He died in Washington, D. C. (*DAB,* XVI, 251-252). He should not be confused with William Hepburn Russell, the overland freighter, who was probably the Russell Waugh met in Lexington (see note 87 above).

113. Mr. Stanley the artist who was going out to collect sketches of Indians. Afterward employed by Genl. Kearney.—WAUGH.

John Mix Stanley (1814-1872) traveled to Santa Fe with the Magoffin party and was attached to Kearny's command on its march from Santa Fe to California. For him consult *DAB,* XVII, 513-514; Kinietz, *John Mix Stanley and his Indian Paintings.*

114. Mr. Wietelzenius, a gentleman of great learning and science. He accompanied Col. Donophan from Chihuahua, on the remainder of his expedition.—WAUGH

Frederick Adolph Wislizenus (1810-1889) was born in Germany and came to America in 1835. He made his first trip over the western plains in 1839; his account of these travels was published in German in St. Louis in 1840; a translation by his son was published by the Missouri Historical Society in 1912: *A Journey to the Rocky Mountains in the Year 1839.* For the present journey he had left St. Louis on 4 May, arrived at Independence 9 May, left town for the camp on the Big Blue River twenty miles west on 14 May. He was traveling with Speyer; the caravan actually started on 22 May. His *Memoir of a Tour to Northern Mexico, connected with Col. Doniphan's Expedition in 1846 and 1847* was published in Senate Miscellaneous Document 26, 30th Congress, Ist session. Consult *DAB,* XX, 430-431.

115. Bryant, author of "What I saw in California."—WAUGH

Edwin Bryant's book was published by Appleton in New York in 1848. He arrived in Independence on 1 May and left on the 5th. Waugh has been taking licence with time: actually Bryant was gone from Independence before Wislizenus arrived there. Note, too, that six weeks have elapsed between the opening of this paragraph and the reference to Russell et al.

116. Poor Meredith who was afterward murdered by Harper in a very cold blooded and treacherous manner.—WAUGH

provided with ellegantly constructed weapons for the chase, with a plentiful supply of the luxuries of life to render the trip agreable. The baggage, equipages and equipments of the various parties, were as diversified as their owners. Here you saw the large waggons of the Santa Fe trader, there the smaller one of the individual who was merely going out to see the country of the disputed territory, (Oregon), and anon the medium size, fitted up in a novel, but comfortable manner to serve as a domicile for a whole family.[117]

The hotels and boarding houses were thronged to overflowing with every variety of the genus homo, whose costumes, selected according to the fancy or taste of each individual gave a decided dash of interest to the scene. Nothing could exceed the originality of their appearance. Here stood a tall weather beaten fellow with long, dark elflocks reaching to his shoulders, dressed in a suit of buckskin, fancifully ornamented with needle-work, looking with perfect contempt upon the city-bred amateur hunter whose travelling coat displayed a row of enormous bronze buttons, and an endless variety of pockets. There lounged the pale valetudinarian who is going to seek in "change of scene" that relief which cannot be granted him by his physicians. But who have we here? Why! he looks out of place in that superb morning gown, and yellow slippers, but what am I talking about, never mind the dress, the tailor made hat,—look at the creature's face, that was the work of madam nature, and certainly we must give her credit for her handywork. She has given a pretty face, a fine complexion and an abundance of superbly flowing hair, but, in the bestowal her kindness was displayed on the externals only, and what few brain she may have given him at first, have long since been expended in the nourishment of his darling, lady killing tresses.[118]

There, do you see that small, spare man, with a wirey figure and thin,

---

In his last chapter Waugh reports at length on this murder. Bryant noted, before he left Independence, that "A party of gentlemen from Baltimore, bound for Santa Fe on a pleasure excursion, among whom were Messrs. Hoffman, Morris, and Meredith, arrived" (*What I Saw in California*, 17-18). Francis Parkman had traveled on the same boat from St. Louis to Westport with this party; they made a poor impression on him: "On board the boat are a party of Baltimoreans—flash genteel—very showily attired in 'Genteel undress,' though bound for California. They make a great noise at table, and are waited on by the Negroes with great attention and admiration. . . . The Baltimoreans got shamefully drunk, and one of them, an exquisite in full dress, tumbled into the water" (Wade, *Journals of Francis Parkman*, II, 415-417, entries for 29 April and 2 May). For the murder see note 143 below.

117. One emigrant to Oregon, had so ingeniously contrived his waggon in its construction that it served for every household purpose; it had a cooking stove, and was large enough for his whole family to live in.—WAUGH

118. This was a young fellow from New York or Philadelphia who was placed by his father under the charge of Mr. Spyre to see something of travelling, but the creature was so great a ninny that Spyre sent him back to his parent.—WAUGH

sharp visage, him with the sallow complexion and dark moustache you percieve what a keen deep set eye he has got, and a nose so aquiline that he might pass for a roman. The firm compression of his thin lips, indicate a strong determination of purpose. He is a man of great energy of character—nothing daunts his courageous spirit. That man lost in one night, during a snow storm, on the prairies, last November upwards of three hundred mules, they were killed by the cold. Which misfortune led to a loss of thirty eight thousand dollars. Every person believed him to be a ruined man; they thought he could not possibly recover himself, but he did, however and now is master of twenty two waggon loaded with merchantdize for the Chihuahua market, and is likely to reallize one hundred thousand dollars by the trade this year.[119]

Hallo "what's the matter is Lucifer let loose with all this clatter". What a racket—Who are they just come in? they must be bent upon a spree as they appear a real devil may care set of fellows. Ah! I know who they are, he with the long dutch pipe is Bryant from Luisville, going to California, with the intention of collecting materials for a book on that out of the way country. He is a man of talents "a fellow of infinite jest," a merry wag of the first water, possessed of the happy faculty of extracting mirth from every thing. That gentleman beside him with glazed oil cloth cap, and indian rubber poncho which he has so gracefully raised over one shoulder, is an officer of the United States navy.[120] He has had leave of absence, and for the sake of novelty will cross the plains, and join his ship at San Francisco. His friend Bryant has mischeivously circulated the report that he is the bearer of despatches from the government to the commodore in the Pacific. As a matter of course this has exalted the navy lieutenant into a lion, and excited the curiosity of all the small gentry about town, but it is only a quis, and has been done for the sake of creating a little fun.[121]

Oh! let me draw your attention to that tall, man who wears a panama

---

119. Mr. Spyre, or as some say he is, Baron Spyre. He is an exceedingly energetic, enterprising man, whom obstacles can not conquer. The late Samuel Owens disliked him very much and spread many reports to his prejudice, for instance Col Owens said that Mr. Spyre was carrying out arms and ammunition to the Mexicans, which was subsequently proved to be incorrect.—WAUGH

Albert Speyer was active in the Santa Fe trade between 1843 and 1848. For him consult the index to Bieber, *Southwest Historical Series;* he figures especially in the first volume: Webb's *Adventures in the Santa Fe Trade.* Wislizenus (note 114) traveled with Speyer. There is no doubt that Speyer was running a cargo of arms on this trip, for he later submitted a claim against Mexico for seizure of arms and ammunition (Drumm, *Down the Santa Fe Trail,* 246).

120. Lieutenant Fitzgeral Beale, attached to the Ship Ohio, at this time in the Pacific.—WAUGH

121. Bonsal in his life of Beale makes no mention of this overland journey. Bryant does not record this episode.

hat covered with oil'd silk. Now, I would say he is a lawyer and politician—anxious for place and power. Do you observe how very courteous he is to all around him,—how kindly he takes every man who is introduced to him, by the hand, seemingly delighted to have the pleasure of his acquaintance;—that gentleman, I am told is colonel Look-a-head,[122]—bound for California with bright visions of prosperity—and eminance in that far off region. That young man standing beside him is a young Kentuckian, still in his minority—full of the wild spirit of romance. His object in going out is merely to see the country and gratify his taste for adventure.[123] Near this group stands an other, composed of three persons carrying on a conversation in the german language. He, with a thin figure, sharp looking face, richly frosted with the small pox,—is a Dane, remarkable for his exactness in buisiness matters, and so close in his dealings, that his prudence verges on meaness.[124] That mild, gentlemanly, and benevolent looking person on his left, is a Prussian, and is the very soul and essence of good breeding.[125] The third, is a very learned and scientific physician whose soul object in travel is to gain knowledge. He is amply furnished with philosophical instruments and accompanied by a countryman of his own, a saxon who acts as curator. A book of much interest, no doubt will be the result of his researches.[126] There stands the author of the Commerce of the Prairie, a gentleman of great truth, but of no poetry in his writings. His book will, hereafter, be quoted as authority, so correct is he in all his statements.[127] Mr. Gregg is talking to young

---

122. Col. Wm. H. Russel.—WAUGH

123. Ewing son of Dr [blank in ms] Ewing of Louisville.—WAUGH.

R. Ewing had come with Bryant from Louisville. On the overland journey he changed his mind about California and joined, Bryant heard, a party of traders bound for Taos or the headwaters of the Arkansas (*What I Saw in California*, 13, 115). Parkman saw him at St. Louis on 25 April; he describes him as "Ewing, the impulsive, unobserving ardent Kentuckian, who lays open his character to everyone, and sees nothing of those about him" (Wade, *Journals of Francis Parkman*, II, 415). According to the *Weekly Reveille* (14 September 1846—dateline 8 September—p. 996) he went as far out as Fort Laramie, then went to Bent's Fort; on 22 August he was at Council Grove on the Santa Fe trail headed homeward with Waugh and others.

124. Mr. Weaks, a small trader to the spanish country.—WAUGH

Weick or Weicks and Blumner were to be in the Ralston party with which Waugh was to travel to Santa Fe; see p. 113 below. Wislizenus (*Tour to Northern Mexico*, 39) mentioned him as "Mr. Wiek, a merchant from Chihuahua."

125. Charles Blumner formerly an officer in the Prussian service, and now a resident of Santa Fe & called Don Carlos Blumner.—WAUGH

Blumner was named treasurer of the Territorial Government set up by Kearny for New Mexico, 22 September 1846 (Bieber, *A Soldier under Kearny and Doniphan*, 242, n. 376).

126. Dr. Wilselzenius.—WAUGH. See note 114 above.

127. Gregg's *Commerce of the Prairies* had been published two years earlier; a lengthy review of it appeared in the *Independence Journal*, 19 September 1844. His diaries and letters have recently been published in two volumes by Maurice Garland Fulton.

Stanley the artist, who is now, no doubt recieving some information about the plains. Mr. S has already a large collection of Indian portraits, and in the tour which he is about to commence, it will be greatly augmented. It is his intention to form a gallery of greater extent than that of Catlin.[128] I think he is a very clever fellow and wish him every success. Indeed, if I were to sketch all the characters at present in this town, I would have no time for any thing else, so let them rest in their spheres and we will look at other things.

This same town of Independence is rapidly growing into considerable importance and if the citizens properly understand their own interests they will, at all times keep the road from the landing in good repair, otherwise they will be apt to loose the Santa Fe trade.[129] It is a pleasant little town whose citizens behave in a kind and hospitable manner to strangers. And, although so many foreign faces make their appearance among them every season, yet, they are not meanly suspicious of their visitants, nor, do they trouble themselves with that silly *ape* called *fashion,* to divide them into classes of cold and heartless,—mushroom aristocracy.

It has three Hotels, the largest of which, the Noland house, lately created by Wood Noland, or, as the young men call him—Uncle Wood.[130] When finished it will be capable of accommodating between four and five hundred boarders. The Independence Hotel, kept by Mr. West, is a new and handsome building. The other is owned by a Mr. Thomas, it is more of a boarding house than a hotel. Independence was formerly the stronghold of the Mormons, but in consequence of these fanatics becoming obnoxious to the citizens at large, they were driven off. When we first

---

128. More than one hundred and fifty pictures by Stanley, almost his entire collection, were destroyed in the Smithsonian fire of 1865.

129. Since the above was written, a rail road has made constructed from the landing to the town.—WAUGH

130. "The large brick Hotel recently built by our worthy old friend, Southwood Noland, better known by the appellation of 'Uncle Wood,' is now about completed, and opened for the accommodation of the public. This is the largest and most commodious Hotel in the State, except those of St. Louis. It has a front of one hundred and eighty feet, and two stories high. 'Uncle Wood,' who keeps this fine house, is known from the Atlantic to the Pacific. He has kept a public house in this place for the last eight years, but was so unfortunate as to get his old hotel burnt down about eighteen months ago. He now 'Phoenix like, comes out with increased brilliancy and splendor.' Travellers are here splendidly accommodated with the substantials of life, tipped off with all the extra good things of the season, and then can wash them down with the most choice liquors, with which his bar is well furnished; after which, they can amuse themselves by listening to 'Uncle Wood's' tales of the Mormon war, as he was one of the principal actors of those momentous times. His details, particularly in his *own peculiar style,* are very interesting. He was one of the number of five who escaped being drowned on the Mormon ferry boat, by swimming the Missouri river. Five others, including Mormons, were drowned at the same time" (letter signed *B,* dated Independence, 26 June 1846, in the St. Louis *Missouri Republican,* 3 July 1846). Both the Magoffins and Parkman stayed at Noland's Hotel.

reached here, a store stood at SW corner of the Court House square which had been what these poor creatures called "The Lord's store." It is said that a larger amount of goods were to cross the plains this year than was ever known, amounting in the agregate, to about one million, three hundred thousand dollars, and there will be employed to carry them, upwards of three hundred waggons. Some persons of small capitol are embarked in the trade, but the great majority have large capitols.

Dr. David Waldo,[131] who has been a trader, gave me a great deal of information relative to the plains and the Mexican country—and also introduced me to Dr. Gregg, who was polite enough to present me with a copy of his work. This gentleman so interested me with his remarks on the prairies and the Mexican country that I began to feel a desire to cross the great Desert of America. But what immediately led to the consumation of my desires was, meeting with a son of Governor Boggs,[132] who was about starting with his father to California. This young gentleman who was just married, gave me an invitation to accompany him—and promised a great many kind things if I would so do, but, as California at that time was, comparatively, an unknown region, and not a likely place for one of my profession to go to, I declined accepting his proferred kindness and by the representation of a man of the name of Ralston the spanish country was selected for the field of my opperations. I had frequently met Samuel Ralston in the office of Genl Lucas and elsewhere, and he appeared to be rather a well behaved man; was polite in his intercourse with me, and seemed in every respect a worthy fellow. He hailed from North Carolina and cultivated a farm a short distance from town, where he had an exceedingly interesting wife and family. Finding from his representation that I could probably do very well in my profession there, and as he was engaged to haul goods for a couple of small traders, and moreover wanted a group of his family painted I soon arranged with him to take me to Chihuahua (i e) he was to haul my baggage and furnish

---

131. David Waldo (1802-1878) came to Missouri from Virginia in 1820. A graduate of the Medical Department of Transylvania University, he presently gave up medicine for the Santa Fe trade. For nearly fifty years he was one of the most prominent citizens of western Missouri.

132. Former governor Lilburn W. Boggs (1792-1860) was one of the principal figures in this season's California emigration—there is much concerning him in Bryant's *What I Saw in California*. He was born in Kentucky, moved to St. Louis at eighteen, married (1) Julia Ann, daughter of Silas Bent, and (2) Panthea, daughter of Jesse Boone. By the first marriage he had two sons; by the second he had ten children, including William (born 1826) who was married near Fort Osage in 1846 just before leaving Independence for the West Coast. Lilburn settled in Independence in 1832 or 1833 and was governor of Missouri from 1836 to 1840. In 1842 the Mormons attempted to assassinate him. In 1846 he went to California; he died in Napa Valley. Consult Boggs, "A Short Biographical Sketch of Lilburn W. Boggs," and "Reminiscences of William C. Boggs."

me with food along the route, I riding my own horse and [furnishing] every equipment necessary.[133] I soon purchased a rifle, a pair of pistols, and a supply of powder and lead. It is usual to carry a short knife stuck in the belt for the convenience of cutting up meat and other purposes. Instead of procuring one of the usual shape and size, I purchased a carving knife and fork and got the saddler to case them after the manner of a Hilander's dirk, the scabbards being placed one over the other. I now bought an indian rubber poncho and hat of the same material, got a pair of long boots made to order, with spurs that were let into the heel, and a good supply of colored calico shirts, flannel undershirts and woolen socks, with a supply of blankets for bedding and other articles of minor importance, besides laying in a good supply of writing paper, quills &c, black lead pencils, for I intended to make notes and sketches during my travels, from which I afterwards purposed to prepare a book for the dear public. As I was not a monied man, I intended to make my pencil act as my fiscal agent and furnish me with the means of travelling over Mexico and the whole of South America, and when my wanderings should be ended, I would then return to London and there prepare my work for publication. All this was very well arranged—in theory, and could have been carried out but for the war which stopped me in my career. I was amply furnished with every thing requisite for collecting materials for an illustrated book of travels, and it is more than probable I could have accomplished my designs had not the war interrupted the amiable relation of the two countries. At this time, however, hostillities had not commenced and I had no reason to apprehend any difficulty in the undertaking which I had laid out for myself.

As soon as it was understood that I was about to leave, many commissions poured in upon me, and I painted pictures for several persons who heretofore had not thought of getting any thing of the kind.

Among the emigrants were several belonging to the Masonic fraternity and the Lodge here, wishing to shew them how much they were held in esteem, determined on having a procession and oration previous to their departure. Accordingly on saturday the 2nd of May 1846,[134] a very

---

133. ". . . Our townsman, Mr. Samuel Rallston, has just returned from Santa Fe, after an unprecedented trip of eighty days. He, in company with Messrs. Weick, Blumner and others, left with their goods in May, and arrived in Santa Fe, making a journey of forty days. After completing their arrangements, a small company, consisting of Messrs. Rallston and Hill, of our place, and Mr. Hutchinson and Jno. McKnight, from Chihuahua, started in, and are now here, in thirty-seven days from Santa Fe" (unsigned letter dated Independence, 13 August 1846, in *Missouri Republican*, 20 August 1846). According to Webb (*Adventures in the Santa Fe Trade*, 181) he was the father-in-law of Jesse James.

134. It must be remembered that Waugh is not keeping a journal but writing a

imposing procession was formed, preceded by a band of music, and closed by a portion of warm hearted ladies, of Independence who stood in near relationship to the members of the order, some of whom wore the regalia of Heroines of Jerrico. The object of all this was to give a parting God speed to their emigrating brethren who were leaving for foreign lands.

The procession on arriving at the Methodist Church, opened to the right and left, and the ladies in the rear, preceded by the Master of the Lodge, R. R. Reese Esgr. first entered, the fraternity following in the usual order on such occasions. As soon as the fraternity and the citizens had taken their places, the brethren seated themselves at the sound of the gavel, and the band gave forth its cheering strains.

The exercises were now opened by prayer after which music followed, and then the worshipful Master rose and in a feeling manner addressed us for the space of half an hour, during which the eyes of many, both old and young were mositened with the tears of sympathy. Music followed and during its performance I had time to collect myself for the part I had to play. A short time before the procession was formed I had shut myself up in my room, to read over my address and while doing so, it occurred to me that I would not be able to deliver it intelligibly, for I found my feelings were getting the best of my utterances. I now said to myself, my brethren have reposed confidence in me, and I am bound in honor, to exert myself to the best of my abilities to please them, so I will not suffer my feelings to master my actions. Just as I had come to this conclusion the music ceased,—a solemn silence pervaded the assembly, and but for the innumerable faces which were turned toward the pulpit I could have fancied myself alone in some uninhabited house, so perfectly still was every thing around me. Nerved to the task by my soliloqy, I stoutly arose, advanced to the front, and bowing to the worshipful Master and brethren, commenced speaking, to a most attentive and patient audience. I found that I got along much better than I expected, for instead being overcome myself I had set my audience to crying.[135]

---

narrative; in this chapter he has taken some slightly confusing liberties with time and has jumped back and forth rather carelessly. Of principal travelers in Independence during this season it may be noted that Bryant arrived on 1 May and left on the 5th: Wislizenus arrived on the 9th and left on the 14th; Parkman arrived on the 2nd and left on the 9th; Webb left on the 9th; Gregg was in town in mid-April and left on 13 June with Owens; the Magoffins (who had been staying for an unknown number of days or weeks with James Magoffin near Independence) pulled out on 1 June. Waugh himself must have left town about 15 May if he traveled with Ralston and reached Santa Fe in forty days, for he arrived there on 24 June.

135. "The masonic lodges of Independence commemorated the departure of their brother masons, connected with the Santa Fe and emigrating parties, by a public procession and address, with other religious exercises. The lady-masons, that is, the

Colonel WH Russel followed in a few striking remarks and the exercises were closed with Burns's farewell, rather murdered in the singing, I being Particips crimines in the foul deed.[136] Nothing occurred save this, to mar the proceedings, and all left the house doubtless with better feelings then they had entered it,—not a heart, perhaps, that was not softened, and those who went there enemies, returned friends to the order.

---

wives of the members of the fraternity, walked in the procession to and from the church. A large audience was collected to hear the address, and participate in the exercises. The address was delivered by Mr. Reese, the grandmaster, or principal masonic officer in the place. It was appropriate to the occasion, except, as I thought, that it was rather overstrained in pathos. The orator, at the close of his discourse, consigned us all to the grave, or to perpetual exile. He was responded to in suitable and eloquent terms, on behalf of the Santa Fe traders and the emigrants to Oregon and California, by Col. Waul [*sic*] and Col. Russell. After the addresses, an original hymn, written for the occasion, as I understood, was sung with much feeling by the whole audience, to the tune of 'Old Rosin the Bow.' These farewell ceremonies were concluded by an affecting prayer and benediction. The ladies of the auditory, I thought, were the most interested in and excited by these proceedings. Some of them wept, and manifested strong emotions" (Bryant, *What I Saw in California*, 14-15).

136. Robert Burns' poem "The Farewell to the Brethren of the St. James' Lodge, Tarlbolton" was written in 1784 when he intended to emigrate to Jamaica. Apparently it was sung to the tune of "Good-night, and joy be wi' you a'."

CHAPTER X

THE ARTIST TAKES LEAVE OF FRIENDS IN LEXINGTON—DESULTORY REMINISCENCES OF HIS EARLY LIFE—ENTERTAINMENT IN INDEPENDENCE—A LADY POET—THE MURDER OF MEREDITH—PREPARATIONS FOR THE JOURNEY—ABOUT TO START

THE MORNING AFTER THE CEREMONIES described in the last chapter, happening to go into a store on the Court House square, I met Dr. Troust[137] and his lady who had attended the day before to our observances in the Methodist Church. Mrs. T who is a lady of great vivacity, good humoredly asked me "if the ghost of Burns did not haunt the Masons for the foul murder they had committed on that his beautiful ode of his for you most certainly murdered it, and ought all of you to be hanged for the deed, that too, without benefit of clergy." "Ah! Madam," said I, "we are not as guilty as you suppose, and I think, that the law, if we should be tried in open court, would deal more mildly with us,—our sentence would be "*justifiable homocide*" for we made but *an attempt*, and that only in "our own defence" as the *ode struck* us in the first instance we could not resist an encountre, without running the risk of being considered cowards, and that, you know, is a title which no man fancies under any circumstance whatever.

Bryant, in his "What I saw in California" says that it was sung to the good old tune of "Rosin the Bow." That only shews the incorrectness of his ear, for I defy any one in the least acquainted with music to tell what air was adopted to the words; indeed, it was a strange mixture of various tunes, both sacred and profane, and could lay claim to no particular rank in the science of music. However, we did our best, and everybody knows that the best can do no more.

Every arrangement being made for my departure, I rode down to Lexington to take leave of Tisdale, and Dr. Ruffin, and found that during the month I had been away that Jack had exerted himself manfully in miniature painting, in fact, had been more industrious after my leaving him, then while we were together. I found that he had produced some

137. A card in the Independence Journal, 12 September 1844, announced that "Doctor B[enoist] Troost has located himself permanently in Independence, and offers his services in the various branches of the practice of Medicine; and hopes, after an experience of forty-five years in its practice and study, to merit a share of public patronage. Office on North Liberty Street." However, in 1846 he bought a lot in Kansas City and the following year settled there (Whitney, *Kansas City*, I, 472). A native of Holland, he was a brother of Gerard Troost, the geologist.

really fine paintings on ivory, very superior to any thing from his pencil which I had seen before. He was not at home when I arrived, but the room being open I entered and took a chair by the fire to await his return. Scearcely had I sat down when Jack's pets, some half dozen kittens introduced themselves to my notice by climbing up my legs, four remaining in my lap while two, more aspiring than the others, never stopped until they reached my shoulders, and commenced playing with my hair. Each one had a string around its neck to five of which were appended a piece of card, and the sixth, a five cent piece. This humor of Jack I could not divine until going over to the table I saw—what do you think—eh! why! a register of their births! each one having a given name, as as *queen of hearts, ace* of diamonds, Jack of clubs &c and the one around whose neck was suspended the small piece of money was called *Hard Currency.* This piece of drollery on his part, set me laughing heartily, in the midst of which, master Jack made his appearance. He had taken a particular fancy to the mother of these kittens, and that poor cat, in grateful remembrance of the notice he took of her, paid him the compliment of ushering her progeny into the world in his room, hence the patronage he bestowed on that interesting family.

Friend Ruffin, Tisdale, and myself spent the evening together very pleasantly. The doctor gave me some directions about certain enquiries I was to make into the climate, soil, botany and diseases of the countries I was about to visit and then gave me good medical advice about the management of myself during my travels, all which I promised to pay attention to. Next day I purchased a large dutch pipe to be used along the road, as my splendid mereschaum was not to be taken out of its case until I had reached a halting place in Mexico. With a heavy heart I shook hands with my friends and mounting my horse bid adieu to them and left Lexington for Independence, for the last time, as I supposed. I need not say that our parting was sad, Jack and I had been companions for some time; it was principally to gratify him, that I thought of going with Fremont, and for him I would have done almost any thing. We had come thus far together, and now, we were seperated, perhaps for ever. In future *he* was to paddle his own canoe, and I to continue a *Wandering Artist* with no relative on the whole continent of North America to make me forget that I was a stranger in the land. Reader, unless you are similarly situated, you can form no idea of the feeling of utter loneliness, which I then experienced,—pshaw, why what a fool I am making of myself to talk in this silly way! but, I can't help my nature—As an artist, I am necessarily sensitive, and being thus sensitive, am, occasionally extremely dejected, so much so, indeed, that I absolutely become hateful to myself. Would I were less so, how much more pleasantly could I glide on through the world; there would not be so many cloudy days in the callender of my existence; I would not then be entitled to the appellation of disagreable old fellow. No! I would be more like the rest of mankind, consequently more happy. Well! well! after all, I dont think that I could be induced to make an exchange with some who seem to take the world easier? What? give up the exquisite pleasure of communing with Nature, —of conversing with the master spirits of antiquity,—enjoying the voice of song and drinking in the rich melody of creation,—No! not for all the gold of California. It is true that my annoyances are severe, but then, as a consequence, my enjoyments are exquisite.

The day was one of those peculiarly pleasant ones, which sometimes seem to make us forget that we have passed through a disagreable winter; it was clear, balmy and calm as heart could wish, and I tried my best to shake off the gloom which had pressed down on my spirits for some time, gradually they became lighter, and finally I fell into a train of quiet reflexions, on the past, and speculations on the future. It is astonishing with what rapidity thought travels through time and space. In a moment I fancied myself back to my school-boy days, my steps were wandering along the sea beach in search of shells or clambering the mountains of my native land. At one moment I was studying from the antique, and, in an other, contending for the prize in the life school of the Royal Academy. Now, I was walking through the gallery of the Louvre, and then standing before the Apollo of the Vatican; then again, I was crossing the Alps, and anon, sailing up the Rhine, for I have travelled much and am familiar with the antiquated scenes of the old World; the ivy mantled towers; the moss grown castles; the delapidated churches, and ruined monasteries of the feudal ages, have each in their turn, arrested by attention, and claimed the homage of a sigh as I passed beneath their mouldering walls. Within the deep shades of the forest solitudes whose sylvan recesses were once vocal with the gleesome sports of the bold hunter, have I spent many an hour, picturing in my young fancy, scenes of loveliness and peace; of foray and battle; of tilt and tourney, such, as have long since been immortalized by both historian and poet, and I became, as it were, transplanted back to the days of romance and chivalry, when

Each bearded warrior, strong at heart
Threw the long spear or hurl'd the rankling dart.
With mighty arm, and matchless strength
They stretched the foman at full length

Upon the field in crimson gore
And the vanquisher's arms in tryumph bore
Back to the fort or fensive castle
And shew'd the spoils to each chief & vassal,

Oh! I have dreamed in many a venerable pile, aye! dreamed as youth, and youth only can dream, for, life to me then, was but a long, sweet dream. It was in the spring tide of my existence, when the bouyant spirit looks at the drama of life through a roseate atmosphere, and clothes each passing scene with the bewildering charms of romance. It was at that time of life when the heart, still soft, is easily touched by either joy or sorrow, e'er intercourse with a cold and selfish world, has paralyzed its noble impulses by its deceitful *wiles* and closed the natural avenues to its finest sympathy. Yes! mine was a dream!—a long,—a pleasing dream. I dreamt of success, of—fame!—fame!—ha! ha!—oh ye gods!—and now I find that

"Twas all but a dream at the best,
The happiest, soonest o'er.
But, Oh! in a dream to be blest
Is so sweet that I ask for no more."

And echo answered from the surrounding woods.

"no more"

for I found that, lost for a time, in my own reflections, I had unconsciously given utterance to these beautiful lines of Moore, and was only recalled to myself by the mysterious repetition of the concluding words of the stanza.

Well! thinks I to myself, I have seen most of the old world, and a good deal of the New, and mankind is pretty much the same every where. Madame de Stael was quite correct when she said, "I have seen a great deal of the world, and have found only two classes,—men and—women." It is a matter of no consequence what the form of government may be under which we live, man remains the same every where, he only has a different way of shewing himself off, tha's all. Nations like individuals, are very apt to fancy themselves great,—Man is only a boy of a larger growth. When a mere child, his school mistress gratifies his "young ideas" of honors and distinction, by ornamenting his pinafore with a blue ribbon and a thin piece of silver, and when he takes to wearing beard and moustaches, his full grown notions are confirmed by a decree from the members of the senior class, that his bravery and good conduct on *that* great play ground,—the battle field, is worthy of a badge of distinction, so a gold medal is voted, and this big boy is as much tickled with the last bauble as with the first. Wonder if the Indians have any kind of aristocracy among themselves, and whether it is, an aristocracy of wealth, or talent, or of first family blood—should like to know. Don't think Madame De Stael knew anything about the aborigines.

During my ride, I ran over my past life, and found that its review produced only one regret—that I had not obeyed the command of High Heavens by remaining unmarried. I had now arrived at middle life, a useless member of society, and felt that I had no claim upon the world and when I asked myself the question why I had not selected a partner, I am sure I must have looked very ridiculous, in the attempt I made to justify myself for my neglect of duty. And yet it was not altogether my fault I have tried often enough to induce some fair one to take me for a life partner, but, I'm afraid, nay! I know it, my matrimonial game was played too much like the way I manage a game of billiards. I began, always very well, but some way or other, I never won the game, for, just as I came to the final stroke, I made a miss cue which my opponent taking advantage of, collected himself for the final blow,—took steady aim,—made a carrom—and I lost.

Now reader, I'll let you into a secret, if you are a young man, my advice may be of some service to you, depend upon it, to make a miss cue is a very dangerous thing. Be steady in all your actions; nerve yourself like a man; throw your whole heart into the game; never say fail; and my word for it your after life will be all the happier. Doctor Samuel Johnson says, "Marriage hath many cares, but celebacy no enjoyments." He said truly, and I know it to my sorrow. Whoever you may be, I pray you for God's sake, dont follow my example. Here I am, wandering about the world, a perfect cosmopolite, following the bent of a wild fancy, running after a shadow, always having something in view, but never obtaining the object of my pursuit. Now, my going out to Mexico is solely for the purpose of procuring me some employment for the mind; were I a married man I would stay at home, for then I would have a home, but now I have no home, no old bachelor has a home, be he rich or poor but, I must make a virtue of necessity, and become reconciled to my fate.

I stopped that night at Mr. Hamilton's and the next day reached Independence, where I found the Brittingham family delighting the citizens with their vaudevilles. When the head of the *interested* family told me that he was travelling in a very novel and original manner, in a pair of canoes, lashed together, I wrote to Tisdale that Mr B expressed himself highly flattered by having a gentleman like Mr T to coppy after him in any particular. Jack, who prides himself a good deal upon his originality, did not like this, for he soon abandoned his scheme of travel.

At a performance which was held that evening in an upper room of the Noland House, our little friend Hovey amused the audience, exceedingly, with an extempore and impromptu display of his comic powers. As his services were not regularly engaged by the manager, he played his part in the midst of the spectators, leaving the stage for the use of the members of the travelling company. This *irregular* interlude, was, perhaps, the most amusing part of the evening's entertainment, and drew forth rapturous applause. The piece was *Low Life above Stairs,*[138] and Hovey acquitted himself admirably, and, were it not for the demon of jealousy, he might have kept the audience in roars of laughter for the remainder of the night, but, Brittingham, fearing that he would be stripped of his well won laurels, shewed signs of impatience, wishing to have this brilliant star shorn of his beams, made some illnatured remarks, when a few, no doubt, in the interest of the manager, managed to spirit the great J. Hovey away, leaving the field to the regular performers, and the chagrin of a large number of the admirers of the renowned captain.

The next evening the Robin's Brothers gave a concert at the Independence House, and were assisted by Miss Brittingham, who possitively enchanted all the young fellows about town. This young lady is so extremely *modest, bashful,* and *retireing* in her manners that it is not to be wondered at that she should lead captive so many, noble, high spirited, and gallant young men as she did. Indeed her powers of fascinating are so great that I was possitively affraid to go a second time to any performance where she appeared, least I would fall a victim, thus rendering myself an object of mirth to others, "for, there is," it is said, "no fool like an old fool."

Independence can boast of having some among its inhabitants, of a very superior order of intellect, whose talents would adorn any community. At present Mrs. Mary Kyle Buchanan,[139] known as a poet and prose writer, is giving instructions in music, to the young ladies. This lady whose effusions have adorned the pages of the Southern Literary Messenger, and other periodicals, adds by her presence, an indescribable charm to the circles of private life. Indeed I do not well know how to

---

138. William G. B. Carson suggests that this was probably a burlesque of Garrick's *High Life Below Stairs.*

139. It is possible that Waugh wrote this name incorrectly. A Mrs. Maria G. Buchanan contributed four poems to the *Southern Literary Messenger* in 1844 (X, 103, 228, 583, 734). These were dated Wetumka, Alabama, 18 October and 4 December 1843, Memphis, Tennessee, 4 July 1844, and Holly Springs, Mississippi, 1844. Another poem published in February 1846 had been sent to the editor from Holly Springs. In the next volume (XIII, 472) there was published in August, 1847, a poem sent from Independence; still other poems from that town appeared in the following volume XIV, 89, 365).

speak of the citizens of this town, for, I have never met more intelligent, kind, and hospitable people, anywhere. Less then twelve month from my entrance into their midst, and I find myself on the footing of an old friend, and it is, really, with regret I am now about to take my leave, and if my life is spared I will return here, and for a time, sojourn among them.

Every day for some time past small companies have been passing through this place to their several rendezvous previous to their final departure for Oregon or California.[140] It is really curious to witness the display of taste and talents of the individuals who thus emigrate. One goes decked out in all his finery—an other is accoutred in a manner as eccentric as possible. One is furnished with a comfortable Jersey waggon curtained so nicely that it will serve him instead of a tent,—an other prefers a small carriage with out springs of any kind. One goes out furnished with ample camp furniture, and an other, despising every thing like effeminacy, is determined to take the broad canopy of the heavens for a covering. There is a young matron with her "jewells" stowed away in a canvass covered waggon and there, the blushing bride just going to spend the honey moon on the plains,[141] peeps modestly forth from behind the cover to get the last sight of the last house in the last town, this side of the Rocky Mountains. But the equestrians who can describe them?—I can not! Just immagine to yourself all sorts of immaginable dresses on all sorts of queer looking fellows and then you will have some idea of the men who are about to cast themselves upon the vast ocean of wilderness which lies between civilization and the Pacific.

Before I go any further, I ought to say, that the Missouri river, which takes its rise in the Rocky Mountains, and passes within three miles of Independence, is an exceedingly muddy stream, frequently carrying on its surface quantities of pumice stone, thrown out on its waters by volcanoes in the region from which it comes. In the autumn of the year, many parties of trappers and hunters belonging to the American Fur

140. The road to Santa Fe was clogged with travelers. A Mr. McKenney who arrived in St. Louis on 24 June informed the *Missouri Republican* (25 June 1846) that his party, which had left Bent's Fort on 13 May and made Westport in thirty-three days, had ". . . Met Messrs. Webb, Doan and others at Ash Creek, twenty days from Independence. Met a part of Armijo's company at Walnut Creek; the remainder, and Mr. Prewitt, at Plum Bute; Mr. Speyers at Little Arkansas; a small party of Dragoons, under Colonel Howard, at Cotton-Wood Fork. Met Mr. Harmony at Council Grove; Capt. Moore with one hundred and eighty dragoons, at Big John Springs; Messrs. Branham and Hickman and Col. Davis near Rock Creek; Messrs. Ferguson, Glasgow & Clark at One Hundred and Ten; Messrs. Magoffin, Leitensdorfer, Masure, Owens, McKinistry and others, at and near Black Jack; and straggling parties, including twenty-five provision wagons, for the United States, bound to Bent's Fort, were daily met until their arrival at Westport."

141. This could be Susan Magoffin whose diary Stella Drumm edited: *Down the Santa Fé Trail and Into Mexico.*

Company of St. Louis, pass down on the steam boats, and by their half civilized appearance, ellicit remarks from those who have never before seen those bold and reckless men. From the length of time these men spend in those far off wilds among wild animals and wilder Indians they have assumed some of the dress and manners of their savage neighbors. As a boat containing a party of these hardy and fearless fellows approaches the landing, the inhabitants of Wayne City are saluted with the war whoop, and other frightful yellings of the savage denizens from whose country they have just returned. Packs of buffalo robes and peltries of all sorts lumber the deck on which these adventures repose during their voyage. Most of them are fine looking fellows, and with their picturesque dresses and long unshorn locks, are capitol subjects for the pencil of such an artist as Bingham.[142] From them the curious in such matters may procure a rare collection of Indian costumes and accoutrements. If I were not leaving the borders of civilized life I would have availed myself of the oppertunity and formed a museum, for I am fond of such things.

As I was on the prairies at the time of the death of a gentleman who was going out to California, and I knew the parties, I may as well insert the account here, which is taken from the Independence Expositor, as it goes to shew to what dreadful lengths a man is carried by "the green eyed monster."

"Unfortunate Affair.—Our town was in a state of excitement about two weeks past on the subject of William Wirt Meredith of Baltimore, who was shot dead on the evening of the 27th of May, by John Henry Harper, attorney at law of this town. The place, the time, and a deck of cards which lay upon the table in Mr. Harper's office, proved on first sight to an excited community which gathered in as soon as the report of a pistol was heard, that a misunderstanding over the card table was the cause of Mr. Meredith's death. Mr. Harper eagerly seized this pretext to justify himself, believing that it would be credited upon mature reflection. It is truly unfortunate that he did not in the first place assign the real cause, but none can appreciate his feelings or justify him in resorting to the subterfuge which appeared to be so generally believed by the public, save he who is a *husband* or a *father* of *daughters.* Neither will the laws of our country justify the shedding of blood, but public sentiment has

142. For George Caleb Bingham (1811-1879) consult Rusk, *George Caleb Bingham The Missouri Artist* and Christ-Janer, *George Caleb Bingham of Missouri.* Bingham was popular and well-thought of in St. Louis. Probably Waugh met him there on some of his visits to that city; certainly Waugh had ample opportunities to see Bingham's work on display in St. Louis.

in all cases acquited the man who signally avenges a wrong attempted by an other upon his family and all reflecting husbands will see that Mr. Harper's motive for assigning a quarrel at the card table as his reason for shooting the deceased, was a sensitiveness concerning his wife's name being brought before the public in so delicate a subject. If the true cause of the killing had been assigned, Mr. Harper would now have been at liberty: as it is he will remain in confinement to await his trial before the circuit court."

"We do not speak without consulting others, we know that we have spoken the language of public sentiment.

"Mr. Harper has been a citizen of our town for nearly two years. He is from Greensboro, Georgia."

The foregoing does not enter into the full particulars of this unhappy affair. It appears from what I can learn from the citizens, that Mrs. Harper who had taken quite a fancy to young Meredith, who was a very fine looking young man, sent him a boquet from her husband's garden with some complimentary remarks upon his appearance, and subsequently a few billet-doux passed between them, which coming to Harper's knowledge the death of Meredith was decided upon. As soon as Harper had arranged the cards on the table of his office in such a way as to indicate a recent game, he went into the street and meeting his victim accosted in a very friendly manner, asked him to go and take something to drink; then putting his arm within that of Meredith's walked into a grocery and pledged him in a bumper, after which he invited him to his office,—locked the door and deliberately shot him with a revolver. When the citizens rushed in Harper tried to make it appear that they were playing cards and that Meredith had cheated in the game for which dishonest and dishonorable conduct Harper took his life. Some of the friends of Meredith being present pronounced Harper's statement false, for that Meredith never played cards and was totally unacquainted with games of chance of any sort. This at once created ill feeling toward Harper, who was forthwith examined before a magistrate and committed to the county jail to await the due course of law.

While in jail Mrs. Harper visited frequently and through her assistance he was enabled to make his escape, by cutting a hole through the wall. Mrs. H carrying out the rubbage under her cloak, thus concealing the work that was being done from day to day. He was subsequently taken in Arkansas as appears from the following which is taken from The Expositor.

"Arrest of Harper,—We learn from the Cherokee Advocate, of the 10th

Inst., that Wm H Harper, the Murderer of young Meredith, at Independence Mo., last spring, has been apprehended.

"On the 31st of August he was arrested by Marcellus Du Val Eqr. agent for the Seminoles, at Mr Ayrd's store, on little river in the Creek nation; and has been conducted probably to Van Buren Ark's where he will be committed to await the requisition of the governor of Mo., who we believe has offered a reward for his apprehension.—Harper is a young man, and said to be possessed of considerable shrewdness, which he summoned to his aid in efforts to prevent being arrested. He passed through the northern part of this (the Cherokee) nation some time since, on his way to the south-west. While travelling, he was guided by a Frenchman, calling himself Harris, was well armed with shot gun, pistols and Bowie-knife and said he was a bearer of important dispatches from the government to General Kearney, &c since his arrest, he has acknowledged that he killed Meredith, but alleges that he did so because Meredith persisted in making improper advances to his wife, whom he acquits of even suspicion."

After his restoration to the jail at Independence, Mrs H visited him and said, "now sir, you have suffered yourself to be taken after I got you clear, so abide the consequences, woman as I am, if I once got out they could not catch me again. You deserve to be hanged."

Shortly after this, the father and sister of the prisoner came on to attend the trial. Much sympathy was felt for the venerable, grey headed man, and the beauty of the young lady had a powerful effect on the public feeling. Harper changed his venue, to Platte county, was bailed out, I believe by Mrs. Owens, his mother-in-law, and finally got clear.[143]

Shortly after my farewell visit to Tisdale I received a letter from him, in which he speaks feelingly and makes his adieu. He says, "Your letter of the 3d May, I should have answered last night that it might have gone by to day's mail but I got home after dark from hunting — tired and sleepy,—totally unfitted for answering your letter as it deserved, for it breathes the spirit of the good Col Waugh of Mobile, instead of the cross, crusty *old* bachelor of Missouri, it was an effort of the pen of the friend of *Auld lang syne*, and I read it with much pleasure. . . . I was one week painting the scenes for the Thespian Society, and on the second day I had a high fever (which did not leave in fact for twenty four hours) I

143. Some accounts of this affair appeared in the St. Louis *New Era*, 1, 3, 12 June 1846, and the *Missouri Republican*, 1 June. The trial was finally held in Platte County, Missouri, in November, 1847, with Colonel Doniphan as chief defense attorney. Harper was acquitted. For accounts of the case consult *History of Jackson County, Missouri*, 641; Connelley, *Doniphan's Expedition*, 26-29. For Harper and Meredith see notes 64, 116 above.

painted however until I lost control of my mind,—lay down on the floor for about three hours—got up at the expiration of that time and, leaning with one hand on a chair, painted with the other — gradually getting stronger until I could stand without an effort. After I had finished, *White* and an other fellow came down to clean up and would you believe it, this daub of a *house painter*, took it upon himself to *improve* my work, laying on strong light and shadow upon the distance, thus as it were suspending it in the air in the foreground. I was extremely vexed, and so much astounded when in answer to my enquiry, he told me that he did it, that I knew not what to say. But a few hours afterwards meeting him at the City Hotel I gave him such a cursing that he will not easily forget me, which will, I hope, effectually prevent his meddling with the work of an artist for the future.

"Last Thursday night I killed half the audience with laughter in the character of Numps in the farce "Tis all a Farce"—forgot more than half my part, bid farewell to the prompter and rattled away on my own hook until I got ready to give the other fellow his 'cue', and judging from the continued and prolonged applause, I did not miss it far after all.—All the other characters were well sustained and the evening went off finely. Previous to the farce Douglas was performed; Martin as Norval, Yeomans as Randolf; Barnett as Glenalvan; and Mills as Lady Randolf.—Mill's performance was classically fine; Martin and Yeomans played remarkably well and Barnett tolerably.[144]

"My cats are all up on my lap, scratching squabling and biting.

"I rejoice at your departure and sorrow at it too. I rejoice as it will be productive of constitutional, mental and, probably pecuniary benefit to you, and grieve that it will perhaps turn out a final seperation,—at any rate for some years.

"I am at leisure now, and will not work for any one, I owe nothing and am ready to start at a moments warning—I am relaxing, taking some pleasure, in fishing, hunting &c and do not know when I shall leave.

"Remember me to all those who may value my friendship, and to Genl Lucas and each member of his family tender my kindest regards, and most sincere wishes for their health and happiness.—And now for yourself dear fellow, here is the hand of affection and esteem, I bid thee a sorrowing farewell, yet the future is filled with bright visions of hope for your prosperity.

"God bless you. J.B.Tisdale"

---

144. Carson ("Diary of Mat Field," 180) identifies "Tis all a Farce" as by John T. Allingham. John Home's tragedy *Douglas* was now in its ninetieth year of popularity.

Lexington Mo.

May 6th 1846

I could not but be touched with this letter, it spoke feelingly of me, and shewed one thing at least that, Jack remembered the kindness which he received from General Lucas and his family when he sick in the house of that most worthy gentleman. It is always pleasing to find a grateful recollection of good deeds, and more particularly so when those deeds spring from disinterested benevolence. As a matter of course I laid the letter before the general. I am now drawing my stay in Indepen[den]ce —I may say in the United States,—to a close, but before I do so, I must not omit to mention one or two circumstances which tend to shew the natures of some men.

Among the young men who are now here, is a Mr. Ruben Creel, from Kentucky, whose father was the early friend of Colonel Sam'l Owens. Mr. Creel, when Owens was a young man, furnished him with capital to start in buisiness with, and by his patronage young Owens commenced a career which soon enabled him to amass much wealth. But fortune, with all that fickleness for which she is renowned, played one of her tricks upon the generous Mr. C and, while she helped the protegee to an ample store of riches, her frowns were cast upon the benevolent patron —the positions of the two individuals were changed, one became a millionare, the other sank down to poverty, and his son, a young man of fine talents and splendid education now comes to this frontier town, to seek some means of getting out to the spanish country, in the hopes of obtaining a situation in which he may constitute himself the architect of his own fortune.

Owens is now preparing to start to Chihuahua,[145] with a large amount of merchandize, in the transportation of which, he must of necessity employ a number of hands, and when applied to for any situation to enable the applicant to reach that country, Mr Owens had no place to bestow upon the indigent son of his early friend. Nay! he did not even invite the young man to his house. Mr Creel is cousin to a family of the highest respectabily in this town and bears an excellent character. He went out in some humble capasity in the employment of [blank in ms.] of New York and afterwards got a good situation in Chihuahua.

Ralston who is a great admirer of Col Owens, seems to me to be a

---

145. "Col. S. C. Owens has not yet left [11 May]. He has a very large amount of goods directly imported from England, thereby having the duty taken off at this point, if they pass through in the original packaging" (*Missouri Republican,* 18 May 1846). Actually he did not start until weeks later; he caught up with his wagons on 16 June (Fulton, *Diary and Letters of Josiah Gregg,* I, 198).

different man from what he has been heretofore, he is more gruff then formerly and at times is extremely rude, but as he is about embarking in a new line of buisiness, it may be, that his mind is perplexed with the troubles attendant upon the undertaking. Messrs Weicks and Blumer are anxious to start, but R says he will not go until *he* is ready. Indeed he is very insolent to those gentlemen, and has said to an acquaintance, "these men think that I am their servant, but I'll show them the difference before long. Let me only get their goods into my possession on the plains and I will soon shew them that they are in my power." In these remarks the inate meaness of the fellow is made manifest, for none but a low contemptable coward would ever think of taking an undue advantage of any one, more especially when immediate redress is impracticable.

Speaking with this man one day,—he has never been on the plains—[I] said, "I understand that on the plains a man shews his real character, if the dog is in him, it is sure to come out." I mention these things now because, hereafter I will have to refer to them. Ralston passes himself off as a native of North Carolina, when in reality he is from Belfast in the north of Ireland, and the peculiar fun of the joke is that this misarable humbug prides himself on belonging to the *native American party*. He is a dirty bird that fouls his own nest. Not having done anything to make Ireland ashamed of me, *I* am not ashamed of Ireland. His partner [blank in ms.] Hill, is a very worthy, honest and respectable farmer and blacksmith and quite the reverse of him. One gambles and drinks, while the other does neither one nor the other. One neglects his wife, the other is an excellent husband and a good father.

About this time (10th May) news reached us that Colonl Taylor has changed his position on the Rio Grande, and I recollect that many persons sneered at him as a coward, but it occurred to me that the old hero was determined on a master stroke, if war should break out. I never dreamed however, that such a thing would occur, and when the press spoke of such a possibility I looked upon the matter as merely a war of words. The difficulty between Great Britain and the U States was just settled,—two powerful nations had come to a good understanding, and it never occurred to me that such a contemptible country as Mexico would have the impudence to cross swords with us. Or at least if hostilities should begin, the probability was that the whole matter would be settled by deplomacy long before I should reach Santa Fe. At last news of a declaration of war reached us. A requisition for troops was made by the Govt and General Lucas was called upon by Gov. Edwards of Mo. to raise seven hundred troops to hold themselves in readiness, for immediate service, still I thought it might all be arranged without coming to blows. Dr. David Waldo met me in the streets one day and said, "Now Waugh as you and I are old bachelors, I think the best service we can do our country is to fight for her, suppose you give up the idea of going to Mexico in your present capacity, and volunteer. I am about to get a commission to raise a company and will be able to procure one for you." I am sorry now, that I did not take the doctor's advice.[146]

The last day but one of my stay in Independence I was seized with a high fever. I had been unwell for some time previously, had some blood taken from my arm and was salivated in my gums from the effect of medicine. I was in my bed when Ralston called, he was extremely rude and vexed me very much. I did not know what to make of his conduct for he had assumed a tone and bearing altogether different from his usual civil manner, but as I was suffering so much from indisposition, I was willing to suppose that in consequence of that I looked at everything in the wrong light. Feeling better toward evening I arose, finished the painting which I was doing for him and completed all my arrangements for a start the next day.

The waggons had left a few days before with my luggage, some few things which I was obliged to retain were still with me, and they puzzled me not a little to know how I should be able to carry them out to the camp, but by dint of contrivance and perseverance I did manage to pack them in such a way as to take them behind me on the horse. I now rode out and took leave of Mrs. Ralston for whom I really entertained much respect, for she was a lady of great amibility and gentleness. In parting with her I little thought that I should never see her again in this life, but so it was, it was my last interview.

The evening I spent in company with Genl and Mrs. Lucas at the house of Mrs. Buchanan and heard some of the melodies of my own dear Ireland performed upon the piano by this charming little poetess, who, I am happy to say is my countrywoman. I left with her the following lines, which I had written some years ago in North Carolina, for which she afterwards composed a delightful air, and taught her lovely pupils to sing them.

---

146. David Waldo served as captain of Company A, First Regiment Missouri Mounted Volunteers (Connelley, *Doniphan's Expedition*, 133, N. 18, and *passim*). He married Eliza Jane Norris of Culpeper, Virginia, in 1849.

"Serenade

Lady my home is far o'er the sea
And night winds around me are flying
But the heart of the minstrel who now sings for thee
Is cheerless as tho' it were dying.

Though he sings to awaken thy slumbers
As he bends o'er his "plaintive guitar,"
He thinks of those pure flowing numbers
That waked his young heart when afar.

And the voice of his once early love,
Comes breathingly 'long the dark sea,
Like the whisp'rings of form from above
Whilst, Lady, he now sings for thee.

Then O, dearest fair one I pray,
Reject not the sighs of thy lover
Refuse not his hand on that day
On which she shall ask you for ever.

The wandering Artist

End of the first vol.

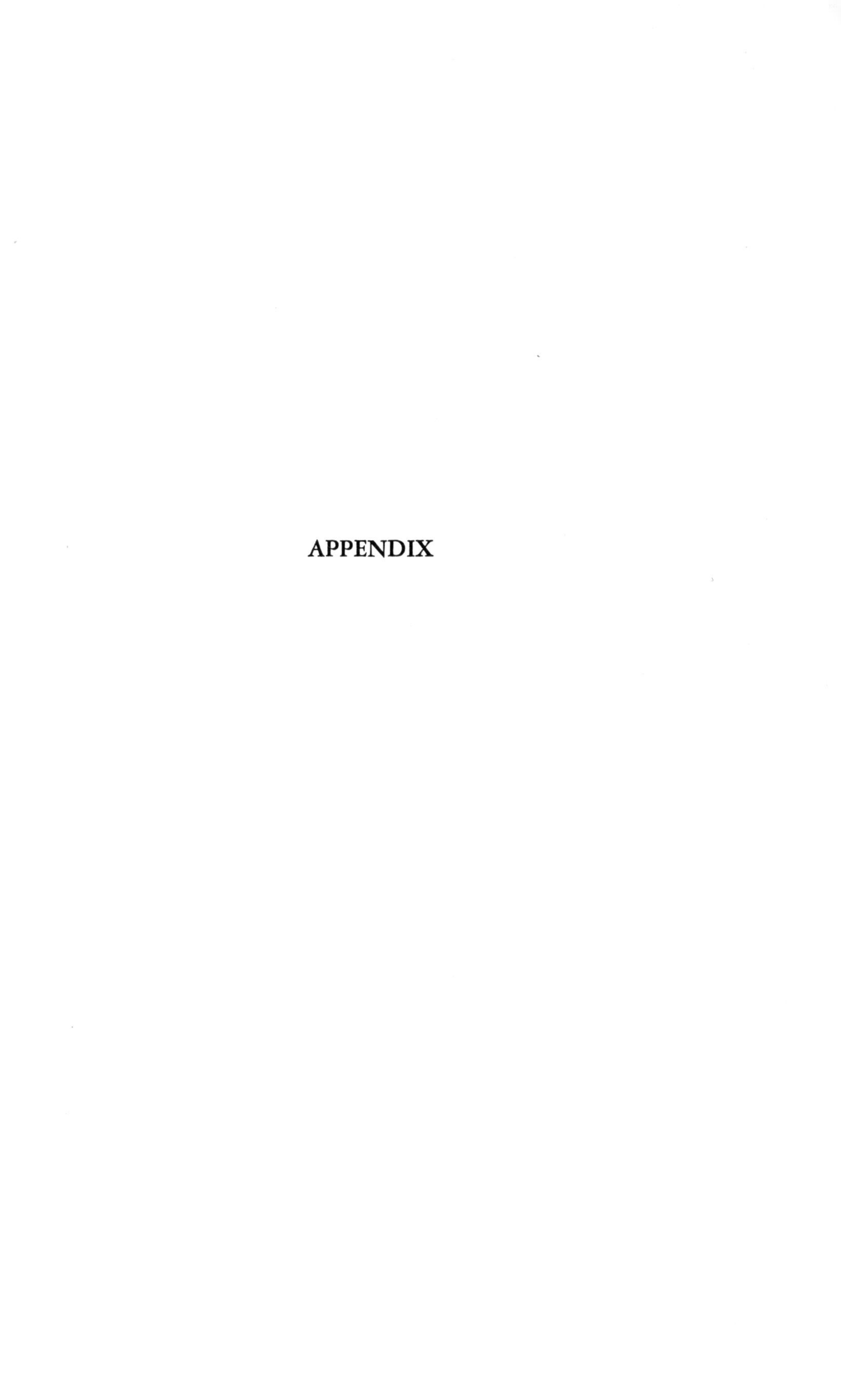

APPENDIX

A TRIP TO MEXICO[1]

By Don Alfredo, El Artista Viajante

A correspondent in the "Far West" has been so kind as to procure for the Messenger, a long contribution, "*A Letter from Don Alfredo, El Artista Viajante. To his friend and pupil, J.B.T.*" He says, "it was not intended for publication; but it will not be less interesting in consequence of the unreserved, conversational style of master to pupil." The author is an artist, who made a tour to New Mexico, during the last summer, for the purpose of collecting materials for an illustrated work on that country. He reached Santa Fé the 24th of June, and commences his letter, from that place, "beneath the hospitable roof of an excellent son of the 'Emerald Isle,' on the eve of the festival of American Independence, and amid innumerable rumors of war." But its length, with the time at which it was received, precludes the publication of the whole of it, in the present number; whilst the posture of our affairs toward Mexico, especially since the Expedition of Gen. Kearny, renders it desirable to avoid delaying it. We have, therefore, determined to omit the description of the journey from Independence, and with our Artist-Traveller we enter at once into

Santa Fe: The Capital

The New Mexicans, like many members of the modern sects of Christians among us, who call their sons and daughters by scripture names, give to their cities and towns sacred and pious appellations, thereby giving you to understand that they reverence the faith which they profess, and that you are travelling in a Catholic country. But what's in a name? This city of Santa Fé, or Holy Faith of St. Francis, would smell as sweet by any other; it certainly would still be what it really is, for among its inhabitants you may look in vain for sanctity or holiness! Its morals, to say nothing of its piety, are sunk so low, and so perfectly reckless and degraded are its Priests, that I am told the Sovereign Pontiff refuses to acknowledge the church here as the Roman or Apostolic. It stands alone in the world, and its ministers pay no allegiance to the Holy See whatever![2]

The city lies in a valley of a spur of the Rocky Mountains, at an elevation of more than seven thousand feet above the level of the ocean, and is possessed of, perhaps, one of the most salubrious climates on the face

---

1. *Southern Literary Messenger*, XII (December, 1846), 755-762. Don Alfredo, of course, is Alfred S. Waugh and "J.B.T." to whom he addressed the letter is Tisdale. Unfortunately the original letter cannot be found.

2. A slight exaggeration, since there was a vicar-general (J. F. Ortiz) in Santa Fé. For two other contemporary accounts see Gregg, *Commerce of the Prairies*, I, 245-260; Davis, *El Gringo*, 227-231. For a twentieth century view consult Twitchell, *Old Santa Fé*, 357-365; Twitchell, *Leading Facts in New Mexican History*, II, 188.

of the globe, giving to man an existence far beyond "three score years and ten." Here life's brittle thread is spun out to a length unenjoyed in other parts of the world, and disease is almost unknown. The soil around it is not fertile, and with the exception of a few trees in the public square, can boast of nothing of interest to the botanist. It is nearly encircled with lofty hills, sparsely covered with dwarfish pines, and a few varieties of other trees, giving them the appearance of having been sprinkled with a house-painter's brush, in imitation of some particular kind of stone. Red granite abounds in the neighborhood, and although this fine building material is so convenient, yet for want of mechanical skill, or as is more likely, through pure laziness, the miserable beings who exist here, have not constructed their homes, or even their churches, of any other substances than sun-dried bricks. Their dwellings do not rise above the ground more than twelve or fifteen feet; they are flat-roofed and devoid of taste or ornament of any kind; the windows are small and placed low in the walls, and altogether present an appearance which is anything but pleasing to the eye. His Excellency, General Don Manuel Armijo, the present governor,[3] dwells in a *palacio* whose externals differ very little from those around it, only it has larger windows, is whitewashed, and a sentry keeps watch and ward at the entrance.[4] The door is not larger than any other, and a tall man would have to stoop as he crossed its threshold. This building occupies one side of the *Plaza*, with the *calabozo* and guard-house at one end, and the office of the Secretary of State at the other. The Legislative Hall and the Custom-House occupy another side, while the remaining two contain the shops of the merchants and traders. All these are of the same general appearance, and are mean and dirty-looking in an eminent degree. The whole is surrounded with *portals*, or as we would call them, piazzas, the supporting columns of which are rude trunks of trees, scarcely divested of their native roughness. Under the shade of the *portals*, facing the *palacio*, may be seen men, women, and children, vending meat, bread, onions and a few other vegetables, and a kind of small round cheese made from goat's milk. These *petit merchants* literally block up the way, and oblige the passerby to step into the dusty streets to avoid tumbling over the venders, or the *leperos*[5] that

3. Manual Armijo was not an admirable character. For a very sharp contemporary biography and description of him see Kendall, *Texan Santa Fé Expedition*, I, 295-297, 315, 346-361. Many glimpses of him are to be found in Webb, *Adventures in the Santa Fé Trade* (consult index, Southwest Historical Series). For a twentieth century evaluation of him see Stella Drumm's note, *Down the Santa Fe Trail*, 96-98. Waugh has more to contribute later in this letter.

4. For a full description, consult Anderson, "The Adobe Palace."

5. Beggars or peddlers, not lepers.

are continually congregated in its shade. One is obliged to look well to his pockets as he moves along, for it is a notorious fact, that the people of this misnamed *Republic,* have a strong desire to make love to their neighbors' property, without once imagining there is any harm in so doing. As to the morals of the place, they are of the lowest description, and I have heard it said that *the women deem chastity no virtue.* Gambling is practised by both sexes, and by none more than the Governor himself.[6]

There is now living in Santa Fé a certain *lady* known as La Tules, who has made a handsome fortune by keeping a *monte table.* Although her early history cannot reflect much credit on her character, yet she is received into the highest circles of society, and, perhaps, there is not a female in that *high-toned* community, who exercises more sway than she does. With this *lady,* who now assumes the more patrician title of *Señora Doña Gertrudes Barcaló,* his Excellency is very intimate; indeed, I believe, he is a partner in her business, and she still pursues *the intellectual* and profitable amusement with as keen a relish as in her younger days. To this Señora, the Governor communicates all the affairs of the State, she then gives them to her adopted daughter, who is married to an American resident, and from the daughter they go to her husband, and thus they go from one to another until every movement becomes known to our people in the capital.[7]

Athough the people of New Mexico live under what they call a Republican form of government, it is, to all intents and purposes, an *absolute monarchy,*—the Governor acting in all respects just as he pleases, the department only paying a nominal allegiance to the *centralismo,* or general government of Mexico. He makes the laws, imposes taxes, levies contributions, and fixes the duties to be paid by the traders; appoints all his officers, civil and military, and in all things exercises the sway of an absolute sovereign. When this man either goes forth or returns to his *palacio,* the sentinel at the door proclaims the fact to the great world of Santa Fé, and calls out the *guard royal,* who do him honor by presenting arms under a grand flourish of trumpets and rolling of drums. On Sundays and festivals, he is accompanied to church by his staff and officers of State, and followed by the troops with their *brass band,* composed of two very antiquated trumpets and a couple of drums. His Excellency, on these occasions, wears the cross of honor, which Santa Anna gave him for murdering the Texans, in 1841.[8] By the way, I must say a few words

6. On the subject of morals most travelers had something to say; see, for instance, Gregg, *Commerce of the Prairies,* I, 221-223, 231. On the passion for gambling, see Gregg, *Ibid.,* I, 238-241; Davis, *El Gringo,* 184-185.

of these same soldiers; but to give any thing like a description, is a thing beyond my powers. When first my wondering gaze fell upon them, I could not help exclaiming, "did any eye ever see such scare-crows." They have dresses certainly, but it would be a misnomer to call them uniforms, for they are piebald, ragged and filthy. Their coats are somewhat military, as they fit like sentry boxes, and are not at all likely to encumber the wearers on an occasion of emergency; indeed, they seem as if the men were not at home when their measures were taken. Altogether, they look like supernumeraries, who had been hired by the manager of a theatre to turn the militia into ridicule. They are not neat, trimly dressed fellows, but a set of worthless vagabonds, possessed of no moral courage whatever; at the same time, I must say, that I think they would fight, provided they had commanders in whom they could place confidence, and the enemy were in fewer numbers than themselves. I can scarcely tell the officers from the common soldiers, except by a little gold or silver lace on their shoulders, and occasionally an epaulette. Enough for the present. I intend to make some sketches of them in their various costumes, and in that way I can convey a better idea of their martial appearance, than by any language of mine whatever.

I have Gregg's "Commerce of the Prairies,"[9] and Kendall's Texan "Santa Fé Expedition" with me, but do not intend reading either book until I have made my own observations; at the same time, I would recommend both to your perusal, for I am told they are interesting and graphic. Now, as I am writing only for your gratification, I scribble on without that attention to style which I ought to observe were I to come before the public; you will, therefore, imagine that I am talking to you face to face, and enjoy my glib nonsense just the same as if you and I were sitting by our own fireside as of old. This same writing is a glorious thing, it enables friends to talk across "the deep blue sea" and boundless plains.[10] I find I am quite a curiosity here, particularly when I am making my notes, but whether it is surprise at my rapidly running pen, or anxiety

---

7. Gregg (*Commerce of the Prairies*, I, 239-240) wrote that this woman came from Taos to Santa Fé in the 1830's and in 1842 sent $10,000 to the United States to be invested in trade goods. "She is openly received in the first circles of society," he wrote. Mrs. Magoffin, who met her at a ball, wrote her down as "the old woman with false hair and teeth" (*Down the Santa Fé Trail*, 119-120, 145). Davis (*El Gringo*, 185-188) reported that she died about 1851 and had a fine funeral.

8. Rosenbury, Howland, and Baker, who were shot at San Miguel (Kendall, *Texan Santa Fé Expedition*, I, 163n., 301-305, 309-310).

9. Given to him by Gregg at Independence; see page 95 above.

10. Waugh left Independence for Santa Fé before Tisdale joined Company A of the Mounted Volunteers; he assumes here (and in the direction of his letter) that his friend is still in Independence or Lexington. They were not to meet in the Southwest, for Waugh left Santa Fé before the Army of the West arrived.

to know what I may be saying about them, I do not know, but this I do know, from the information of my friends, that very few of the inhabitants can *read and write:*—this part of education not being deemed at all necessary to any but priests, lawyers and a few others.[11] Too much learning only makes a man abhorrent to the "powers that be," and brings down suspicions of the clergy and authorities. By the way, the former gentlemen can boast of but a small share of this commodity—not enough to make them mad. Their time being principally occupied with gambling and other immoral practices, they have not leisure for the acquirement of Latin and Greek, or any of the mental accomplishments for which the Catholic priesthood in our own land are so justly celebrated; take them, all in all, a more worthless set of scamps the world can not produce.

I went, a day or two after coming here, to witness the funeral of an infant, and observed the whole ceremonial, from its appearance in the street, until the earth closed over the mortal remains in the grave-yard; and when I shall have given you the sketch complete, you can form your own opinion. I was sitting in the store of a friend, when the sounds of music in the street drew me to the door: on looking out I saw a very novel procession, to me at least. A few young girls were carrying a bier, on which was placed the body of a child, of a few months old: it was dressed in the clothes which it wore in life; its little frock was decorated with artificial flowers, and in its pale, cold hands, which were tied together at the wrists, it held a colored paper ornament somewhat resembling a fan; the mattress on which it reposed in unconscious sleep was uncovered, and simply showed its coarse, dark fabric. Immediately behind, two musicians performed on a guitar and violin, and a few friends and relatives brought up the rear. I was instantly struck with the appropriateness of this mode of conveying to its last home the body of an innocent child, and thought at once how much more the survivors had to rejoice than mourn at its departure from this world, so soon after having crossed its threshold! Anxious to witness the whole ceremony, I followed, with a couple of gentlemen, who were almost as great strangers in Santa Fé as myself, and overtook it just as it reached the church-door. The bearers laid it down on the path-way at the foot of the steps, and we stood respectfully, with uncovered heads, with our backs to the wall, waiting for the door to be opened, the musicians all this time performing a lively air. Presently I heard an angry voice speaking to the poor people who had gone after the priest. After a delay of some minutes, we heard some person within the church taking down the bar, and soon after its ponderous

---

11. *Cf.* Gregg, *Commerce of the Prairies,* I, 197-202; Davis, *El Gringo,* 193-195.

gates stood open. We now entered and had full time, while they were waiting for the priest, to examine the interior. It was cruciform, and had statues of some ecclesiastics painted to resemble the life,—as no doubt the artist supposed.[12] The great altar was bedizened with a multitude of very paltry pictures and a profusion of the commonest looking-glasses—such as you can buy in the States for a few dimes, and the drapery was extremely shabby. Another altar in the great aisle resembled the first in tinsel splendor; and nearly opposite, was an enclosed seat of considerable length, terminated by another of more ample proportions and covered with crimson cloth. We had the audacity to sit near this, but did not remain long, when I saw a gross fat man enter very hastily, followed by an attendant who helped the first put on vestments that looked really as if they wanted washing, and were, indeed, any thing but clean. As soon as he was uniformed, and with a little four-cornered black cloth cap on his head, he took hold of a ragged dirty looking book, — the tattered remains of a quarto bound volume,—and proceeded in great haste to the door, and his attendant after him with a vessel of holy water. We, of course, went out also, for the corpse had not been brought into the church. This priest, who was the vicaria, scarcely gave himself time to reach the body of the child, before he began to read, and from his very rapid delivery and quick turning over of the leaves, I concluded he had skipped those parts that were missing. Occasionally he threw some water towards the corpse, without reaching it, and in a few minutes he wheeled round and entered the church, followed by the whole funeral procession. In the aisle the body was again laid down, a few more sentences were read, and the ceremony closed in a very abrupt manner. In a short time the priest was divested of his sacerdotal garments, and went away to his own house, while we followed to the grave-yard. Here the body was lowered into a pit about eight feet deep, a cloth placed over the face,—it had no coffin,—the women threw in a few handfulls of earth and then retired to the other side of the *campo santo,* where they formed a circle on the ground, drew their *rebozos* over their heads, and sat in solemn silence until the grave was filled up. The man who officiated as sexton pounded in the earth with a large piece of rock, which so excited my horror, that I came away as quickly as I possibly could. The coarse-looking priest, who performed the services at the church, went through his routine with a grudge, because the poor people were not able to pay him his fee, and seemed, by his haste, as if he were anxious to get to a more agreeable

12. For other descriptions of the church see Gibson, *A Soldier under Kearny and Doniphan,* 227; Emory, *Notes of a Military Reconnoissance,* 34; Abert, *Examination of New Mexico,* 754 (*i.e.,* 454).

occupation. Although he leads a very unrighteous life, and his irregularities are known to all, yet every head is uncovered the moment he appears in the streets.[13]

Now, as I have given you a sketch of a funeral, let me give you one of a wedding. But I cannot carry you on to the conclusion, for I had not the honor to be invited to the house of joy.

A few days after this, happening to hear music of the same kind I have been speaking of, I looked out and saw a party of people coming towards where I was; on enquiry, I learned that it was a new married couple and their friends returning from the church. First in the procession came the *bride* and her maid, followed by the *groom* and his man: immediately behind those, were two musicians with guitar and violin, and in their rear, an indiscriminate medley of all ages and sexes. On closely observing the passing throng, I could not but be struck with the bridal dress here and with us; the fair one wore a robe of striped silk, white and green; over her head and round her shoulders she wore the *rebozo,* or long scarf, common to all the females of Mexico; but to my great surprise, it was black as dyestuff could make it,—fringed with lace of the same sombre hue, which covered her face and concealed her modest blushes, if she really did blush. Her attendant wore a colored dress also,[14] but her *rebozo* was not black. Not an article of the apparel of either did I see that approximated to the gleesome white. The groom was dressed in the usual costume of his class, for the parties belonged to the peasantry. His attendant being a soldier, wore his uniform. The whole passed so rapidly, that further observations could not be made, and you must therefore be content with this half-finished sketch.[15]

The day we entered Santa Fé was the festival of St. John, or midsummer's day, and the whole town was alive with mirth and jollity; business seemed to be suspended, and the inhabitants gave themselves up to amusements of all sorts with a perfect abandonment of rational feeling. The principal sport on this occasion appeared to be riding, or, I should rather say, *racing;* for this purpose, every kind of animal, on whose back a saddle could be placed, was in requisition; and men, women and boys

13. Abert (*Examination of New Mexico,* 447): "I was much surprised with the manners of the Mexicans at a funeral. They marched with great rapidity through the streets near the church, with a band of music. The instruments were principally violins, and these were played furiously, sending forth wild raging music. The corpse, that of a child, was exposed to view, decked with rosettes and flaunting ribands of various brilliant hues, and the mourners talked and laughed gaily, which seemed to me most strange. I was told, too, that the tunes played were the same as those which sounded at fandangoes." *Cf.* also Gregg, *Commerce of the Prairies,* 263-266.

14. The bridal dress among all classes is invariably colored.—WAUGH.

15. *Cf.* Gregg, *Commerce of the Prairies,* I, 261-263; Davis, *El Gringo,* 281-283.

scampered through the streets, jostling and tilting against each other, frequently to the destruction of the principles of equilibrium. Many Señoras gaudily dressed, sat behind the gentlemen and enjoyed the fun as much as any body. Stop! Stop! I am too fast: having read this part of my letter to a friend, who has just now called upon me, I find I did not observe quite close enough,—the *ladies* sat in front of the *caballeros*; now only think of this! Why, how could I be so stupid as not to have noticed so strange a fact? By George, I thought I had seen sights of all sorts, but this beats all I had ever seen or heard of before,—no matter, let me proceed. What is most strange, the *caballero* although having his lovely burden thus before him, will keep his feet in the stirrups, and this may be the reason why the Mexicans place the leathers in the centre of the saddle-trees. You must have observed how very uprightly they all ride.

As I closely observed every thing around me,—for we are apt to pay more attention to objects on first sight, than when we become more familiar,—a friend gave me a passing history of many of these same *Señoras,* and although they occupied respectable stations in Mexican society, almost every one had a blot on her fair name, indeed, as I have said before, chastity is not esteemed a virtue; nor does the want of it incapacitate a female from mingling in the highest ranks of the *aristocracy!*

What amused me most of all, was the donkey riding. On one of these patient, serviceable animals I saw no less than three stout boys, urging the poor creature to his speed with clubs, while three or more were trying to retard his movements, by holding on to his latter end appendage; still the *burro* "took it with a patient shrug, for sufferance is the badge of all his tribe"; and as he turned in obedience to whatever set was in the ascendant, he reminded me of a political candidate, puzzled between two contending parties, only waiting for one to obtain power that he might obey the will of the majority. His submissive looks drew forth roars of laughter from the crowd.

"In the evening a great crowd were assembled in the *plaza.* From their uproarious" mirth I expected fun, and being a sort of knight-errant in search of adventures, I of course went to see what was going on. In the centre of a circle of men, composed of almost all ages and stations, I beheld the head of an unfortunate domestic fowl peeping out of the ground, and eyeing, with a fierce gaze, the motley throng that surrounded his prison-house, for he was buried alive, and his head well-greased. I had scarcely found a place among them, when there was a cry raised of "make room," and a man on horseback instantly dashed past the captive, and stooping as he did so, tried to pull him by his caput from his place of confinement, but failed in the attempt, for which he was saluted with laughter and jeers; another and another followed in quick succession with the same success and greeting; at length a stout young fellow, mounted on a mule, rode swiftly past, and bending low, dragged master chanticleer from the earth, and as swiftly rode off with his prize, followed by all who were mounted, in hot pursuit; each one vieing with the other who should regain the victim. But the captor stoutly belabored every one who came near him with the body of the chicken, until it died a very unnatural death.[16] Other sports, equally refined, were carried on, and thus the good people of Santa Fé honored the memory of the holy St. John. The priests enjoyed it as much as any body else.

Being invited to a *fandango*, I gladly accepted the proffered civility, because I was anxious to see one.[17] It was something I had often heard of, but never witnessed. Our party consisted of five persons, each one from a different country; one was from old Spain, one from Prussia, one from Germany, one from *auld Scotia*, and one from the land of the shamrock so green.[18] Every one spoke English tolerably well. Now, in a group composed of such different materials, it could not but afford an ample fund for shrewd observation, and, if we consider the different tastes of each nation thus represented, it is a strong evidence of the grace of the dancers, when I tell you we were all highly delighted with the "poetry of motion" there displayed.

In a long room, of the usual size and shape to be found in almost every house here, were assembled a crowd of people of various degrees of station and respectability. It was lighted by a rude chandelier pendant from the centre of the ceiling, and by tin sconces on the walls. Benches were arranged around the room. On them sat the fair Señoras—Oh, Heaven! forgive me for telling such a falsehood!—they were any thing but fair, and exhibited a variety of hues almost as great as those displayed on your palette after a month's use, and the accumulation of dust arising from carelessness in not turning it down when you quit painting a miniature. As to the beauty I had been taught to expect among the *ladies* of this country, I must confesss I did not see a single one of the sex that could lay claim to a single particle, or at least not one of them came up to

16. *Correr el gallo.* For another description of this pastime see Gregg, *Commerce of the Prairies*, I, 241-242.

17. Every traveler wrote up the *fandangos*. Gibson went twice in August (*A Soldier under Kearny and Doniphan*, 215-216, 224-225). Mrs. Magoffin saw two of them the next month (*Down the Santa Fé Trail*, 118-124, 142-145).

18. The Spaniard was undoubtedly Manuel Alvarez (see note 27 below). The two Germans might have been Wiecks and Blumner with whom he had traveled to New Mexico: the latter, a Prussian, at least remained in the territory (see note 124, p. 95 above). The Irishman was himself.

my ideas of that attractive quality; but you will say, "tush, tush, you are no judge; I knew exactly what you would say; you're a crustly old bachelor, and cannot see as clearly as a younger fellow, who is all alive to the charms of dear woman." It may be that I judge too hastily, and should not form my opinion from the specimens I see here; nevertheless, I do reckon myself a judge, and although it is a thing rarely to be met with, I have met *some* who came fully up to my conceptions of the beautiful. You perceive how I have digressed,—it is my nature; I have been digressing all my life, and am now almost past the chance of reformation. Well, but let us get back to the *fandango.*

The ladies, as with us, kept close by themselves; but oh, horrible to relate, they smoked *cigarittos!* a *vicio inocente,* which our dear ones would not indulge in, although I must confess they do sometimes use *snuff.* They smoked, and chatted, and laughed, as women will do all the world over, and gave as many roguish glances out of their bright black diamond eyes, as would set a whole village on fire. Each one was wrapped in her *rebozo,* and kept her seat until asked to take her place on the floor. Dancing now began, and as they whirled through its mazes, I was perfectly delighted at the ease and grace with which each one performed his or her part; here were high and low, rich and poor, the officers of the army and of the government, mixing in the same dance with the common soldiers and peasants, on a perfect footing of republican equality, yet every one moving with equal grace, and keeping most excellent time to the music of two violins and a guitar. Although there were many couples waltzing at the same time, and, consequently, obliged to move in a limited space, yet I did not see the least confusion arising from their circumscribed sphere of action; all went on smoothly, and put me in mind of the groups of wooden figures which we see on the tops of German organs that we sometimes meet with in our streets. They all moved as if by clockwork. Some of my companions joined in and did themselves no discredit. P.[19] proposed to some of the *foreigners* to have a contre dance, and distinguished himself by cutting the "pigeon wing"; this brought forth great applause from the natives, and when the dance was ended, he moved an adjournment, for, like a man who leaves a party immediately after having said something smart, he was desirous of retiring in the midst of the good impression he had made. After we left the ball-room, I am told, the

19. Could this possibly be Benjamin Pruett? He was a Jackson County (Missouri) man who had kept store in Santa Fé earlier in this decade; in November 1845 he left for Independence in Webb's company, but he returned to New Mexico in 1846 and in August of that year was running a hotel there. He was killed at the Mora settlements during the Taos rebellion in 1847. Consult Webb, *Adventures in Santa Fé Trade,* 139 and *passim*; Gibson, *A Soldier under Kearny and Doniphan,* 215.

natives had a regular row among themselves about us; some siding with, and some against the Americans. Blood was shed, but no lives lost. It appears after we had retired, the Señora who gave the fandango, remarked, "Now the Americans are all gone, I suppose there will be no more money spent to night": upon this hint a row sprang up. I am glad I did not see it, and I care not to go to another such place.

Not many nights after this, an English gentleman coming out from one, was struck in the face with a stone by some concealed villain, just as he reached the open air; his face was most horribly disfigured, and he will probably carry the scar to his grave. He is the gentleman who came up the river on the Henry Bry steamboat when you and I were going to F.'s camp; you may recollect I used to call him Santa Fé.[20]

These *fandangos* are open to all who choose to go, free of charge, but the party making them is remunerated by the sale of refreshments, at a very advanced price. On the arrival of a caravan, these people are certain to get up a few, because the Americans spend their money much more freely than the Mexicans, and during their stay in the city, quite a harvest is reaped by such as provide them for *the foreigners.*

This place is filled with wretches, who would kill merely for the love of taking life; they will smile in your faces, and bow, and declare themselves most devotedly your friend, and stab you the moment you turn your back. I came here with the best feelings toward the Mexicans, for I thought our people treated them too contemptuously, without any just cause, but I had scarcely been in this city of the *holy faith* when my opinion was changed, and I wished myself away from them. They are, almost without an exception, a set of very depraved, unprincipled wretches, from the *ruler* to the *ruled,* and it would be rendering them a signal service to take them under our mild and wholesome government.

Before I close this tedious letter, I will relate a few anecdotes, as tending to illustrate the character of the people among whom I am thrown, and then I will bid you *A-dios* for the present. They may be relied on, for I have them from the best authority.

You are aware of the capture and defeat of the unfortunate Texan Santa Fé Expedition in 1841, and of the subsequent disasters to the prisoners. Lewis Robedoux,[21] a well-known citizen of this town, when he

20. There is no mention of this man in Waugh's narrative, nor does he figure in François des Montaigne's account. Wislizenus (*Tour to Northern Mexico,* 29) mentioned a man named Houghton among the foreigners of Santa Fé; however, if this was Joab Houghton it could not be the man Waugh meant, for Joab was born in New York State.

21. Louis, one of the sons of Joseph Robidoux, was born in St. Louis in 1796. After

received a copy of the newspaper containing young Comb's[22] statement of the *governor's* stealing his buffalo robe at San Miguel, went directly over to the *palacio* and translated it for his Excellency; upon which, the high and mighty ruler of *Mud Town* and the province over which he sways the sceptre, exclaimed in wrath, *"I'm d——d if I did! If I stole it, I do not recollect!"* From the foregoing, you can form an estimate of his majesty's character. The following will shew how far the schoolmaster has been abroad among these people.

The Señor Maranda,[23] private Secretary to Armijo, was in the habit of calling every morning on the gentleman at whose house I am staying, to enquire the news, in the pursuit of which he was most assiduous. Mr. S.[24] growing tired of these inquisitorious visits, and being, moreover, a very great wag, thought of an expedient to get rid of him and have some fun in the bargain. Almost immediately after conceiving the plan, he was enabled to put it in execution, for the Secretary just then made his bow, and his usual question of "any news this morning, Don Juan?" followed as a matter of course. Don Juan, with a very serious face, which he can command at will, told the *escritor* that he was glad he had called, as he had just received an important dispatch from his foreign correspondent, but of such a nature, that unless the other would promise to keep it a profound secret, he would not communicate the information which he had obtained! The face of his visitor grew elongated, and his mouth opened as if he would swallow anything, no matter how marvelous. S. seeing him thus prepared, began by saying—"I am credibly informed, that the '*Dutch have taken Holland.*' "

"Dear me," cried the other, elevating his eyebrows, "is it possible? will it injure us in the slightest degree? will it interfere with our commerce?" Now, up to this moment, Mr. S. never fancied it possible that an old hackneyed joke, which he thought all the world knew, would so terrify any one, and which he intended merely as a hint to the Secretary to leave off his annoying habits for the future,—but he shook his head very knowingly, and said, "I am not sure but it may, it is really a dreadful

several years residence in Santa Fé, in 1846 he removed to California where he founded Riverside.

22. The son of General Leslie Combs of Kentucky (Kendall, *Texan Santa Fé Expedition*, I, 20). Combs (*Niles National Register*, 5 March, 1842, pp. 2-3) had declared: "The governor himself took my blanket and buffalo robe, cursing and striking the prisoners and raving like a madman."

23. This could be a misprint for (Guadalupe) Miranda, but it does not sound like the same man. Miranda was secretary for the Department of New Mexico rather than Armijo's private secretary.

24. This is the "excellent son of the Emerald Isle" mentioned in the introductory note to the letter. He was John Scolly, who had opened a store in Santa Fé in the 1830's and who died in 1847 (Webb, *Adventures in the Santa Fé Trade*, 97, n. 141).

piece of business, and God only knows where it will end." The Secretary instantly took his leave, and in all haste made his way to the *palacio,* where he, like a true and faithful servant of the State, communicated what he had heard, at which *His Highness* was perfectly thunder-struck, and seeing, with the eye of a wise ruler, into the future, determined to guard against the worst, by issuing commands to the captain of his host to have the troops ready at a moment's warning to protect the province over which he ruled. Indeed, I could give you many more, as going to prove the extent of geographical knowledge of many in high places, but the above is sufficient in *such a letter as this.* I cannot, however, refrain from giving you the following, to which I was an eye-witness, and I am sure if Mr. Clay only knew that he was canonized by the Mexicans, he would use his mighty eloquence in the Senate of his country to save this people from the ruthless hand of their invaders. A poor fellow came into the store of mine host the other day, to buy a pocket handkerchief: many patterns were shown without meeting his approval; at last Mr. S. opened a package of very neatly printed calicoes representing the flag of our country, and containing the head of the great statesman with his name in full below it: this pleased the man very much. "But who is that?" said he, pointing to the portrait.

"Ah," said S, "now as you are naturally a bad man, you ought to do all in your power to prevent the devil from leading you astray,—it is only right you should guard against witchcraft and evil spirits, by having the picture of a holy man about your person; here, you must take this, it will be a sure charm against all evil, and protect you wherever you go. This, my dear friend, is the likeness of the best of saints,—it is no less than the greatest of all American saints, whose likeness every good Christian in that country keeps about his person as a safeguard from the assaults of the arch-enemy of the human race; this is the great! the good! and the holy *Santo Henrico,* of most pious memory!" Whereupon the *paisano* rummaged all his pockets, and producing his whole store of twenty-five cents, and a small bundle of corn-shucks, for making *cigarittos,* said, "that's all I have got; if you will take it, *I* will have the blessed saint and thank the *Santisima Guadalupe* for sending me such a treasure!" Mr. S. folded it up, handed it over and received his pay, and away went the man with the canonized Henry Clay in his bosom. These people can be made to believe anything, if it is only connected with their holy faith.

Once I start with anecdotes, you know how hard it is to stop me; I will tell you another; it will serve to show what a high sense of honor dwells in the breast of the Mexican *caballero.*

A swarthy-looking member of the dragoon corps came into the same store, and calling for a measure of *aguardiente,* it was handed to him, and drunk by himself and the *Señora* who accompanied him; but upon putting his hand into his pocket, he found he was without the means of paying for it; this was a very awkward predicament for any *gentleman* to be placed in,—he was very sorry indeed, but he had forgotten his purse,—was in the pocket of his other coat, &c., &c. The young gentleman who attends to the store, knowing the tricks of such *gentry,* told him that Mr. S. did not do a credit business; upon this assurance, the face of the warrior grew crimson with indignation, he pulling off his coat. I thought he was going to fight,—no such thing, I was mistaken,—it was for the convenience of taking off his *shirt* also, which he did, and giving it a dash upon the counter, exclaimed, as he turned half around in scorn, "take that in pledge—I will redeem it immediately"; then striking his right hand upon his left breast, said, "Don Henrico, I am a *caballero,* my honor is at stake!" but Don Henrico, touched with deep humiliation for the wrong which he had done a *Mexican gentleman,* in doubting *his honor,* refused to receive the pledge, and told him *his* word was sufficient. This pacified the brave dragoon, who instantly replaced his under garment, and coat, took his helmet from his brow, politely bowed low, and departed. In a few minutes he returned, paid the money, and said, "Be good enough to let me have twenty-five cents worth more *on credit,*" which was granted. This member of *his majesty's* body-guard, I am told, holds the commission of lieutenant in that distinguished corps: think of that Horatio.

Having given you quite enough of anecdotes, let me come now to other subjects. When I started from Independence, I had heard of war, and Gen. Lucas told me that he had orders from the governor of Missouri to raise seven hundred men for the protection of the frontier; there was a good deal of excitement in town, and volunteers were anxious "to follow to the field some warlike lord." I heeded it not, but kept to my purpose of going, and looked upon it only as a war of words for the employment of editors, and believed it would be settled with the *pen* between the two cabinets, without any appeal to arms, long before I should reach the Spanish country. We were on the road only a few days when we were overtaken by some wagons; from the owner of which I learned that three thousand troops were being raised for the purpose of taking Santa Fé and chastising the "insolent foe" for their many insults offered to our flag. When Speyer overtook us at the crossing of the great Arkansas,[25]

25. "On the afternoon [of 9 June] we arrived at the usual fording place of the Arkansas, and, to our great satisfaction, we perceived on the other bank of the river,

the number was still further increased, and on entering the city of the Holy Faith, they had reached the full number of ten thousand. All people here were expecting an invasion of their country. Reports were in circulation daily of what might be expected in such a case, and the troops of Armijo were constantly engaged in martial exercises. Trumpets sounding and drums beating, morning until night, kept us all in a state of feverish anxiety. Sometimes we would hear that the wagons of the traders who were at hand would be confiscated with all they contained, then again, that all foreigners would be ordered to leave the country forthwith. Indians would come in and make report of troops seen at various places; Americans would meet each other in the streets and stores and enquire the news,—"well! what's going on, anything fresh?" "Yes, the boys are coming! and maybe I'll not *haw! haw!* when I see the stars and stripes flying from yonder hill top." But of all persons here, perhaps the most anxious is a very excellent old Frenchman, Doctor Pieretan, whose life had been attacked by a party of three or four soldiers in his own store.[26] They had come in under pretense of buying some articles, and while the doctor was engaged in serving them, fell upon him and left him for dead, plundered the store and made off; this was at night, and next morning Pieretan was found insensible, with his head in the fire-place, with no less than *sixteen wounds* inflicted by the dastardly wretches. It was a long time before he recovered; ever since he has occupied a room in the house of Mr. S., is always well armed, and only waits an opportunity to be revenged on the villains. On one occasion, after he had given me a minute account of the whole affair, he unbottoned his great coat, and pointing to a belt of pistols, said, "*See here, Monsieur Le Colonel, I say to one Mexicun, jus you liff your fingere just so high, I kill you ver dead, Messieurs Les American sall giff you let petit hell you god dam. Ah, mon ami, I sall be very much rejoice to see dey troop, I sall die content; vell! dey may be come to-morrow, yesterday, las a week, some day, don't know.*"

I saw the Consul,[27] delivered my letter of introduction, learned from him, of a surety, that our troops were on the road. He looked gloomy, talked of the peculiar position he occupied, not only as Consul, but as a

a corrál of wagons, belonging to some smaller companies that had started before us" (Wislizenus, *Tour to Northern Mexico*, 11).

26. Webb, who was writing the story of his adventures late in life, apparently did not remember this incident too vividly or accurately (*Adventures in Santa Fé Trade*, 98).

27. Manuel Alvarez, born in Spain in 1794, went from Missouri to New Mexico in 1824, and established himself in Santa Fé as a merchant. He was appointed U. S. consul in 1839, was elected lieutenant-governor of New Mexico in 1850, and died in Santa Fé in 1856 (Bieber, ed., Webb's *Adventures in the Santa Fé Trade*, 97, n. 142).

native of old Spain, (you must know that the *Gachupins*[28] are even more obnoxious to the Mexicans than the Americans; on one or two occasions, the mob here have attempted his life,[29]) and drew such a picture of Santa Fé as quite disgusted me with the place, and made me wish myself elsewhere. This gentleman was polite enough to accompany me, the day after my arrival, to the *palacio,* when I called to deliver my letter of introduction to the governor. During the interview, I arranged with his Excellency to take his likeness for my *own* collection; it is now completed, and gives great satisfaction; it is a cabinet size picture, a full length figure in full uniform, with the cross of honor given by Santa Anna, on his breast, and the sword, presented by the people of Chihuahua, at his side. He was so much pleased with it that I had to make a copy of it for his family. He says I am the only artist who ever took his likeness.[30] I shall get it engraved.

The other day a courier arrived from the country with some dispatches; in a few minutes after, all was bustle and confusion in town; soldiers were scampering about in every direction; the poor miserable peasantry were ordered to be numbered, from twelve to fifty years old; many were collected on the moment, and with their long spears, bows and arrows, made a very curious appearance. I noticed a small young man, who had been pointed out to me a day or two ago as a *prisoner at large,* running hastily from place to place, then enter one of the public buildings and come forth again, carrying his sabre under his arm; this looked as if "the boys" were close at hand sure enough, and the next morning I saw this fellow, in full uniform, inspecting the troops in the public square! This young man, who is a lieutenant of cavalry, for a couple of cold-blooded murders which he had committed was condemned to be shot, but governor Armijo, for some reason of his own, intends sending him down to Chihuahua for execution, and to day gives him up his sword and uniform, which looks strange, and leads me to think the various reports which

28. Gachupin, a native of old Spain.—Waugh or Editor, *SLM.*

29. One incident was reported by Gregg (*Commerce of the Prairies,* I, 231); it occurred apparently in 1841.

30. On 30 July 1851 Waugh addressed a note to George W. Kendall, then passing through St. Louis: ". . . If you will do me the honor to call at my quarters, I will show you a sketch of your *very par[ticular] friend Don Manuel Armijo,* taken by me a very short time before that absolute monarch abdicated the throne of his realm in 1846. It is, I believe, the only likeness of him in the United States, and was copied from the one I painted for that august ruler during the last day[s] of his authority. The sketch represents him [in] his *grande* uniform of brigadier general in the army of Mexico. His left breast is decorated with the cross of *honor* given him by Santa Anna for the cruelties which he practised in 1841. As a work of art it is nothing, its only interest lying in its resemblance to the last Mexican governor of Santa Fe and, as such may possess some value in your eye" (Waugh Mss., Missouri Historical Society).

we hear have truth in them. Immediately an express is sent down to the low country in all haste, and another arrives from the Pass. Then an edict was published, forbidding any one to discuss the subject of the *war*. In the mean time, the news from Matamoras arrives, and the account of the battle of the 8th and 9th and defeat of the Mexican troops not contradicted by even the governor himself. The Comanches come to pay their regular visit to his Excellency, and receive their annual presents; they stay a couple of days and depart. A rumor was afloat of a treaty between this tribe and the government, to annoy our troops on the march, but I do not know whether it was true or false. All this time, no insults have been offered to the Americans; but should anything occur to give them the slightest pretext, then it may be expected we will be butchered. It was proposed by some one in council, the other morning, to confiscate the goods of the traders, but his Excellency instantly rejected it, and yesterday, (the 13th,) a party of Apaches came to town to obtain leave of the governor to meet and rob our soldiers, but Armijo would not receive their chief into the house nor see any of them. This I was told this morning; my opinion is, that the story was only circulated to raise the governor in our good opinion! What could those Indians do with our troops? why, nothing; and the whole of the tribes fear the long guns of our brave fellows. I scarcely know what to think, however, for we are told of a large invading force now on their march from the States, and that four thousand Mexicans are coming from the low country to meet them.[31] At all events, the peasantry are reluctant to give them battle, for they are leaving their homes and betaking themselves to the mountains. At the gold mines there are scarcely a dozen people left; goods are not purchased this year as freely as they were twelve months ago; the *Rancheros* tell you plainly that they do not like to part with their money, as they cannot tell what will come to pass. Some will say, "we would rather be Americans, for then we could have a good government, now we have none, or worse than none, a very bad one." The governor told a friend of mine, the other day, that *he* would not go out to meet the Americans, but send another officer with the command, and stay in Santa Fé to regulate matters, as became a governor! That same day he parted with his wagons and goods to Mr. Speyer, and remarked to the gentleman, "I am sending off my property, as I can not foresee what change will occur in the present state of affairs." I think that this same high and mighty captor of the Texans,[32] who was

31. The American Army, 1650 strong, had left the frontier at the end of June and entered Santa Fé on 18 August.

32. The following is on the gold plate of the belt which accompanies the sword, presented by the government of Chihuahua to Governor Armijo, June, 1846, [*sic*.].

rewarded by Santa Anna with a cross of honor, and a sword from the government of Chihuahua, is preparing to make a timely retreat.[33]

I am low spirited at not being able to secure a passage in any of the caravans that have left for the south, and at the same time satisfied to be here at this important crisis, as, most undoubtedly, I will turn it to account if I live. I will make such sketches of the passing events as may interest the people of the United States, and my notes, thus far, furnish me with ample materials to fill a volume already. If other traders come in, I may be able to go on with them, if not, I do not well know what I shall do, but in all events, I will make the most of my time while in this mighty city of the Holy Faith. Thus ends the chapter. I hope you may not be as tired of reading as I am of writing.

Farewell.

Santa Fé, July 14th, 1846.

TRIUMFO DEL GRAL. D. M. ARMIJO SOBRE LOS TEJANOS

The Triumph of Gen'l Don Manual Armijo over the Texans.

The plate is of pure gold, but the workmanship rather coarse. The sword is mounted with gold and chased with the national devices, &c. The cross is about the size of the decoration worn by the companions of the Bath in England; it is of pure gold, and enameled white, and bears an inscription to the same effect as the sword. This was given by Santa Anna, the god of Armijo's idolatry, and was blessed by the priest previously to his being invested with it.—WAUGH.

33. On 17 August Emory noted in his journal: "As we approached the ruins of the ancient town of Pecos, a large, fat fellow, mounted on a mule, came toward us at full speed, and extending his hand to the general . . . said, with a roar of laughter, Armijo and his troops have gone to hell. . . . This was the alcade of the settlement, two miles up the Pecos. . . ." (*Notes of a Military Reconnoissance*, 29).

Mora Valley[1]

The Prairie Dog

ONE MORNING WHILST RAMBLING OVER THIS VALLEY,[2] I was led to make some researches among the dog towns of the neighborhood. I had made many attempts to get some of their inhabitants into my possession, but without the slightest success. Shooting seemed to be of no use, for they were always close to their houses, and, whether killed or wounded, they invariably disappeared the moment I fired at them, and some way or other, none of them gave me a chance in their open streets. Weary with my fruitless efforts, it was at once determined to enter upon the business of exploration among their subterranean abodes, and if possible, capture them in their own homes. Accordingly, I set our little friend Mickey Whelan, who, by the by, was returning to the United States on his own hook, as the Kentuckians say, and another fellow traveller to work with pick-axe and spade, in order to come at the correct knowledge of the domestic manners of those strange little animals. But before we began our excavations, it was proposed to try the experiment of inundating their houses, and by so doing, drive them out into the open air where we hoped to be able to catch them as they would come forth. One barrel after another of water had been hauled from the creek and poured into the entrances, but no sooner did we empty each vessel than the water disappeared, without producing the slightest effect whatever. Again and again did we repeat the experiment, yet not a solitary dog raised his nose above the ground. At last coming to the conclusion, that the extreme droughtiness of the earth militated against our operations, it was determined, as we could not drown them out, we would dig them up *nolens volens*. Mickey freely lent himself to the task, and displayed in all his movements a perfect acquaintance with the instrument he was using. He worked with as much energy and devotion as if life and death depended upon his individual exertions; nor was his co-laborer behind him in the pursuit of knowledge. It would have rejoiced the heart of the great Belzoni himself, to have seen the labors of those men. First they made

1. This extract from "a forthcoming work, entitled 'Travels in search of the Elephant, or the Wanderings of an Artist, by Alfred S. Waugh, Esq.'," labelled Chapter XXIII, Volume II, was published in the *Western Journal and Civilian*, VII (October, 1851), 33-38.

2. The "settlements" on the Mora River (a branch of the Canadian) were to the northwest of Santa Fé, about one hundred miles by trail. Possibly Waugh investigated the prairie dogs while on his way back to Missouri.

a descent by a perpendicular opening to the depth of six or eight feet, then they ran a level to the distance of fourteen or fifteen more, and following the windings of the passages extended their researches far and wide; the deeper and more extensive they made their way, the further they seemed to be from the attainment of their object. Still, Mickey and his comrad continued their labors without a moments cessation; sometimes the passage would continue straight on, then it would turn to the right and anon to the left, now it would make an upward course and again descend, but no inner chamber could be found. *"Ah! thin by the powers of Moll Kelly, but ye'r Kute crathers, and sure the ould boy himself couldn't find out yer parlor if he was to try, for there's no ind to yer krucked hall, bad screen to you for kontrary brutes"* exclaimed Mickey as he paused for a moment to contemplate the field of his labors. "I tell you what it is, *Kurnel,* the only way you could get hould of thim is to earthquake thim out." How is that I asked. "Oh, the sorra an easier thing in life sir, all you have to do is to dig a big hole in the ground, bury a can of gun-powdher and blow thim up sky high as they do the rocks in the quarry, and sure if you don't git thim alive and kicking, praps you'l git thim dead and may be that'l do as well." Not exactly, I replied, I am more anxious to find out how they live when at home than to capture their dead carcasses. "Ah! thin, he replied, ye'l have to travel a long way before ye come to their bed-rooms. Arrah musha! sir, did you iver hear tell of the great king of Egypt who built his palace away down in the ground in order to keep people from botherin him whiniver he wished to be all alone by himself? Well sir, he give directions to his bricklayer to build the entrance in sich a kurus manner, that none but himself, and the queen, and the prince, could find their way into the room where he used to sit upon a great big goolden *trone,* smokin his pipe like a Christian man, all as one. Now sir, do you see, the bricklayer or builder, or whativer ye plase to call him, was a mighty cunnin man in all sorts of schaming (scheming) and by the same token he was a great magicianer likewise also, who could trick owld Nick and give him odds into the bargain. Well, the same betoken, he put on his considerin cap, lit his pipe and made himself a tumbler of hot whiskey punch, and sot down over his big book, to invint a puzzle that wouldn't be found out by morthal man—barrin he was let into the saycret, so he sot up all night smokin his dudgheen to keep his nose warm—for it was a could night—and drinkin the hot consolation before him from time to time, just to keep the wind out of his stomack—for he was subject to the kolic, and more betoken the punch used to help him mightily to a clear way of thinkin wheniver he got bothered by too much study. So ye see sir, after spending the whole blessed night in the way I tell ye of, he goes to the king in the mornin, "God save yer majesty" says he to the king, save ye kindly, the king says back again to him—for ye must know that the king was a mighty p'lite man and prided himself on his jintility. "Ye look as if ye'd been up all night my man" says the king; troth, ye may say that, says the builder, and I've done a power of thinkin' for yer majesty, but I've made an invintion that'l beat the world for kuteness, intirely, so it will, and isn't it myself that's wake with fastin and study, so if yer plase my lord, I'l take a drink of wather to refresh me." The sorra, a taste of that same dirty stuff ye'l get here my man, says the king. "*Ooh musha, a worra sthruc* thin, if I dont I'l not be able to stand up and insince your majesty into my plans, for it's going to faint I am, sure enough, if I dont git somethin to wet my lips with, says the builder. "No, no, my gossoon" says the king, no wather is iver drunk in my house; arrah masha, do ye think that I'm a haythen brute to let a christian crayther drink wather, whin I've loads and lashins of the real mountain dew in my cellar." With that the king rings the bell and whin the ould butler made his appearance, he was tould to bring up a bottle of pottheen from below stairs, with the rest of the materials for makin punch. Well now, as luck would have it, the punch revived him like—the builder I mean, and he began to talk mighty p'litely and showed the king his plan, and whin the king saw it all beautifully pictured out on paper, his eyes began to sparkle and says he, "be jabers yer a great man intirely, and if ye only carry out the work as ye planned it, I'll make a lord of ye—and there's my hand on it." Well, lo and behould! the builder wint to work, he, and his min, and they made the completest job of it ye iver clapped yer two eyes upon, it was easy enough to git into the place, but it would puzzle the fairies to git out of it, for, first there was one passage and thin there was another running off in every direction so that ye got lost before ye could say Jack Robinson. And unless ye knew the saycret the dickens a bit ye could tell where ye were going to. The king himself got bothered the first time he wint there, and only for the builder, who kept close behind him, the sorra scran to the bit if he iver could find his way into daylight again. At last all was right and the king was mightily plased whin he learned the saycret, and was as good as his word, so the builder was made a great lord of immediantly."

"The great saycret of the whole affair was this sir, do ye see, all the rooms and passages run into each other in such a kurus manner that in case of an insurrection among his people, while the inimy would be groping about in the dark to find him, the king who could hear thim coming in at one door, could make his escape by an other, so he called the place a *labor-in,* by reason of the trouble they would be in to find him. And now, sir, do ye perceave? I'm thinkin the place we've got into is a *labor-in,* for there's no tellin whether we're goin right or wrong, and praps while we're working our lives out here, the inhabitants, as ye call thim, have made escape by some other intrance."

This singular story of Mickey's, although conveyed with all the absurdity of a legend, not only served to amuse me, by the peculiarity of the delivery, but led me to speculating upon the possibility of a general communication between all the domiciles of this interesting little animal whose territories we were then invading. The few hours experience we had had in our exploring expedition allowed me to come to the conclusion that such might possibly be the case, for there appeared to be a perfect *labyrinth* of passages to which there seemed to be no end; and as the greater part of the day had been consumed in the work without producing the desired end, I called off the labor to refreshment, fully satisfied in my own mind at least that I had acquired some information. Upon speaking of the experiment to Mr. James Bonney,[3] I was told that others had tried to ascertain the knowledge which I had sought to gain, but with no success, and that some had even gone so far as to find out that a general communication actually did exist. So, after all, the imaginative mind of Master Mickey had not strayed far from the truth when a vague recollection of the story of the Egyptian *labyrinth,* which he must have heard, led him to suppose a similar state of affairs might be the case in the present instance. Of this curious little animal Gregg says:

"The prairie dog has been recorded[4] by some naturalists a species of the Marmot (arctomys ludoviciana;) yet it seems to possess scarce any other quality in common with this animal except that of burrowing. Some have supposed, it is true, that like the Marmot, they lie torpid during the cold season; and it is observed in 'Long's Expedition,' that, 'as they pass the winter in a lethargic state, they lay up no provisions' &c., but this is

3. James Bonney, an Englishman by birth, was a resident at the Mora, an excellent, good-hearted fellow and very much esteemed by the Santa Fé traders. He was murdered by a Mexican shortly after I returned to the United States, in 1846.—WAUGH.

Bonney settled on the Mora in 1843. Webb met him there the next year: "I think he had a wife or housekeeper and three or four children, the eldest a son, I should think, fourteen or sixteen years old" (*Adventures in the Santa Fé Trade,* 74). Lieut. Emory met him on 13 August 1846: "Six miles brought us to the first settlement we had yet seen in 775 miles. . . . Mr. Boney . . . is the owner of a larger number of horses and cattle, which he manages to keep in defiance of wolves, Indians, and Mexicans. He is a perfect specimen of a generous, open-hearted adventurer, and in appearance what, I have pictured to myself, Daniel Boone, of Kentucky, must have been in his day" (*Notes of a Military Reconnoissance,* 25).

4. *Reckoned* in Gregg.

no doubt erronious; for I have the concurrent testimony of several persons, who have been upon the prairies in the winter, that, like rabbits and squirrels, they issue from their abodes every soft day; and therefore lay up, no doubt, a ho[a]rd of hay (as there is rarely anything else to be found in the vicinity of their towns) for winter's use."

"A collection of their burrows," continues this author, has been termed by travellers a 'dog town,' which comprises from a dozen or so, to some thousands in the same vicinity; often covering an area of several square miles. They generally locate upon firm, dry plains, coated with fine short grass, upon which they feed; for they are no doubt exclusively herbivorous. But even when tall grass surrounds, they seem commonly to destroy this within their "streets" which are nearly always found "paved" with a fine species suited to their palates. They must need but little water, if any at all, as their 'towns,' are often, indeed generally, found in the midst of most arid plains—unless we suppose they dig down to subterranean fountains, at least they evidently burrow remarkably deep. Attempts either to dig or drown them out of their holes have generally proved unsuccessful."[5]

Kendal in his "Narrative" gives a very graphic description of the habits of these creatures.

"In their habits," says he, "they are clannish, social, and extremely convivial, never living alone like other animals, but, on the contrary, always formed in large villages or large settlements. They are a wild, frolicsome, mad-cap set of fellows, when undisturbed, uneasy and ever on the move, and appear to take especial delight in chattering away their time, and visiting from hole to hole to gossip and talk over each other's affairs—at least so their actions would indicate.[6] On several occasions," he says, "I crept close to their villages, without being observed, to watch their movements. Directly in the centre of one of them I particularly noticed a very large dog, sitting in front of the door or entrance to his burrow, and by his own actions and those of his neighbors it really seemed as though he was the president, major, or chief—at all events he was the big dog of the place. For at least an hour I secretly watched the operations of this community. During that time the large dog I have mentioned received at least a dozen visits from his fellow dogs, which would stop and chat with him a few moments, and then run off to their domicils. All this while he never left his post for one moment, and I thought I could discover a gravity in his deportment not discernible in those by which

5. *Commerce of the Prairies,* II, 229-230.
6. One sentence omitted here.

he was surrounded. Far be it from me to say that the visits he received were upon business, or had any thing to do with the local government of the village; but it certainly appeared so. If any animal has a system of laws regulating the body politic, it is certainly the prairie dog."[7]

When I first saw these cities of the desert, I was for a moment or two rather disappointed in my expectations. From all which I had heard or read, I had formed an idea that they were a variety of the canine species, and looked as a matter of course to see a small dog; but what was my surprise when startled by a variety of sound resembling the noise made by those dutch toy dogs of the shops, I looked down from my horse to ascertain what it was, that was saluting me in so novel a manner, *tcheip, tcheip—tcheip* sounded in every direction,—*tcheip, tcheip—tcheip,* was repeated by hundreds of voices, I looked to the right hand and then to the left,—*tcheip, tcheip—tcheip,* still saluted my bewildered ears! I turned in my saddle—*tcheip, tcheip—tcheip*—swelled up around me—there was no end to *tcheip, tcheip—tcheip*—it was incessant and reached me no matter how I turned about. Now, whether this was the voice of welcome or warning to be cautious in my progress through the settlement, I could not tell, for I was entirely ignorant of the language, in which they addressed me, and could make no reply to what they were saying. At length at some distance from which I was, I saw a few small animals of a yellowish color, somewhat resembling the common squirrel in shape, running about from cone to cone, and either taking up a position on the top of it, or at once descending into the earth. Sometimes a venerable looking fellow would sit on his hind quarters on the roof of a large house, while others would collect around him on the ground, and with all the gravity of Indians in council, sit in silence as if listening to the talk of a chief. On such occasions it is very rarely you ever hear more than one speaking at a time. I have watched them for hours and could have almost fancied them rational creatures, they behaved with so much propriety. Now and then I observed a larger house than others in the town, which might lead one to suppose that grades of society existed amongst them, and that this was the palace or white house of a king, a president or perhaps a governor; but how they are governed, or what form of government they live under, whether a monarchy or a republic, I am unable to say, not having sufficient time to stay and make myself intimately acquainted with their manners and customs. I have no doubt, however, that a great deal of curious information might be obtained by any person who had taste and opportunity to study the "domestic manners" of these free-born citizens

7. *Narrative of the Texan Santa Fé Expedition,* I, 192-193.

of the desert. They are said to be a very social people, and moreover, not bigotted in their ideas of aristocratic exclusiveness, for they allow the *Rattle-snake, the owl,* and *the Rabbit* to share their dwellings in common with themselves. That these different creatures live in peace with each other, I cannot for one moment suppose, and how animals so totally distinct in their natures can possibly manage to live under the same roof is to me a most unaccountable matter. The *owl* is a bird of prey, the Rattle-snake is voracious and venemous, and the rabbit herbivorous and the very opposite of the others. I am unable to say upon what the Prairie Dog feeds—indeed I am puzzled to know how they exist at all, for their towns are always in high, dry latitudes, and perfectly barren, or at least they look so. There can be but little hesitation in saying that the snake preys upon some of his neighbors, as a rattle-snake was killed to-day while in the act of swallowing a young dog, and it is more than probably the owl feasts off the same dish, and it is possible the poor rabbit is also sacrificed upon the same altar. The owl and rattle-snake are smaller than those found in the southern states, and what is most remarkable is that all these animals, except the rabbit, resemble each other in general color; namely a yellow or dun, or what painters might term, a dirty tawney.[8]

Dr. Wizslizenius when going out to Santa Fé was fortunate to procure a few specimens, which were preserved by his curator for him.

8. For a recent detailed account of the prairie dog see Scheffer, "Historical Encounter and Accounts of the Plains Prairie Dog."

SOURCES CONSULTED

BOOKS AND PERIODICALS

Abert, J. W. *Journal of Lieut. J. W. Abert, from Bent's Fort to St. Louis, in 1845.* 29th Congress, 1st Session, Senate Document No. 438.

Abert, J. W. *Report of Lieut. J. W. Abert of His Examination of New Mexico in the Years 1846-47.* 30th Congress, 1st Session, House Executive Document No. 41.

Anderson, Clinton P. "The Adobe Palace." *New Mexico Historical Review,* XIX (1944), 97-122.

Atherton, Lewis E. "James and Robert Aull—A Frontier Missouri Mercantile Firm." *Missouri Historical Review,* XXX (1935), 3-27.

Bay, W. V. N. *Reminiscences of the Bench and Bar of Missouri.* St. Louis, 1878.

Bieber, Ralph P. (editor). *Adventures in the Santa Fé Trade, 1844-1847* (by James Josiah Webb). *Southwest Historical Series, Volume I.* Glendale, California, Arthur H. Clark Co., 1931.

Bieber, Ralph P. (editor). *Journal of a Soldier under Kearny and Doniphan, 1846-1847* (by George Rutledge Gibson). Southwest Historical Series, Volume III. Glendale, California, Arthur H. Clark Co., 1935.

Bieber, Ralph P. "Letters of James and Robert Aull." *Missouri Historical Society Collections,* V (June, 1928), 267-310.

Boggs, William C. "A Short Biographical Sketch of Lilburn W. Boggs, by his Son." *Missouri Historical Review,* IV (1910), 106-110.

Boggs, William C. "Reminiscences of William C. Boggs." *Missouri Historical Review,* VI (1912), 86-90.

Bonsal, Stephen. *Edward Fitzgerald Beale. A Pioneer in the Path of Empire, 1822-1903.* New York, Putnam's, 1912.

Brown, T. Allston. *The History of the American Stage.* New York, Dick & Fitzgerald, 1870.

Bryant, Edwin. *What I Saw in California . . . in 1846, 1847.* 2nd edition, New York, Appleton, 1848.

Carey, Charles H. (editor). *The Journals of Theodore Talbot, 1843 and 1849-52.* Portland, Oregon, The Metropolitan Press, 1931.

Carson, William G. B. (editor). "The Diary of Mat Field, St. Louis, April 2 - May 16, 1839." *Missouri Historical Society Bulletin,* V (1949), 91-108, 157-184.

Chick, W. H. "A Journey to Missouri in 1822." *Missouri Valley Historical Society Publications,* I, No. 1 (1921), 97-103.

Chick, W. H. "The Vicissitudes of Pioneer Life." *Missouri Valley Historical Society Publications,* I, No. 2 (1922), 207-218.

Chiles, Henry C. *One Hundred Years of Freemasonry in Lexington.* Lexington, Missouri, 1940.

Christ-Janer, Albert. *George Caleb Bingham of Missouri.* New York, Dodd, Mead and Company, 1940.

Conard, Howard L. *Encyclopedia of the History of Missouri.* 6 volumes, St. Louis, 1901.

Connelley, William Elsey. *Doniphan's Expedition and the Conquest of New Mexico and California.* Topeka, 1907.

Cowell, Joe. *Thirty Years Passed among the Players of England and America . . . .* New York, Harpers, 1843.

Cullum, George Washington. *Biographical Register of the Officers and Graduates of the United States Military Academy.* 3rd edition, 3 volumes, Boston, Houghton Mifflin, 1891.

Dana, Charles A. (editor). *The United States Illustrated in Views of City and Country. With Descriptive and Historical Articles.* [Volume I] *The West; or the States of the Mississippi Valley, and the Pacific.* New York, Herrmann J. Meyer (ca. 1853).

Davis, W. H. H. *El Gringo; or, New Mexico and Her People.* New York, Harpers, 1857.

Dictionary of American Biography.

Dictionary of National Biography.

Dellenbaugh, Frederick S. *Frémont and '49.* New York, Putnams, 1914.

Donaldson, Thomas. *The George Catlin Indian Gallery in the United States National Museum.* Part II, Annual Report of Smithsonian Institution for 1885. Washington, D. C., 1886.

Drumm, Stella M. (editor). *Down the Santa Fé Trail and into Mexico. The Diary of Susan Shelby Magoffin, 1846-1847.* New Haven, Yale University Press, 1926.

Edwards, Richard, and M. Hopewell. *The Great West and Her Commercial Metropolis.* St. Louis, 1860.

Emory, W. H. *Notes of a Military Reconnoissance from Fort Leavenworth, in Missouri, to San Diego, in California. . . .* 30th Congress, 1st Session, House Executive Document No. 41.

Firkins, Ina Ten Eyck. *Index to Plays, 1800-1926.* New York, H. W. Wilson Company, 1927.

Frémont, John Charles. *Memoirs of My Life.* Chicago and New York, 1887.

Frémont, John Charles. *Report of the Exploring Expedition to the Rocky Mountains in the year 1842, and to Oregon and North California in the years 1843-'44.* Washington, 1845.

Fulton, Maurice Garland. *Diary and Letters of Josiah Gregg, 1840-1850.* 2 volumes, Norman, University of Oklahoma Press, 1941, 1944.

Garraghan, Gilbert J., S.J. *Catholic Beginnings in Kansas City, Missouri.* Chicago, Loyola University Press, 1920.

Gibson, George Rutledge. See Bieber, Ralph P. (editor).

Gregg, Josiah. *Commerce of the Prairies.* 2 volumes, New York, Langley, 1844.

Gregg, Josiah. See Fulton, Maurice G. (editor).

Heitman, Francis. *Historical Register and Dictionary of the United States Army, 1789-1903.* 2 volumes, Washington, 1903.

Hill, John B. *The Presbytery of Kansas City and Its Predecessors, 1821-1901.* Kansas City, 1901.

The History of Jackson County, Missouri. Kansas City, 1881.

Hughes, John T. *Doniphan's Expedition; containing an account of the conquest of New Mexico. . . .* Cincinnati, James, 1848.

Hyde, William and Howard L. Conard. *Encyclopedia of the History of St. Louis.* 4 volumes, St. Louis, 1899.

[James, Thomas Horton] *Rambles in the United States and Canada During the Year 1845 . . . by Rubio.* London, 1847.

Journal of the Proceedings of the Fifth and Sixth Annual Conventions of the Protestant Episcopal Church in the Diocese of Missouri held in Christ Church, Saint Louis . . . November . . . December, 1844, and . . . April, 1845. Saint Louis, 1845.

Journal of the Proceedings of the Seventh Annual Convention of the Protestant Episcopal Church in the Diocese of Missouri held in Christ Church, St. Louis . . . May, 1846. St. Louis, 1846.

Journal of the Proceedings of the Eighth Annual Convention of the Protestant Episcopal Church, in the Diocese of Missouri, held in Grace Church, Jefferson City, May . . . 1847. Saint Louis, 1847.

Kendall, George Wilkins. *Narrative of the Texan Santa Fé Expedition.* 2 volumes, New York, Harpers, 1844.

Kinietz, William Jermon. *John Mix Stanley and His Indian Paintings.* Ann Arbor, University of Michigan Press, 1942.

Lyell, Sir Charles. *A Second Visit to the United States of North America.* 2 volumes, New York, Harpers, 1849.

McDermott, John Francis. "Another Coriolanus: Portraits of Keokuk, Chief of the Sac and Fox." *Antiques,* LIV (1948), 98-100.

McDermott, John Francis. "An Upper Mississippi Excursion of 1845." *Minnesota History,* XXII (1941), 13-34.

McKenney, Thomas L., and James Hall. *The Indian Tribes of North America.* New edition, edited by Frederick Webb Hodge. 3 volumes. Edinburgh, John Grant, 1933.

Magoffin, Susan. See Drumm, Stella M. (editor).

A Memorial and Biographical Record of Kansas City and Jackson County, Missouri. Chicago, 1896.

Miller, W. H. *The History of Kansas City.* Kansas City, 1881.

Montaignes, François des. "The Plains, Being a Collection of Veracious Memoranda, taken during the Expedition of Exploration in the year 1845. . . ." *Western Journal and Civilian,* IX (1852-53), 71-73, 146-148, 221-222, 290-293, 366-368, 433-436; X (1853), 69-73, 149-152, 222-226, 295-301, 370-375, 441-445; XV (1856), 289-295.

Nevins, Allan. *Frémont, Pathmarker of the West.* New York, Appleton-Century, 1939.

Norman's New Orleans and Environs. . . . New Orleans, B. M. Norman, 1845.

Parkman, Francis. See Wade, Mason (editor).

Portrait and Biographical Record of Lafayette and Saline Counties, Missouri. Chicago, 1882.

Rusk, Fern Helen. *George Caleb Gingham, the Missouri Artist.* Jefferson City, Hugh Stevens Co., 1917.

Sage, Rufus. *Scenes in the Rocky Mountains.* Philadelphia, Carey & Hart, 1846.

(Green's) St. Louis Directory for 1845. St. Louis, 1844.

(Sloss's) St. Louis Directory for 1848. St. Louis, 1848.

(Green's) St. Louis Directory for 1850. St. Louis, 1849.

(Green's) St. Louis Directory for 1851. St. Louis, 1850.

(Morrison's) St. Louis Directory for 1852. St. Louis, 1852.

(Montague's) Saint Louis Directory for 1853-4. St. Louis, 1853.

The St. Louis Directory for 1854-5. St. Louis, 1854.

Scharf, J. Thomas. *History of St. Louis, City and County.* 2 volumes, Philadelphia, 1883.

Scheffer, Theodore H. "Historical Encounter and Accounts of the Plains Prairie Dog." *Kansas Historical Quarterly,* XV (1945), 527-537.

Thwaites, R. G. (editor). *The Original Journals of the Lewis and Clark Expedition, 1804-1806.* 7 volumes and atlas, New York, Dodd, Mead and Co., 1904.

Tuckerman, Henry T. *Book of the Artists.* New York, Putnams, 1867.

Twitchell, Ralph Emerson. *The Leading Facts in New Mexican History.* 2 volumes, Cedar Rapids, Torch Press, 1912.

Twitchell, Ralph Emerson. *Old Santa Fé.* (Santa Fe, 1925).

Vital Historical Records of Jackson County, Missouri, 1826-1876, collected, compiled and published by the Kansas City Chapter of the Daughters of the American Revolution. Kansas City, 1933-34.

Wade, Mason (editor). *The Journals of Francis Parkman.* 2 volumes, New York, Harpers, 1947.

Wagner, Henry R. *The Plains and the Rockies, 1800-1865.* Revised and extended by Charles L. Camp. San Francisco, Grabhorn Press, 1937.

Waugh, Alfred S. "Mora Valley—The Prairie Dog." *Western Journal,* VII (1851), 33-38.

Waugh, Alfred S. "A Trip to Mexico" by Don Alfredo, El Artista Viajante. *Southern Literary Messenger,* XII (1846), 755-762.

Webb, James Josiah. See Bieber, Ralph P. (editor).

Webb, W. L. *The Centennial History of Independence, Missouri.* (Independence) 1927.

Whitney, Carrie Westlake. *Kansas City, Missouri, Its History and People, 1808-1908.* 3 volumes, Chicago, 1908.

Wilson, Arthur H. *The History of the Philadelphia Stage, 1835-1855.* Philadelphia, University of Pennsylvania Press, 1935.

Wislizenus, Adolph. *Memoir of a Tour to Northern Mexico, connected with Col. Doniphan's Expedition in 1846 and 1847.* 30th Congress, 1st Session, Senate Miscellaneous Document 26.

Young, William. *History of Lafayette County, Missouri.* 2 volumes, Indianapolis, 1910.

NEWSPAPERS

Boonville Commercial Bulletin, 1846-1847.

Independence Journal, 1844.

Lexington Appeal, 1847.

(St. Louis) *Daily Bulletin.*

St. Louis Intelligencer.

(St. Louis) *Missouri Republican.*

(St. Louis) *New Era.*

(St. Louis) *Weekly Reveille.*

Weston Journal, 1845.

MANUSCRIPTS

Waugh Manuscripts, Missouri Historical Society.

INDEX